ity

writing

making the transition

Pearson Canada
Toronto

Library and Archives Canada Cataloguing in Publication

Marshall, Steve, 1964–
Academic writing : making the transition / Steve Marshall.

Includes index.
ISBN 978-0-13-610390-5

1. Academic writing. 2. English language—Rhetoric. 3. Report writing.
4. Critical thinking. I. Title.

PE1408.M387 2011 808'.042 C2011-901057-7

ISBN 978-0-13-610390-5

Vice-President, Editorial Director: Gary Bennett
Editor-in-Chief: Ky Pruesse
Acquisitions Editor: David S. Le Gallais
Marketing Manager: Loula March
Senior Developmental Editor: Madhu Ranadive
Project Manager: Richard di Santo
Production Editor: Claudia Forgas
Copy Editor: Melissa Churchill
Proofreaders: Claudia Forgas, Marnie Lamb
Compositor: Aptara®, Inc.
Permissions Researchers: Beth McAuley and Nadine Bachan, The Editing Company
Art Director: Julia Hall
Interior Designer: Anthony Leung
Cover Designer: Anthony Leung

9 10 11 12 13 V0UD 19 18 17 16 15

Printed and bound in the United States of America.

PEARSON

CONTENTS

PREFACE

The ideas in this textbook have come to fruition over 18 years of teaching academic writing, first at the University of London, in the UK, and then at Simon Fraser University, in Vancouver, Canada. Over this period, I have seen students from diverse social, cultural, and linguistic backgrounds study together in my classrooms, usually with different ideas about what is expected of them in academic writing. These students have been undergraduate and graduate students, international students with English as an additional language, multilingual students who are the children of immigrants, native English speakers who want to improve their academic writing, and mature students returning to higher education after several years in the workplace. When students from different backgrounds share the same classroom, they want teachers and classmates to respect and understand their individual ideas and perspectives. At the same time, they need to learn and apply in context the norms and rules of academic writing to become successful students.

The way students learn and write is affected not only by their social, cultural, and linguistic backgrounds but also by the internet and social media. Students use online search engines and databases for research, and maintain contacts with friends across the world via social networking sites. Formal academic writing is, therefore, only one literacy practice in a very broad spectrum of writing for today's students. This is the complex and multi-layered space in which *Academic Writing: Making the Transition* has been conceptualized.

MAKING THE TRANSITION TO WRITING AT COLLEGE OR UNIVERSITY

The focus of this textbook is on teaching foundational academic writing skills, through taught courses or through self-study, to four groups of students making the transition to writing at college or university:

- Students making the transition from writing at secondary school to writing at college or university
- Mature students making the transition from several years in the workplace to writing at college or university
- International students making the transition to writing in English as a second or additional language
- Students making the transition from undergraduate to graduate studies who require a review of the foundations of academic writing

Audience, Genre, and Context

In most contexts of higher education, students take courses in a wide range of disciplines where they are required to write in different ways. To help students make informed decisions about how they should write across the disciplines, three key concepts run through this textbook: audience (who you are writing for and their expectations), genre (what type of text you are writing), and context (the purpose and situation of your writing—e.g., for assessment or as a non-assessed part of the writing process).

Reading, Thinking, Writing, and Reflecting

The origin of many students' success in academic writing can be found in how they read. Accordingly, effective reading is recognized in this textbook as an integral component of effective writing. In each chapter, reading samples and writing tasks unify active and critical reading, critical thinking, and effective writing in different academic contexts. Reading samples include authentic excerpts from academic journal articles, documents from news media and non-governmental organizations, and authentic samples of students' writing on different topics. Chapters also include self- and peer-review activities, which students use to read and analyze their own writing and that of peers. Each chapter ends with a review of the content studied.

THE WRITING PROCESS AND WRITING PRODUCTS

This textbook focuses on the *writing process*, that is, the stages that writers go through in creating texts, such as reading and note-taking, organizing ideas, writing, and editing. Important *writing products* that students need to master for success are also studied in depth: summaries and critical summaries; essay sections (introductions, main body paragraphs, conclusions, and references); and different modes of writing across the disciplines (e.g., expository writing, and writing about arguments, comparisons, problems, solutions, causes, and effects).

Learning to Write and Writing to Learn

The aim of most academic writing courses and textbooks is to teach students to write, or *learning to write*, with a focus on the norms and rules of different forms of academic writing through practice activities and review. An additional focus of this textbook is learning through writing, or *writing to learn*, through exploratory writing activities (in free-style forms) as part of the writing process and to generate ideas and practise concepts.

A CLEAR EXPLANATION OF THE FOUNDATIONAL ASPECTS OF ACADEMIC WRITING

Some of the philosophical, organizational, and contextual ideas behind academic writing are complicated. In this textbook, the explanations are written in sufficient detail and in language that is accessible and easy to understand.

DETAILED APPENDICES FOR REFERENCE AND FURTHER STUDY

Ten appendices at the back of the book can be used in different ways. Students can refer to Appendices 1, 2, and 3 for further study of MLA and APA referencing styles, and common linking words in academic writing. Appendices 4 to 10 can be used by students who need to work on punctuation, sentence structure, style, and grammatical accuracy/variety. Appendices include description and practice activities that can help students with their academic writing.

SUITABILITY FOR VARIOUS COURSES

Academic Writing: Making the Transition is suitable for use as a textbook in any of the following types of courses:

- First-year college and university courses in foundational academic writing and composition;
- Pre-college and pre-university courses in English for academic purposes and academic writing;
- In-sessional university courses that give students additional support in academic writing during their college or university studies, at an undergraduate or a graduate level.

ORGANIZATION OF THIS TEXTBOOK

Academic Writing: Making the Transition provides comprehensive coverage of the aspects of academic reading and writing, critical thinking, language use, and sentence structure required at a foundational level. Instructors and students will not need to spend endless hours searching for authentic texts that exemplify ideas studied, for online sources that explain the rules of citation and referencing, or for activities on academic language and writing styles. Everything is included in a single teacher-friendly, student-friendly textbook.

The textbook is organized into three sections.

Part 1: From Reading to Writing comprises Chapters 1 to 5 and looks at active and critical reading, thinking and writing critically, and key aspects of writing successful research essays: introductions, main body paragraphs, conclusions, referencing and citation, and avoiding plagiarism.

Part 2: Writing Modes across the Disciplines comprises Chapters 6 to 10 and focuses on the different forms of academic writing that are common across most disciplines: expository writing; and writing about arguments, comparisons, problems and solutions, and causes and effects.

Part 3: Appendices comprises 10 appendices on the following: MLA and APA citation style, linking words, punctuation, improving style, sentence structure (independent and dependent clauses, complex and compound sentences, relative and participle clauses, sentence fragments, and comma splices), the passive voice, and article usage in noun phrases.

The chapters and appendices can be taught and studied in any order and over different time periods, depending on the context. For example, as a one-semester introduction to the foundations of academic writing over 13 weeks, the organization would allow for between four and five hours classroom contact per week, or for two to three hours a week for a similar course over two semesters. This time frame would lend itself to either a first-year introduction to university/college writing or a one or two semester pre-college or pre-university course in which an introduction to academic writing is a major component.

Where a classroom is made up of a mixture of students with English as a first and additional language, the language-oriented appendices in Part 3 can be incorporated into the course through additional guided self-study. For groups made up exclusively of English-language learners studying English for academic purposes, the appendices can be taught in class, for example, to examine the grammar of academic writing and sentence structure.

SUPPLEMENTS

The following supplements are available:

- mycanadiancomplab

  Visit MyCanadianCompLab (*www.mycanadiancomplab.ca*) to access diverse resources for composition in one easy-to-use place:
  - Sections on writing, research, and grammar cover all the key topics in the text, providing additional instruction, examples, and practice.
  - An online composing space includes tools such as writing tips and editing FAQs, so that you can get help as you need it, without ever leaving your writing environment.
  - The portfolio feature helps you create an e-portfolio of your work that you can easily share with your instructor and peers.
  - Access to MyCanadianCompLab can be purchased separately, from your bookstore or from Pearson Canada.
- Answer Key (ISBN 0135110424)

  A separate Answer Key is available to instructors and students, for instruction and self-study, with clear explanations of answers. The separate Answer Key means that instructors can use the textbook in class without students jumping to the back of the book for answers. At the same time, students can do chapters and appendices as self-study activities, correct their own work, and bring questions to class or to their instructor's office hour. The Answer Key contains answers, clear explanations, and sample answers/models for writing tasks. Instructors can download the Answer Key from the Pearson online catalogue. A print version of the Answer Key is available to students on demand.
- Instructor's Manual (ISBN 0135110416)

  For no additional charge, instructors who use *Academic Writing: Making the Transition* in their classrooms can download an instructor's manual. The manual gives guidance on how best to use the activities in each chapter as well as ideas for additional activities that can consolidate student learning.
- CourseSmart for Instructors (ISBN 0132604531)

  CourseSmart goes beyond traditional expectations–providing instant, online access to the textbooks and course materials you need at a lower cost for students. And even as students save money, you can save time and hassle with a digital eTextbook that allows you to search for the most relevant content at the very moment you need it. Whether it is evaluating textbooks or creating lecture notes to help students with difficult concepts, CourseSmart can make life a little easier. See how when you visit *www.coursesmart.com/instructors*.

- CourseSmart for Students (ISBN 0132604531)
  CourseSmart goes beyond traditional expectations–providing instant, online access to the textbooks and course materials you need at an average saving of 60 percent. With instant access from any computer and the ability to search your text, you will find the content you need quickly, no matter where you are. And with online tools like highlighting and note-taking, you can save time and study efficiently. See all the benefits at *www.coursesmart.com/students*.

ACKNOWLEDGMENTS

I would like to acknowledge the following people for their invaluable help in assisting me in the writing of this book: all of the students who have taken my classes in Simon Fraser University's Foundations of Academic Literacy course (FAL X99) for their creativity, optimism, humour, hard work, and moments of inspiration; the large team of FAL X99 instructors in the Faculty of Education at Simon Fraser University, who have participated in detailed discussion about how best to teach foundational academic literacy; Michael Ho, Nam Khong, Candy Lau, Hua Li, and Jake Zuurbier; the following Marshalls—Earl, Helen, Noni, Dave, Miki, Joey, Jamie; those at Pearson Education who offered their much-valued expertise and advice: Suzanne Schaan, Madhu Ranadive, David LeGallais, Christopher Helsby, Melissa Churchill, Claudia Forgas, and Katie McWhirter. Finally, sincere thanks go to the many reviewers who read through sections and manuscripts of the book in its various stages, many of whose suggestions can be found in the finished product:

Marlene Sawatsky
Simon Fraser University

Nancy Marenick
St. Francis Xavier University

Janice Fiamengo
University of Ottawa

Alison Calder
University of Manitoba

Debbie Gascoyne
Camosun College

Sunita Wiebe
The Art Institute of Vancouver

Roxanne Harde
University of Alberta

Rachel Mines
Langara College

Roger Fowler
University of Ottawa

Gisele Baxter
University of British Columbia

David Watt
University of Manitoba

Sean Johnston
Okanagan College

Jennifer Read
Capilano University

Monika Rydygier Smith
University of Victoria

Karen Inglis
Kwantlen Polytechnic University

From Reading to Writing

PART 1

CHAPTER 1

Active and Critical Reading

In this chapter, you will study the following aspects of active and critical reading:

- ✓ Audience, genre, and context
- ✓ Active and critical reading: Why they are important
- ✓ Assessing reliable sources
- ✓ Reading around the text
- ✓ Skimming and scanning
- ✓ Annotating text
- ✓ Locating different voices and opinions as you read
- ✓ Reading between the lines: Inference
- ✓ Focusing on what is not said
- ✓ Analyzing style and formality
- ✓ Writing summaries
- ✓ Peer review of your work

You can read without writing but you can't write without reading. If you want to be successful in academic writing, you also need to be successful in academic reading. Effective readers write effectively. That said, many problems in academic writing are related to reading. For example, writers may suffer from writer's block and be unable to get any words down on paper or on a computer screen, or they may receive essays back from instructors with comments about weak argument or inappropriate style. In each case, the root of the problem may be found in the way writers are reading academic texts; they may be reading passively or uncritically.

In this chapter, you will learn about the importance of *active* and *critical* reading skills, and how these skills are an essential starting point for successful academic writing.

AUDIENCE, GENRE, AND CONTEXT

Academic reading and writing require awareness of *audience*, *genre*, and *context*. Awareness of these three aspects can help you to engage actively and critically with texts. It can also allow you to organize your ideas effectively, and help you to make informed choices about how to write in appropriate styles with clarity, precision, and persuasion.

Audience

When you read and write, it is important to be aware of the audience.

Academic texts are written in different styles for different audiences. For example, writers of academic journal articles are expected to follow strict rules about structure and style and to write with a lot of specialist language. The intended audience is a reader who has expert knowledge in his or her specialist area. Whenever you write, it is important to remember that your reader will also have clear expectations about how you should write.

When you read and write academic texts, you should begin by asking yourself the following questions:

- Who is the intended audience for this text?
- What are the audience's expectations?

Genre

Another important aspect of reading and writing academic texts is genre.

The term *genre* can be used to refer to a type of text, for example, a reflective journal, a lab report, an argument essay, or a literary critique. Each genre comes with certain conventions, or rules, about how you are expected to write. If you are writing a reflective journal (in which you reflect on your learning experience in a course), you will be actively encouraged to express your voice using the personal "I" and to write in a less formal style. However, if you are writing a lab report in physics, use of the personal "I" may be discouraged by instructors who feel that it gives your writing an overly personal and less scientific focus. You need to find out what is appropriate for each genre.

Moreover, the term *genre* can also be understood in a wider sense in terms of the academic communities that produce texts in similar ways. There are some generally accepted norms of practice, or rules about how to write, that are common to academic fields, for example, English, education, biology, law, and engineering. In each of these fields, there are shared common practices that determine how academic texts are written. For example, people in an English department will have very different ideas about how introductions should be written compared with their colleagues in the engineering department. There may be as many differences as similarities between fields. The rules are often a little loose and flexible as not every individual within a field will agree entirely on what constitutes appropriate writing style.

Again, you need to find out what is appropriate in the different academic communities for which you write. Ask your instructor if you are unsure.

When you read and write academic texts, you should ask yourself another question:

- What forms of writing are associated with the genre of the text that I am reading/writing?

Context

The third aspect that you should consider whenever you read or write academic texts is context. Academic texts are produced in relation to many contextual factors. Central to all contexts of academic writing is the writer's purpose in writing. The next questions to ask yourself when reading and writing academic texts are the following:

- Reading: What was the purpose of the writer in writing this text?
- Writing: What is the purpose in my own writing? (Is my text a first draft, an examination, or a text written to generate ideas or for a grade?)

Making Decisions Based on Audience, Genre, and Context

Imagine that you are a guitarist playing a piece of classical music (genre) for a group of middle-aged professionals (audience) at a local arts centre for $100 per hour (context). How will you play the guitar?

What if you are playing a piece of popular music (genre) for a group of university students (audience) for free in the student bar (context)? Will you play the guitar in a different style?

It is very likely that you will perform the music in a different style on each occasion, depending on your preferences and on how you interpret the expectations associated with the particular genre, audience, and context. Academic writing is the same. You need to consider your personal preferences about writing styles and also make informed choices about what is expected of you when you write in a specific genre, for a specific audience, and in a specific context.

Now imagine that you are writing a summary of lecture notes (genre) for a classmate who missed the lecture (audience). Your classmate may be a close friend, but may have little knowledge of your subject (context). In this case, you will probably decide to write the summary in a particular way, maybe less formally and presenting a lot of facts. In contrast, if you are writing a lab report (genre) and your reader is an instructor who is an expert in her field (audience), and is going to assign a grade for the work (context), you will write in a different way, perhaps more formally and critically. The interrelationship between the writer, reader, genre, and context will determine how you write.

ACTIVE AND CRITICAL READING: WHY THEY ARE IMPORTANT

Active reading means engaging with a text actively and critically, not passively.

Passive Reading

When you are reading a novel for pleasure or a newspaper to pass the time, the way that you read, process, and internalize information can be quite passive. This is usually because you are not required to link what you are reading to another task, for example, writing an assignment that your instructor will assess, or giving an oral presentation to a class.

Active Reading

Active reading involves active engagement with the text that you are reading—you are reading for a specific academic purpose, analyzing and evaluating, rather than reading for pleasure or to pass the time. Reading an academic journal article, a book, a webpage, or a newspaper article for a writing assignment demands reading skills that are much more active.

When you read actively, you need to be selective and search for specific information that you require for your task. You cannot sit back, relax, and wait for the information from the text to come to you. You need to go to the information.

However, active reading is not just about being active and seeking out specific information. It also relates to what you do with the information when you find it. When you find information that is relevant to your task, it is not always enough to just highlight it and carry on reading. You will need to engage with the ideas more actively by taking notes and organizing the information as you read, in ways that will help you when you start the writing process.

Critical Reading

You also need to engage critically with the information that you read. Critical reading demands more than just reading and understanding the words on a page or screen. It also involves the following:

- Determining the reliability of the source
- Understanding who the writer is
- Understanding multiple voices and opinions in a text
- Thinking about what is missing from a text
- Inferring meaning when it is not stated clearly
- Considering the relevance of ideas to your writing task
- Expressing your opinion

Reading critically relates to critical thinking, which you will study in more detail in Chapter 2.

ASSESSING RELIABLE SOURCES

A quick internet search on almost any topic will find a wide range of websites with articles that discuss the topic. Any of the following may appear, in any order:

- Newspaper articles
- Academic journal articles
- Policy documents or reports from governmental and non-governmental organizations

- Policy documents and reports from political lobby groups
- Product information from commercial organizations
- Informal blogs

All are worth reading as, together, they will offer you a comprehensive overview of your subject. However, if you are intending to use information from such sources for your writing assignment, you need to ensure that the sources you use, and the information presented, are reliable. Doing this involves some basic investigative work on your part.

Why Might a Source Be Unreliable?

There are many reasons why a source might be unreliable:

- An academic journal may not have rigorous controls about what is published and what is rejected. This may be the case if the journal is not peer reviewed. (*Peer reviewed* means the articles are refereed, or reviewed, by an editorial board and academic experts before being accepted for publication.)
- A lot of information from websites may also be unreliable for academic assignments. If the website is not linked to a recognized academic, governmental, or non-governmental organization, there may be little control over what is published. In such cases, it is difficult to rely on the website's information as accurate and trustworthy.
- Not all newspaper articles are reliable. Although all newspapers have editors, not all of what they publish goes through a rigorous and scientific process of review. Many newspapers also have affiliations to corporate groups, which affect what they publish. You need to take these factors into account when citing newspaper articles in your academic writing.

Checklist for Reliable Sources

The following is a checklist you can use when trying to assess the reliability of academic journal articles, websites, newspaper articles, and news websites.

CHECKLIST FOR RELIABLE SOURCES

ACADEMIC JOURNAL ARTICLES

- ☐ Is the journal peer reviewed?
- ☐ Are the editors of the journal affiliated with reputable universities or colleges?
- ☐ Does the journal appear regularly?
- ☐ Is the journal linked to a database of recognized academic journals?
- ☐ Does the article have a clear abstract?
- ☐ Does the article have an accurate and a comprehensive reference section?
- ☐ Has the article been cited by academics in other journal articles or books?

WEBSITES

- ☐ Is the organization that runs the website recognized in the subject area that you are looking at?
- ☐ Does the organization have links to a recognized government body, charity, or academic institution?
- ☐ Does the organization have a strong political agenda that may make it biased?
- ☐ Does the content or do the statistics have an author, date, and reference section?
- ☐ Is the style of the language used on the site appropriate for serious academic discussion?
- ☐ Are bright colours or sensational images used to attract readers?
- ☐ Does the URL give any indication about the website (e.g., .org, .com, .edu)?

NEWSPAPER ARTICLES/NEWS WEBSITES

- ☐ Does the newspaper/website seem to be one that carries out serious and reliable journalism?
- ☐ Are bright colours or sensational images used to attract readers? (The use of either is often a sign that a newspaper or news website is less than serious.)
- ☐ When was the article published?
- ☐ Are opinions stated with supporting evidence from reliable sources?

TASK 1

Use a search engine to find information about **the nutritional benefits of organic food.** Assess the reliability of one academic journal article, one website, and one news article using the checklist above.

READING AROUND THE TEXT

Before you start reading the content of the text itself, it is a good idea to "read around" it first. Reading around a text involves gaining some basic background information about the text:

- What is it about?
- What do I already know about this topic?
- What is the title and/or subtitle?
- Who wrote it?
- Who published it?
- When was it published?
- What genre is it?
- What do the images, if any, imply?
- Is the writer supporting a particular viewpoint?

This information will give you a useful overview of the text before you decide whether to read it in detail to find the specific information that you need for your task.

TASK 2

See how much information you can find by reading around the newspaper article below, which is about organic food. Take **three minutes.**

1. Topic:

___

2. Title:

___

3. Subtitle:

___

4. Author:

___

5. Publisher:

___

6. Publication date:

___

7. Genre:

___

8. Images:

___

9. Author's viewpoint:

___

Margin Notes

Organic food not healthier, says FSA

KAREN MCVEIGH

Report finds organic food provides no significant nutritional benefit compared with conventionally produced food

1 Organic food is no healthier and provides no significant nutritional benefit compared with conventionally produced food, according to a new, independent study funded by the Food Standards Agency. **2** But its conclusions have been called into question by experts and organic food campaigners. **3** The report looked at evidence published over the past 50 years of the different nutrient levels found in crops and livestock from both types of farming and also at the health benefits of eating organic food. **4** The findings, partly published today in the *American Journal of Clinical Nutrition*, contradict previous work that has found organically grown food to be nutritionally superior.

5 Dr Alan Dangour, who led the review by the London School of Hygiene and Tropical Medicine, said: "Most studies were based on the hypothesis that eating organic food is beneficial to health. **6** Looking at all of the studies published in the last 50 years, we have concluded that there's no good evidence that consumption of organic food is beneficial to health based on the nutrient content." **7** He said that while small differences in nutrient content were found between organic and conventionally produced food, they were "unlikely to be of any public health relevance."

8 Organic food campaigners criticised the study for failing to consider fertiliser and pesticide residues in food. **9** They expressed disappointment at its "limited" nature, saying that without long-term studies it did not provide a clear answer on whether eating organic food has health benefits. **10** A leading food academic went further, saying he found the conclusions "selective in the extreme." **11** Peter Melchett, policy director at the Soil Association, said: "We are disappointed in the conclusions the researchers have reached. **12** It doesn't say organic food is not healthier, just that, according to the criteria they have adopted, there's no proof that it is." **13** He criticised the methodology used by the team, which he said meant they rejected as "not important" some nutritional benefits they found in organic food, and led them to different conclusions from those reached by previous studies. **14** Melchett said: "The review rejected almost all of the existing studies of comparisons between organic and non-organic nutritional differences."

15 Carlo Leifert, a professor of ecological agriculture at Newcastle University and the co-ordinator of a major EU-funded study, which recently found nutrient levels were higher in organic foods, said the conclusions of the study were selective. **16** He said: "I'm worried about the conclusions. **17** The ballpark figures they have come up with are similar to ours. **18** I don't understand why the FSA are not going away and saying, 'Right, there's something you can do on a farm to improve food.' **19** But they are so blocked by not wanting to say positive things about organic farming."

20 The appendix of the FSA report shows that some nutrients, such as beta-carotene, are as much as 53% higher in organic food, but such differences are not reflected in its conclusions. **21** The farming of organic food, which is now worth £2bn in the UK alone, is governed by strict regulations that set it apart from conventional farming. **22** Crops are not treated with artificial chemical fertilisers or pesticides, while antibiotics and drugs are not used routinely on livestock. **23** Gill Fine, the FSA director of consumer choice, defended the scope of the study. **24** She said: "We are neither anti nor pro organic food. **25** We recognise there are many reasons why people choose to eat organic, such as animal welfare or environmental concerns. **26** We specifically checked claims that organic food is better for you.

27 "This study does not mean people should not eat organic food. **28** What it shows is that there is little, if any, nutritional difference between organic and conventionally produced food and there is not evidence of additional health benefits from eating organic food." **29** When asked whether consumers had been misled over the benefits of organic food, she said: "If they are buying organic on the basis that it is healthier, then that is not the case."

30 The EU study co-ordinated by Leifert, which ended in May this year, involved 31 research and university institutes. **31** It found that levels of nutritionally desirable compounds, such as antioxidants and vitamins, were higher in organic crops, while levels of nutritionally undesirable compounds such as toxic chemicals, mycotoxins and metals such as cadmium and nickel, were lower in organic crops.

Source: Karen McVeigh. "Organic food no healthier, says official study." From *The Guardian*, 28 July 2009.

TASK 3

Assess the reliability of the *Guardian* newspaper article on organic food by using the four questions below from the Checklist for Reliable Sources. Take notes in the spaces provided under each question. Give reasons for your answers.

NEWSPAPER ARTICLES/NEWS WEBSITES

1. Does the newspaper/website seem to be one that carries out serious and reliable journalism?

____

____

____

2. Are bright colours or sensational images used to attract readers?

____

____

____

3. When was the article published?

____

____

____

4. Are opinions stated with supporting evidence from reliable sources?

____

____

____

The article on pages 8 and 9 is a British newspaper report of the findings of an American academic study. It is written in a journalistic style and with British spelling conventions. If you are going to paraphrase (write in your own words) information from a newspaper article such as this one in an academic essay, you will need to write it according to the "genre conventions" of an academic essay, not those of a newspaper article. (*Genre conventions* can be understood as rules about how to write different types of text.) Also, you will need to change some of the spelling if, for example, you are expected to use either Canadian or American spelling. However, any direct quotations (using the author's exact words) from the article should remain in the original form.

SKIMMING AND SCANNING

Another feature of passive reading that may not serve you well in academic contexts is linear reading. If you read in a linear way, it means that you read in a straight line, starting at the beginning and finishing at the end of the text. Passive linear reading does not always help you to engage actively with the ideas that you come across.

Two skills that can help you to break the habit of linear reading in academic contexts are *skimming* and *scanning*.

Skimming a Text

Skimming a text is like skimming a stone across a lake. When you skim a stone across a lake, the stone bounces off the surface of the water without reaching the depths of the lake. Similarly, when you skim a text, you are reading for gist, or the general idea of a piece of writing, rather than reading the whole text in depth. You are jumping around the text to get a general idea of what it is about, and whether it is interesting or useful for your purpose.

TASK 4

Take **one minute** to skim the article below, published online by the Soil Association, a UK-based non-governmental organization that regulates and campaigns in favour of organic food, in response to the FSA report. One way to skim the article is by looking for the topic sentence, which states the main idea, in each paragraph. In many cases, you can find a topic sentence at the beginning of a paragraph. In the margin, take note of the topic of the paragraph. Then move on to the next paragraph. Do not read the whole article.

FSA report on organic food—our response

Margin Notes

SOIL ASSOCIATION

1 As you may be aware, the Food Standards Agency (FSA) has just published a report on organic food, which claims that there are no significant benefits to be gained from eating organic. **2** This is a serious piece of research, and the Soil Association will examine its conclusion seriously—however at first glance the research appears to be a fairly limited piece of analysis. **3** For example, the review only looked at research papers with abstracts written in English, it excluded the results of more than half the papers it found, and it ignored more up-to-date research from the European Union, completed in April this year (despite knowing this research was due to be published). **4** You can read our initial response to the report by following the link below, and in due course we will of course respond more fully. PARA. 1

BIGGER BENEFITS

5 That all said, it's a popular myth that people who buy organic food only do so because they think it will make them healthier. **6** Recent EU research has found that regular buyers of organic food (who buy about 80% of all organic products) have a much more sophisticated understanding of the range of benefits that organic farming and food deliver. PARA. 2

7 For example, the review failed to address the issue of the long-term effects of pesticides, herbicides and insecticides on human health. **8** The European Commission, in 2006, reported links between certain cancers, male infertility and nervous system disorders and exposure to pesticides. **9** The average industrially-produced apple may have been sprayed up to 16 times with 30 different chemicals. PARA. 3

10 Buying organic food also promotes a healthy environment. **11** Organic farms have on average 30% more species and 50% more wildlife like birds, butterflies and bees. **12** Compassion in World Farming, the recognised experts, say organic farming has the potential for the highest animal welfare standards. **13** Other environmental benefits are self evident—there's less dangerous waste on organic farms. **14** Artificial nitrogen fertiliser is PARA. 4

banned in organic farming, so there's less run-off of nutrients that cause algae blooms in coastal waters.

PARA. 5 **15** There are more women and younger people involved in organic farming and organic farmers are more optimistic about the future. **16** That future will be dominated by climate change. **17** Here organic farming is leading the way, insisting on using solar powered fertility through crops like red clover that fix nitrogen into the soil for subsequent crops. **18** For our own health and the health of the planet, organic food and farming will play a big part in our future.

Source: "FSA report on organic food—our response." Courtesy of Soil Association. www.soilassociation.org.

TASK 5

Look back at your margin notes from Task 4, in which you noted the topic of each paragraph through skimming the text. Match each paragraph with the related topic below. The first one is an example.

Paragraph 1 → b)	a) Reasons why people buy organic food
Paragraph 2	b) Information about the FSA report
Paragraph 3	c) Organic farming and the future
Paragraph 4	d) Pesticide chemicals and health risks
Paragraph 5	e) Environmental benefits of organic food

Scanning a Text

When you scan something, you are looking for something specific; for example, a medical scan will look for specific things in the body, like a torn muscle. Scanning a text involves looking for and locating specific information or key ideas. These are usually specific pieces of information that will help you to answer a question, develop an argument, or use as an example to support an idea in your writing. The information may be located anywhere in the text.

An effective way to scan a text is to take note of the main information that you are looking for and to search for it by focusing on related key words. For example, if you are looking for information about the specific findings of the FSA report in the Soil Association article above, look for related words: *research*, *conclusions*, *findings*, *results*, etc. When you find any of these related words, you should read the surrounding text in more detail to find out the specific information that you need.

TASK 6

Scan the Soil Association article above for the following information only. You need to find specific information in each of the paragraphs. See how many questions you can answer in **two minutes** by scanning the article.

Paragraph 1:	Did the FSA report cite studies with abstracts written in languages other than English?
Paragraph 2:	Do people who buy organic food buy it only for health reasons?
Paragraph 3:	How many times is the average industrially produced apple sprayed?
Paragraph 4:	What is banned in organic farming?
Paragraph 5:	What topic will dominate the future?

ANNOTATING TEXT

Merely highlighting or underlining important information and then moving on is a passive form of reading academic texts. One way to focus on important information in a more active way is to annotate the text.

Annotation is a useful form of active reading that involves taking notes as you read; it can be used in addition to or instead of highlighting or underlining important information. These notes can be made in the margin of the text. Annotation goes beyond just focusing on the main ideas that you find in a text. It also involves adding more subjective notes. These subjective notes are part of your active and critical engagement with the text. For example, you can add notes that give your opinion of the information, that comment on the validity and relevance of the information, or that highlight new or unanswered questions you may have as you read.

All of these annotations are intended to help you locate information when it comes to structuring and writing an assignment. Moreover, by writing down the annotations, you process and internalize ideas more effectively. Annotating can also be more time-efficient than only highlighting or underlining; this is because it can save you having to re-read highlighted or underlined sections of text and forming opinions at a later stage. It will save valuable time as you plan the initial stages of writing your assignment.

The following six questions will guide you as you practise active and critical reading through annotation.

SIX ANNOTATION QUESTIONS

1. What is the main point of this sentence/paragraph/section?
2. Do I agree with this idea? Why or why not?
3. Is this idea relevant to my focus and task?
4. Does the author back up ideas with reasons, examples, and/or evidence?
5. Is the argument logical and convincing? Why or why not?
6. Do I have any questions about this?

TASK 7

Read and annotate the newspaper article "Organic food not healthier, says FSA," focusing on the six annotation questions. To save time when writing up the notes, you can also highlight or underline in the article the main idea you are referring to.

LOCATING DIFFERENT VOICES AND OPINIONS AS YOU READ

Academic articles, or newspaper articles that discuss academic research, often present the reader with a range of different voices, ideas, arguments, and statistics. An important critical reading skill is to find your way around the multiple opinions, voices, and ideas that can be found in a text. As part of your critical engagement with the text, you need to understand and explain to your reader *who thinks what*, that is, to whom different ideas or opinions belong.

Attribution

As you read and annotate an academic text, it is important to remember "attribution." The term *attribution* in academic writing means making it clear to your reader *who thinks what*. As you read and write, you need to attribute ideas to different people, including yourself. In this way, you allow your reader to locate different voices and opinions in your writing.

Imagine that you are writing a summary of the newspaper article "Organic food not healthier, says FSA." Your reader will need to know if opinions belong to a supporter or opponent of organic food or to you. So, as you take notes, remember to attribute the different ideas and opinions. In Chapters 3 and 5, you will learn more about the language of attribution.

TASK 8

Scan the newspaper article "Organic food not healthier, says FSA" for the information listed below. Attribute the ideas in List 1 (listed by sentence numbers) to the person, organization, or research project in List 2 (listed by letters a to g).

LIST 1

Sentences 1 and 4 — Organic food is no healthier and provides no significant nutritional benefit compared with conventionally produced food . . . The study contradicts previous work that has found organically grown food to be nutritionally superior.

Attributed to ______________________

Sentence 6 — There is no good evidence that consumption of organic food is beneficial to health based on the nutrient content.

Attributed to ______________________

Sentences 8 and 9 — The study failed to consider fertilizer and pesticide residues in food, and it did not provide a clear answer on whether eating organic food has health benefits.

Attributed to ______________________

Sentences 10 and 14 — The conclusions of the study are selective in the extreme . . . The review rejected almost all of the existing studies of comparisons between organic and non-organic nutritional differences.

Attributed to ______________________

Sentence 19	The FSA does not want to say positive things about organic farming.
	Attributed to ____________________
Sentence 20	The appendix of the FSA report shows that some nutrients, such as beta-carotene, are as much as 53 percent higher in organic food, but such differences are not reflected in its conclusions.
	Attributed to ____________________
Sentences 25, 26, and 28	The study is valid as it looked specifically at claims that organic food is better for you, irrespective of animal welfare and environmental concerns . . . and there is not evidence of additional health benefits from eating organic food.
	Attributed to ____________________

LIST 2

a) Dr. Alan Dangour
b) A new, independent study funded by the Food Standards Agency (FSA)
c) Gill Fine, the FSA director of consumer choice
d) A leading food academic, Peter Melchett, policy director at the Soil Association
e) Carlo Leifert, of Newcastle University
f) Karen McVeigh, journalist
g) Organic food campaigners

READING BETWEEN THE LINES: INFERENCE

Inference is another important critical reading skill. You need to infer meaning when ideas and opinions in a text are ambiguous, or not stated in a clear or explicit way.

Authors of academic articles or newspaper articles that present findings from academic studies do not always present their opinions clearly. There may be a number of reasons why this is the case. Some authors may unconsciously write in such a way. Others may intentionally choose to write in a style that expresses opinions implicitly, hoping to make the reader work a little to tease out those underlying opinions. And others may feel that they are not in a position to state a controversial opinion explicitly, perhaps due to expectations that they should present information impartially, without criticizing one side or the other.

When opinions and ideas are expressed implicitly or indirectly, your task as a reader becomes a little more demanding as you are required to *infer meaning*, or *read between the lines*.

TASK 9

Look at the following two excerpts from the newspaper article "Organic food not healthier, says FSA" and answer the questions in your own words. In both cases, the statements have implicit meanings that require inference skills on the part of the reader.

EXCERPT 1

Sentence 19: Carlo Leifert, of Newcastle University
"'But they are so blocked by not wanting to say positive things about organic farming.'"

QUESTION: Leifert's statement about the FSA not wanting to say positive things about organic farming is his opinion, but it also has wider implied meaning about the FSA's research findings. What do you infer from it? Why might the meaning be expressed implicitly rather than in a more explicit way?

____

____

____

EXCERPT 2

Sentence 20: Karen McVeigh, journalist
"The appendix of the FSA report shows that some nutrients, such as beta-carotene, are as much as 53% higher in organic food, but such differences are not reflected in its conclusions."

QUESTION: McVeigh is the journalist who wrote the newspaper article. She states that although the FSA shows that some organic foods have higher nutrient value, this is not raised in the conclusion. What meaning do you infer from this statement? Why might a journalist critique a study in this way and not more directly?

____

____

____

TASK 10

The two excerpts above are from a newspaper article reporting on the findings of a scientific study. Do you think that the implicit way that opinions are stated in these two excerpts would work in an academic essay? Why or why not?

____

____

____

FOCUSING ON WHAT IS NOT SAID

Critical reading is not just about critically evaluating what is said in an article. You may also need to consider *what is not said*: what a writer has chosen not to include in an article and why. What writers do not say in an article can, at times, be as relevant as what they do say.

The reasons why writers may not have included important information in an article cannot usually be ascertained from reading their work. It may be that they simply did not have time or space in the article to cover everything. Or, it may be that they have intentionally omitted information that does not fit with their position. It is your role as a critical reader to look for and consider information that is absent as well as information that is present.

Critiquing by Highlighting What Is Not Said

The Soil Association article on pages 11 and 12 is a response to the FSA report. It focuses on what the FSA report *did not mention* about the nutritional value of organic food. By raising a number of missing factors, the Soil Association is critiquing the FSA report and bringing new ideas and arguments to the debate.

TASK 11

List four factors that the Soil Association article explicitly highlights as being ignored by the FSA report. Include the sentence numbers.

1. ______________________________

____

2. ______________________________

____

3. ______________________________

____

4. ______________________________

____

ANALYZING STYLE AND FORMALITY

The Soil Association response to the FSA report appears on the organization's website and is written in a less formal style than many types of academic writing.

TASK 12

Why do you think the Soil Association article is written in a less formal style than the *Guardian* newspaper article? Think of the *genre* (the type of text) and *audience* (the intended readers).

____

____

____

WRITING SUMMARIES

Writing summaries is a common task in most academic disciplines. You may be asked to summarize the content of an academic article, a book, or a collection of works by one or more authors, for example. The three keys to writing successful summaries are *selecting the main ideas, representing the main ideas accurately,* and *being concise.*

1. **Selecting the main ideas**

   Writing a summary involves making important decisions about what to include and what not to include. As you read and take notes, you need to decide which main ideas will be included in the summary.

2. **Representing the main ideas accurately**

   When writing summaries, it is very important to represent ideas accurately. Make sure that you do not change the meaning of ideas.

3. **Being concise**

   Whenever you write a summary, you need to be concise. Normally, you will be required to stay within a designated number of paragraphs, pages, or words. Part of the skill of summary writing is being able to use language effectively to express ideas in as few words as possible.

Giving Your Opinion?

You would not normally be expected to give your own opinion in a summary unless specifically instructed to do so. Summaries are normally written in a rather objective tone, that is, a tone in which your opinion as a writer is not given prominence. If you are instructed to add your own opinion in a summary (for example, in a critical summary), then you should use a more subjective tone, and tell your reader whether you are convinced by the ideas that you are summarizing.

Guidelines for Summary Writing

Although there is no standard way to write a summary, many writers use a number of common strategies.

1. In the first sentence of a summary, it is common to include the following:
   - The title of the article/book
   - The name of the author
   - The name of the publisher/journal
   - The date of publication
   - The general topic

   EXAMPLE
   In the article "Organic food not healthier, says FSA," written by journalist Karen McVeigh in July 2009 for the *Guardian* newspaper, the nutritional benefits of organic food are discussed.

2. If there is a general statement that sums up the article, it can be included after the first sentence in the form of either a direct quotation (using the original words) or a paraphrase (changing the original words).

> **EXAMPLE: Direct quotation**
> McVeigh begins by stating that the report from the Food Standards Agency found that organic food provides "no significant nutritional benefit compared with conventionally produced food."
>
> **EXAMPLE: Paraphrase**
> McVeigh begins by stating that the report from the Food Standards Agency found that organic food does not provide major nutritional benefits when compared with food that is conventionally produced.

3. After the first sentences, a series of short paragraphs may follow (depending on the required length) in which the main ideas of the article are stated. It is normal to include the idea, and then to summarize any reasons, supporting examples, or evidence that the author provides.

TASK 13

Write a one-page summary, double-spaced, of the article "Organic food not healthier, says FSA." Read through your annotations again and look for the main ideas you think should be included in the summary. You need to be selective. Remember to represent the ideas accurately and to be concise. For this summary, it is not necessary to include your own opinions; therefore, you should try to write in a more objective style. You will practise adding your own opinion to a summary in Chapter 2.

PEER REVIEW OF YOUR WORK

Peer review is a form of peer-based learning, through which you and your peers (in this case, your classmates or friends) read one another's work and comment on it. Peer review can help you to improve your writing in two important ways: you can learn a lot by receiving different ideas from different readers, and you can learn a lot and improve your own writing by reading others' work.

Remember: when you review others' writing, your comments should always be constructive. If you are commenting on strengths and weaknesses, try to do so not only in a friendly way but also in a way that can help other writers develop their writing.

TASK 14

After you have written your own one-page summary, read it through carefully and do a self-review of your work by using the Summary Writing Peer Review Worksheet below. After you have done a self-review, ask a classmate or friend to review your work with the same worksheet. Compare the responses from both peer review worksheets.

SUMMARY WRITING PEER REVIEW WORKSHEET

Name of reviewer: ______________________________

1. **First two sentences**
   Does the first sentence of the summary include any of the following:
   - The title of the article ______________________________
   - The name of the author ______________________________
   - The name of the publisher ______________________________
   - The date of publication ______________________________
   - The general topic ______________________________

   Does the second sentence contain a statement that effectively sums up the article?

   ____

   ____

   ____

   ____

   ____

2. **Content**
   Does the writer select what you consider to be the main ideas from the article? Are any main ideas missing from the summary? Are any ideas present in the summary that you think should not be included? Are the original author's ideas represented accurately in the summary?

   ____

   ____

   ____

   ____

   ____

3. **Style**
   Is the summary written in an objective style? Does the writer of the summary express his or her own opinions? Is the level of formality appropriate? Is there a good range of vocabulary, grammar, and sentence structures?

   ____

   ____

   ____

   ____

   ____

4. **Format**
Is the summary one page and double spaced? Does the writer use separate paragraphs for each new idea?

5. **Accuracy**
Comment on the accuracy of the grammar, spelling, vocabulary, and punctuation.

6. **Strengths and weaknesses**
First describe what you feel to be the strengths of the writing. Then mention any areas that you feel could be improved to make the summary better for you as a reader.

CHAPTER 1 SUMMARY

In this chapter, you have studied the importance of active and critical reading, and writing summaries.

ACTIVE AND CRITICAL READING: WHY THEY ARE IMPORTANT

Reading actively involves seeking out ideas in the text rather than sitting back and waiting for them to come to you. It also involves annotating text as you read, taking notes of the main ideas in a text and noting your opinions and any questions that come to mind as you read. These annotations will help you to organize your essay or summary, and they will save you time, too.

Reading critically is closely tied to active reading. To read critically, you need to read around the text before you read the text itself; assess the reliability of the source as well as the ideas in the text; understand who thinks what and make this clear to your reader as you write your essay or summary; use inference skills when ideas are not clearly stated and ask why when ideas are absent. It is also important to be aware of the writing style and take into consideration whether you should follow that style in your own writing.

WRITING SUMMARIES

Three important things to remember when writing summaries are carefully selecting the main ideas in a text, representing these ideas accurately, and being concise. It is not always clear whether your own opinions as a writer should be explicitly stated when you write summaries: as a general rule, unless you are instructed to do so, you would normally not include your own opinion. If you are unsure, ask your instructor.

PEER REVIEW OF YOUR WORK

It is useful to do a self-review before you ask someone to do a peer review of your work. This will enable you to focus on what you think are the strengths and weaknesses of your own writing. Moreover, peer review will always benefit your writing: you gain insight from others who read your work, as well as by reading others' work yourself.

CHAPTER 2

Thinking and Writing Critically

In this chapter, you will study the following aspects of thinking and writing critically:

- ✓ Understanding critical thinking
- ✓ Stating your arguments
- ✓ Avoiding logical fallacies
- ✓ Exploring critical thinking through writing
- ✓ Writing a critique

Chapter 2 builds upon the aspects of active and critical reading that you studied in Chapter 1. In this chapter, you will learn about thinking critically. You will also study some common forms of "uncritical thinking" that you will need to avoid during your studies.

The information in these first two chapters is also closely related to Chapters 6 to 10, in which you will learn how to organize your ideas in different ways for different modes of writing across the disciplines.

UNDERSTANDING CRITICAL THINKING

TASK 1

What do you understand by the term *critical thinking*?

In the box below, take **four or five minutes** to write down what you understand by the term. This is freestyle writing: you can write in any style you choose. The main thing is to get as many ideas as possible down on paper.

EXPLORATORY WRITING: WHAT IS CRITICAL THINKING?

____

____

____

____

____

____

____

____

____

____

Three Key Learning Skills in Critical Thinking

In order to be a successful writer at university, you need to be able to think critically and to express your critical thinking in your writing. Critical thinking involves complex and challenging processes of thinking that bring together many skills of analysis and evaluation.

Becoming a critical, or more critical, thinker involves developing three key learning skills:

1. **The ability to think about arguments and ideas in new ways**

   First, critical thinking requires "thinking outside of the box." In other words, when you come across arguments, you need to be open to thinking beyond your comfort zone. This will allow you to form knowledge and understand situations in new ways. This learning skill has a long history.

   > **EXAMPLE**
   > In the sixteenth and seventeenth centuries, it was commonly believed that the sun revolved around the Earth. As a result of developing a basic telescopic lens and studying the cosmos, Galileo Galilee argued that, in fact, it was the other way around—the Earth revolved around the sun. His observations allowed him to understand the relationship between the Earth and the sun in new ways. This involved analysis and challenging established ideas about the world.

2. **The ability to look at problems and issues from many different angles**

   We often face difficult issues and problems in our daily lives, and sometimes in our academic studies. There is not always a clear way of dealing with these issues and problems. To find solutions, we usually need to think critically and analyze a situation from different angles.

   > **EXAMPLE**
   > The downtown eastside of Vancouver has a large number of homeless people. One solution to the problem has been for the local government to increase the

number of beds in homeless shelters so that no one has to sleep on the streets. However, the number of people sleeping on the streets has not gone down as much as expected. Why not? To find answers to this question, the problem needs to be looked at from many different angles: Has the increased help for the homeless had the unintended outcome of attracting more homeless people to the city? Are the people who are still sleeping on the streets suffering from addictions and mental illness, which also need to be addressed? Are the new beds in homeless shelters inadequate? Are they safe and clean enough? Only by thinking critically and asking these and many more questions can effective solutions be found.

3. **The ability to recognize the limitations of your own arguments and consider counter-arguments and opposing views**

   It is human nature to disagree on many issues. It is also human nature to think that you are right and others are wrong. How, then, can you persuade your reader, or the person listening to you, that you are right and the others are wrong? Or should you even be thinking in those terms? If you learn how to recognize the limitations of your own arguments, and to consider counter-arguments and opposing points of view, you might actually strengthen your existing view, or you may shift to a compromise somewhere between two opposites.

   EXAMPLE

   You are preparing a presentation on allowing more offshore oil drilling in Canadian coastal waters. You are firmly in favour of offshore drilling as you believe that it will give Canada greater energy independence. However, you know that there are many counter-arguments and that many people oppose offshore drilling on environmental grounds. How can you persuade them to agree with your opinion? One way is to think critically by recognizing their counter-arguments and getting into their minds to understand why they hold their views: Are their concerns justified? Are there alternative routes to energy independence? Considering your own limitations and counter-arguments can strengthen your arguments. You may even end up agreeing with some of your opponents' reasons and moderating your own position as a result.

The three learning skills above will help you start to become a more effective critical thinker when dealing with problems and solutions, causes and effects, and arguments and counter-arguments. Developing these ways of thinking can help you in your academic writing as well as your everyday life.

STATING YOUR ARGUMENTS

When you transfer your critical thinking skills to academic writing, your writing needs to reflect the complex thinking processes you have gone through in forming your arguments. You need to back up your arguments with reasons, examples, and evidence. You also need to recognize and consider a range of counter-arguments.

Supporting Your Arguments with Reasons, Examples, and Evidence

Imagine that you are writing an essay on whether the legal age for drinking alcohol in the United States should be lowered. You argue that lowering the legal age from

21 to 18 would likely result in an increase in deaths caused by drunk driving. If you just state this argument alone, it is unlikely that your reader will be convinced. By adding reasons, examples, and evidence, you can make your argument far more convincing.

> **EXAMPLE 1: Argument**
> I believe that changing the United States Federal Uniform Drinking Age Act, by lowering the legal drinking age from 21 to 18, will lead to an increase in deaths on the road caused by drunk driving.
>
> **EXAMPLE 2: Argument + reason**
> I believe that changing the United States Federal Uniform Drinking Age Act, by lowering the legal drinking age from 21 to 18, will lead to an increase in deaths on the road caused by drunk driving. This is because more young drivers will be tempted to drive while under the influence of alcohol.
>
> **EXAMPLE 3: Argument + reason + example**
> I believe that changing the United States Federal Uniform Drinking Age Act, by lowering the legal drinking age from 21 to 18, will lead to an increase in deaths on the road caused by drunk driving. This is because more young drivers will be tempted to drive while under the influence of alcohol. Many young people in US states travel to social gatherings by car rather than public transport. If 18-year-olds were legally able to drink alcohol in bars and clubs, more drunk teens would find themselves behind the wheel at the end of a night out.
>
> **EXAMPLE 4: Argument + reason + example + evidence**
> I believe that changing the United States Federal Uniform Drinking Age Act, by lowering the legal drinking age from 21 to 18, will lead to an increase in deaths on the road caused by drunk driving. This is because more young drivers will be tempted to drive while under the influence of alcohol. Many young people in US states travel to social gatherings by car rather than public transport. If 18-year-olds were legally able to drink alcohol in bars and clubs, more drunk teens would find themselves behind the wheel at the end of a night out. In fact, it has been reported by MADD (Mothers Against Drunk Driving) that before the legal drinking age was raised to 21 across the United States, underage drunk drivers were involved in more than double the number of fatal traffic crashes.[1]
>
> ---
>
> [1] The statistic in the MADD article is as follows: "For example, before the 21 minimum legal drinking age was implemented by all states, underage drunk drivers were involved in over twice as many fatal traffic crashes."
> *Source:* Fell, James. From "Chapter 2: Federalism: Resolved, the Federal Government should restore each State's freedom to set its drinking age." in Ellis, Richard and Nelson, Michael (eds.) Debating Reform. CQPress Publishers, Fall 2009.

What was originally an argument lacking support and evidence is now, in Example 4, backed up with a reason, example, and evidence from a reliable source. As a result, the reader is much more likely to give the writer's argument serious consideration. However, before you go further, you need to recognize the possible limitations of your argument, and to consider possible counter-arguments.

Recognizing Limitations of Your Own Arguments, and Considering Counter-Arguments

Even if you are convinced that you are right, you should recognize the limitations of your own arguments and consider counter-arguments. This will make your argument stronger and more convincing. In this case, you can ask yourself the following questions:

1. How reliable is my argument?
2. Are there any counter-arguments to my argument?

By asking yourself these questions, you are critically engaging with your own arguments as well as those of others. In the case of Example 4 above, asking these questions broadens your argument as follows:

1. **How reliable is my argument?**

   The argument that a lower drinking age will lead to more deaths involving underage drunk drivers is based on a statistic from MADD (see the footnote in Example 4 on page 26). But how reliable is this statistic?

   Are there other ways to prevent more deaths on the roads from underage drinking? (For example, more effective policing, education programs, improved public transport.)

2. **Are there any counter-arguments to my argument?**

   There are usually a lot of counter-arguments to any argument. In this case, the writer could consider several counter-arguments that those in favour of a lower legal drinking age might raise:

   In most Canadian provinces, the legal drinking age is 19: might there be US-specific factors to consider in this case?

   Would this link between legal drinking age and deaths on the road still be relevant in European countries with low legal drinking ages and advanced public transport systems?

By recognizing the limitations of your own arguments and considering counter-arguments, you can strengthen your own arguments. This is the case whether you stick with your original argument or whether you moderate it somewhat. Either way, you are showing that you have a broad awareness of the issues in the debate, and that you are able to consider the debate from multiple angles and perspectives. You are effectively developing your own position within an ongoing debate.

Positioning Yourself within an Ongoing Debate

Most of the arguments that you present in your writing have already been discussed and debated by others: in tutorial groups, lecture theatres, blogs, newspapers, academic journal articles, and books. Your argument, therefore, is one view within a broad scholarly community. When expressing this view, you need to show clearly where it fits into the ongoing debate within your scholarly community.

Your "position" can be your *personal opinion* about the information you are reading. Which side of the argument do you stand on: in favour, against, or somewhere in between? Wherever you stand, you should let your reader know you have a clear opinion, and that you have developed that opinion through balanced analysis and evaluation.

Your "position" can also relate to *the relevance of the information* you are studying to the specific focus of your study or research. For example, if your essay on lowering the legal drinking age were focusing on the UK, where the legal drinking age is 18, you would need to question the relevance of US-based data such as that from MADD.

TASK 2

Add reasons, examples, and counter-arguments to the two arguments below. Expand upon the counter-argument (possibly with a reason and examples). Then add your position. The first one is an example.

EXAMPLE

Argument
Buying organic food is good for the environment.

Reason
Supporters would argue that organic products do not use pesticides.

Example
For example, non-organic apples are sprayed many times before reaching supermarkets.

Counter-argument
A large amount of organic food is transported long distances.

Expand
The fuel emissions contribute to global warming and pollution.
Organic apples flown from Chile to North America are flown many thousands of miles and thus have a large carbon footprint.

My position
Buying organic food alone is clearly not always good for the environment. Instead, we should be thinking about buying local food, ideally organic, that is not transported long distances.

ARGUMENT 1

Argument
All university tuition fees should be abolished.

Reason
This is because

____

____

Example
For example,

____

____

Counter-argument

____

____

____

Expand

My position

ARGUMENT 2

Argument
School uniforms should be compulsory in all primary and secondary schools.

Reason
Supporters would argue that

Example
For example,

Counter-argument

Expand

My position

AVOIDING LOGICAL FALLACIES

What is a logical fallacy? If an argument is logical, it follows generally recognized conventions of science and thought. The term *logical fallacy* refers to various forms of illogical arguments, that is, arguments that fail to follow the rules of logic. Logical fallacies can be the result of many kinds of *uncritical thinking*. They are often the result of uncritical thinking that relates to the following four factors:

- Inaccurate generalization
- A misunderstanding or misrepresentation of cause-and-effect relationships
- Weak or inaccurate statements about the opinions and actions of others
- Weak logic

Logical Fallacies Based on Generalization

Many common logical fallacies are the result of inaccurate generalization. Two common types of logical fallacy based on inaccurate generalization are *hasty generalizations* and *stereotypes*.

Margin Notes

TASK 3

Read the two numbered descriptions of logical fallacies based on inaccurate generalization below. Then match the descriptions to the examples and explanations that follow. Write the letter for the corresponding example and explanation in the margin.

DESCRIPTIONS

1. **The "hasty generalization" fallacy: reaching a conclusion too quickly**
With a hasty generalization, speakers or writers reach a conclusion too quickly, ignoring important evidence or facts that are needed to make the conclusions valid. Hasty generalizations can be the result of looking at an isolated incident that is not representative, and then reaching an inaccurate conclusion about the incident.

2. **The "stereotype" fallacy: tarring all with the same brush**
Some hasty generalizations result in stereotyping, which involves making a judgmental and non-representative statement about the characteristics of a whole group of people, without evidence to back up the statement.

EXAMPLES AND EXPLANATIONS

a) **EXAMPLE**
An international exchange student is staying with your family for a home-stay. He doesn't like the food he has on his first day with your family. When he phones home to his family the next day, he tells his family that the food in your country is awful.
EXPLANATION
The international student is making a general statement about all food in your country, but basing his statement on only one meal that he had with your family. He has insufficient evidence or experience to make such a statement.

b) **EXAMPLE**
English football supporters drink too much beer and fight a lot.
EXPLANATION
Many people around the world have seen shocking news reports of English football supporters misbehaving at international tournaments. However, the statement is based on the assumption that all English football supporters behave in this way, when of course they do not. Those seen on the news are a small minority that does not represent the larger group.

Logical Fallacies Based on Cause and Effect

Sometimes, logical fallacies are the result of someone making a false assumption about actions or states (*causes*) and their results (*effects*). Two common examples of logical fallacies based on cause and effect are the *post hoc fallacy* and the *slippery slope fallacy*.

TASK 4

Margin Notes

Read the two numbered descriptions of logical fallacies based on cause and effect below. Then match the descriptions to the examples and explanations that follow. Write the letter for the corresponding example and explanation in the margin.

DESCRIPTIONS

1. **The "post hoc" fallacy: A causes B because A precedes B**

   This logical fallacy mixes up a chronological sequence (A happening then B) with causality (A causes B to happen): in other words, because one event occurred before another, the first event is said to have caused the second event. However, in this fallacy, other possible causes have been ignored.

2. **The "slippery slope" fallacy: one bad thing inevitably leads to something worse**

   The slippery slope fallacy suggests that if one event (A) happens, it will automatically lead to a series of consequential events (B, C, and D). According to the logic, or lack of it, in the fallacy, in order to prevent B, C, and D from occurring, A must be prevented from taking place.

EXAMPLES AND EXPLANATIONS

a) **EXAMPLE**
As marijuana is a "gateway drug" that leads to the use of more addictive drugs such as cocaine, crystal meth, and heroin, it should never be legalized, even for medical use.
EXPLANATION
The above argument is based on the view that marijuana users have no control in limiting their drug use and that they will lose their grip and end up on a path of drug addiction. However, the writer has provided no evidence to back up this assumption. It may indeed be the case that many users of hard drugs start with marijuana, but from that premise it cannot be assumed that all marijuana users will become hard drug users.

b) **EXAMPLE**
The municipal government is responsible for the dramatic increase in the number of forest fires in the area because it lifted the ban on campfires.

EXPLANATION

In the example above, the writer is assuming that the first event caused the second event. Indeed, it may be possible that one or two of the forest fires were caused as a result of the lifting of the ban on campfires. However, other possible causes are being ignored, such as drivers discarding cigarettes from their cars, lightning striking, or fires being set intentionally by malicious arsonists. Even though the two events are related in time sequence, the writer has not provided any evidence that A caused B.

Logical Fallacies Based on Others' Opinions and Actions

Another common form of logical fallacy is one that is based on false assumptions or false representations of others' opinions and actions. Three such examples are the *straw man fallacy*, the *ad populum fallacy*, and the *ad hominem fallacy*.

Margin Notes

TASK 5

Read the three numbered descriptions of logical fallacies based on others' opinions and actions below. Then match the descriptions to the examples and explanations that follow. Write the letter for the corresponding example and explanation in the margin.

DESCRIPTIONS

1. **The "straw man" fallacy: misrepresenting others' opinions for your own purposes**
The straw man fallacy involves taking an argument that an opponent would hold, changing or misrepresenting the argument to make it seem weaker, and then criticizing the argument for being weak. You thus create a straw man that is very easy to knock down.
2. **The "ad populum" fallacy: if most people believe it, it's got to be right**
This logical fallacy can come in many forms. The ad populum fallacy involves attempting to strengthen your position by pointing out that the ideas that you support have popular support among a community. You then cite that popular support to justify and support your idea or opinion.
3. **The "ad hominem" fallacy: shooting the messenger, not the idea**
Ad hominem fallacies involve directing your focus or attack on the person who is associated with an idea rather than the actual idea itself.

EXAMPLES AND EXPLANATIONS

a) **EXAMPLE**
Prime Minister: "The Leader of the Opposition comes from a very wealthy family and was educated at one of the country's top private schools. What right does he have to criticize our policies on public education?"
EXPLANATION
Here, the prime minister is making a personal attack on the privileged educational background of the leader of the opposition, and suggesting that because of his background, his views on public education have no value. There is no mention of the actual policies, just an attack on the person.

b) **EXAMPLE**
Politician: "The majority of the people in this country support the death penalty for murder when they are asked in opinion polls. It is now time for us to change the law and to respect the view of the majority."

EXPLANATION
The politician is arguing for the death penalty for murder based on the fact that the majority of people in the country have stated support for it in opinion polls. This is a direct appeal to "popular wisdom" that ignores complex moral and practical issues around the debate: Does a government have the right to take a life? Is the legal system reliable enough to sentence people to death? And does the death penalty provide an effective deterrent against violent crime? Although the popular appeal may be effective in politics, in critical thinking and academic writing the wider issues in the ongoing debate need to be brought into the discussion.

c) **EXAMPLE**
Opponents of extending free public health care want the poor to carry on suffering from curable illnesses. Their opposition is uncaring and threatens the health of the nation.

EXPLANATION
The writer has put forward the view that opponents of free public health care are uncaring and want the poor to suffer. The writer clearly supports free public health care. Yet he or she is misrepresenting the views of opponents, as it is very unlikely, and there is no evidence to suggest, that opponents would be happy to see the poor die from curable illnesses. Opponents may have other concerns about a free system that relate to issues such as health insurance and longer wait times for treatment. The author has clearly set up a misrepresentative weak argument that seems easy to attack and knock down.

3 Other Logical Fallacies Based on Weak Logic

Other logical fallacies are simply the result of weak logic and careless skills of argument. The speaker or writer makes a statement and reaches a conclusion with gaps in the logic. Many such examples of this more general type of logical fallacy exist. Three of the most common ones are the *circular logic fallacy*, the *false dichotomy fallacy*, and the *red herring fallacy*.

TASK 6

Margin Notes

Read the three numbered descriptions of logical fallacies based on weak logic below. Then match the descriptions to the examples and explanations that follow. Write the letter for the corresponding example and explanation in the margin.

DESCRIPTIONS

1. **The "circular logic" fallacy: avoid the question by saying things twice**
When speakers or writers present a fallacy based on circular logic, they make a statement or argument and then back it up simply by restating the same idea.
2. **The "false dichotomy" fallacy: either A or B and nothing in between**
In this logical fallacy, readers or listeners are presented with an argument and then offered two opposite options around which they are expected to form a conclusion. These two opposites are presented as the only two options to consider, when other options exist.
3. **The "red herring" fallacy : distract the audience by presenting irrelevant information**
A red herring was a rotting fish that would be dragged behind horses during a fox hunt. Its scent would distract the hounds, thus prolonging the hunt. A red herring fallacy

involves introducing an irrelevant argument that distracts your reader or listener from the original idea.

EXAMPLES AND EXPLANATIONS

a) **EXAMPLE**

I support the introduction of speed cameras on busy roads to reduce the number of accidents, in spite of civil liberty and privacy concerns. An increase in gasoline prices might also help to prevent accidents.

EXPLANATION

The person presenting the argument above has introduced an argument that distracts attention away from how opponents might object—on the grounds of civil liberties—to speed cameras. Although higher fuel prices may mean that fewer car journeys are made, and thus fewer accidents may occur as a result, this is of little relevance to the discussion on civil liberties.

b) **EXAMPLE**

Legalization of narcotic drugs will neither reduce crime nor free up police time. The government should oppose legalization, because more people having legal access to drugs will lead to more crime and greater demands upon the country's police forces.

EXPLANATION

In the example above, in the first statement and the concluding statement the writer is saying the same thing rather than bringing in examples and evidence to back up the view being presented. The reader needs to be presented with some supporting evidence to be convinced.

c) **EXAMPLE**

George W. Bush, 2001: "You're either with us or against us in the fight against terror."

EXPLANATION

In his speech to the United Nations General Assembly in 2001, US president George W. Bush presented the world with this logical fallacy. In the highly complex debate about the world's response to the 9/11 terrorist attacks, he reduced the argument to two opposite options, ignoring all of the arguments in between supporting and opposing US foreign policy. No other option was offered to the UN audience and to the worldwide TV audience.

EXPLORING CRITICAL THINKING THROUGH WRITING

An effective way to practise thinking critically is to engage with ideas, opinions, and arguments, and with your reactions to them, through exploratory writing. In each of the exploratory writing tasks in this section, you will be required to think and write critically by engaging with one of the logical fallacies you have studied above.

TASK 7

Choose at least two of the exploratory writing tasks below. For each task, try to write the text in a style that is appropriate for the genre. Take **15 minutes** to write each one.

1. **A friendly note**
You overheard the phone call in which the home-stay student staying with your family told his family back home that the food in your country is awful. Write a friendly note to

him, explaining that he is making a *hasty generalization* and that he is mistaken. Use an appropriate writing style.

2. **Email or text message**
You are listening to a radio talk show debate on whether or not marijuana should be legalized. The talk show host asks listeners to send a text message or email with their views on the issue. Write a message on the subject and make reference in some way to the *slippery slope fallacy*. Follow the normal style you would use for this genre of writing.

3. **Free writing**
Should countries that have abolished the death penalty reintroduce it if the majority of the population supports its reinstatement? Answer the question with reference to the *ad populum fallacy*. Write in a more formal academic style.

4. **A two-minute speech**
President George W. Bush famously addressed the United Nations General Assembly after the 9/11 attacks in 2001 and stated, "You're either with us or against us in the fight against terror." Write a short script for a two-minute speech to your tutorial group on the issue. Make sure to refer to the *false dichotomy fallacy*. Write the script in a style that is appropriate for speaking academically.

WRITING A CRITIQUE

In Chapter 1, you wrote a summary on the nutritional benefits of organic food. The summary did not require you to give your personal opinion. When you write a critique of an article, you are required to analyze and evaluate the ideas in the article, which does involve giving your personal opinion.

There is no single way to write a critique. In the tasks that follow, you will learn some common strategies for writing critiques.

TASK 8

In order to prepare your critique, read the following two articles, which present opposing views on the subject of the legal drinking age in the United States. Annotate both articles as you read. Base your annotations on the six annotation questions from Chapter 1:

Six Annotation Questions

1. What is the main point of this sentence/paragraph/section?
2. Do I agree with this idea? Why or why not?
3. Is this idea relevant to my focus and task?
4. Does the author back up ideas with reasons, examples, and/or evidence?
5. Is the argument logical and convincing? Why or why not?
6. Do I have any questions about this?

Margin Notes

ARTICLE 1

Why 21?: Addressing underage drinking

MOTHERS AGAINST DRUNK DRIVING

More than 20,000 lives[1, 2] have been saved in the U.S. thanks to the 21 Minimum Legal Drinking Age.[10, 11]

This law continues to prevent tragedies—decreasing crashes by an estimated 16 percent[9] and keeping young people safer from many risks.[13] Sometimes, without knowing all the facts, people assert that youth shouldn't have to wait until they're 21 to drink. James C. Fell, a public health researcher at the Pacific Institute for Research & Evaluation, responds to their questions.

Why do we make young people wait until 21 to drink alcohol?
Many activities have ages of initiation. A person must wait until age 16 to start driving, age 18 to marry without parental consent, age 35 to become president, and so on. The age limit for alcohol is based on research which shows that young people react differently to alcohol. Teens get drunk twice as fast as adults,[9] but have more trouble knowing when to stop. Teens naturally overdo it and binge more often than adults.

Enforcing the legal drinking age of 21 reduces traffic crashes,[4-6] protects young people's maturing brains,[12,14] and keeps young people safer overall.

Can't parents teach their teens how to drink alcohol responsibly by giving them small amounts—under supervision—before they reach 21?
Some states permit parents to do this with their own child (rarely, if ever, with someone else's child), but there's no evidence that this approach actually works.[3] As [a] matter of fact, there is evidence to the contrary. When teens feel they have their parents' approval to drink, they do it more. When parents have concrete, enforced rules about alcohol, young people binge drink less.

Would lowering the legal drinking age make alcohol less of a big deal, and less attractive to teens?
History says no. When we had lower legal drinking ages in the U.S., the underage drinking problem was worse.[3] For example, before the 21 minimum legal drinking age was implemented by all states, underage drunk drivers were involved in over twice as many fatal traffic crashes.[3]

I thought Europeans have fewer underage drinking problems . . . is it because their kids drink from an earlier age?
That's a myth. European countries have worse problems than America does, as far as binge drinking and drinking to intoxication.[2] Studies show that Europe has more underage drunkenness, injury, rape, and school problems due to alcohol.[1,3] Since alcohol is more available there, it actually increases the proportion of kids who drink in Europe.

Some people propose a 40-hour alcohol education course for teens that would entitle teens to drink before 21. Is this a good idea?
Research shows that education alone doesn't prevent risky behaviors. For example, driver education by itself does not reduce youth car crashes. Beginning drivers need other restrictions in place, such as curfews and passenger limits, to stay safe. In addition, there are clear health risks associated with underage drinking.[7,14]

References

1. European School Survey Project on Alcohol and Other Drugs.
2. DiClemente, Ralph J. et al "Parental Monitoring: Association With Adolescents' Risk Behaviors" Pediatrics 107: 6 June 2001, 1363–1368.
3. Fell, James. From "Chapter 2: Federalism: Resolved, the Federal Government should restore each State's freedom to set its drinking age." in Ellis, Richard and Nelson, Michael (eds.) Debating Reform. CQPress Publishers, Fall 2009.
4. Fell, J.; "Minimum Legal Drinking Age Policy Knowledge Asset," website created by the Robert Wood Johnson Foundation's Substance Abuse Policy Research Program; March 2009.
5. Fell, James C. National Highway Traffic Safety Administration, Oct. 2008 "An Examination of the Criticisms of the Minimum Legal Drinking Age 21 Laws in the United States from a Traffic-Safety Perspective."
6. National Highway Traffic Safety Administration, National Center for Statistics and Analysis "Lives Saved in 2007 by Restraint Use and Minimum Drinking Age Laws" DOT HS 811 049 A Brief Statistical Summary November 2008.
7. National Institutes of Health, "Fact Sheet: Underage Drinking."
8. National Institutes of Health, "Fact Sheet: Alcohol-related Traffic Deaths."
9. National Institutes of Health, National Institute on Alcohol Abuse and Alcoholism, Statistics on Underage Drinking.
10. National Institutes of Health, National Institute on Alcohol Abuse and Alcoholism, "Research Findings on Underage Drinking and the Minimum Legal Drinking Age."
11. National Institutes of Health, Alcohol Policy Information System "The 1984 National Minimum Drinking Age Act."
12. Shults, Ruth A., Elder, Randy W., Sleet, David A., Nichols, James L., Alao, Mary O. Carande-Kulis, Vilma G., Zaza, Stephanie, Sosin, Daniel M., Thompson, Robert S., and the Task Force on Community Preventive Services. "Reviews of Evidence Regarding Interventions to Reduce Alcohol-Impaired Driving." Am J Prev Med 2001;21(4S).
13. U.S. Department of Health and Human Services, The Surgeon General's Call to Action to Prevent and Reduce Underage Drinking 2007.
14. Zeigler DW, Wang CC, Yoast RA, Dickinson BD, Mccaffree MA, Robinowitz CB, et al. The Neurocognitive Effects of Alcohol on Adolescents and College Students. Prev Med 2005 Jan;40(1):23-32.

Source: "Legal Drinking Age: Why 21." As published on the Power of Parents®-MADD® website.

ARTICLE 2

Why we should lower the drinking age to 19

Margin Notes

GENE FORD

Age 21 minimum drinking laws are counterproductive. There is much evidence that reducing the drinking age to 19 would reduce the abuse of alcohol among young people. The U.S. has the strictest youth drinking laws in western civilization and yet has the most drinking-related problems among its young. And there seems to be a connection between these two facts.

When I was a teen in the 1930s my peers drank to physical and mental oblivion on weekends to demonstrate their "manhood," and, to a lesser degree, their "womanhood." Alcohol abuse had received new energy as a result of Prohibition. The harvest of forbidden fruit was bitter and disastrous.

Today, irrefutable scientific evidence supports the fact that the early introduction of drinking is the safest way to reduce juvenile alcohol abuse. Young people in France, Spain, and Argentina rarely abuse alcohol. They learn how to drink within the family, which sees drinking in moderation as natural and normal. Youth in these societies rarely embarrass themselves or their families by abusing alcohol. In Portugal and New Zealand there are no minimum drinking age requirements. In Belgium, most of Canada, Italy, and Spain, young people of sixteen years may consume in restaurants when with parents or another adult. Australia and South Africa have an 18-year minimum.

Researchers have pointed out that minimum drinking age laws in the U.S. are a post-Prohibition phenomenon. Prior to the repeal of the Eighteenth amendment (Prohibition), state laws prohibiting minors from possession or use of alcohol were unusual. Adolescent alcohol consumption was regulated by the informal controls of family, community, peers, and self-restraint. The only drinking controls that have enjoyed any success over the centuries are social and cultural constraints.

I continue to witness the fundamental goodness of our young people and their capacity to be truly adult in their behavior, when given the chance. Despite the dissolution of the nuclear family, the vast majority of young people in America are well-intentioned and upright citizens. The twisted logic of youthful minimum drinking age laws denies them that basic respect. Research has found that restricting access to alcohol doesn't lower its consumption among young people. It just drives it "underground" into undesirable locations that aren't subject to the moderating influence of adults. In short, such efforts are counterproductive.

No one seriously contends that alcohol beverages should be free of societal controls. The question isn't whether there should be controls, but which controls work best. What has proven around the world to work best is a combination of reasonable laws backed by strong social sanctions. But in the U.S. we treat our emerging adults as infants and get infantile behavior as a result.

If adults would learn to temper their patronizing attitudes toward young men and women, more maturity, self-restraint, and social responsibility could be expected of them. Lowering the drinking age to 19 would do much to reduce the youthful abuse of alcohol.

Gene Ford is the founder and publisher, emeritus, of *Healthy Drinking* magazine and the author of five books about drinking, including *The French Paradox & Drinking for Health*, which is an extensively documented analysis of drinking in terms of health and control issues. He is currently completing another book on the health benefits of moderate consumption of alcohol beverages.

Source: Gene Ford, "Why We Should Lower the Drinking Age to 19." Published on *Alcohol: Problems and Solutions*, http://www2.potsdam.edu/hansondj/youthissues/1046348192.html. Reprinted by permission of Professor Emeritus David J. Hanson.

TASK 9

The following is a critique written by Lee, an undergraduate university student. In the essay, he critiques the article "Why we should lower the drinking age to 19" by Gene Ford. Read the critique and fill in the Critique Peer Review Worksheet that follows. As you read, take notes in the margin on how the arguments are critiqued, and on the general strengths and weaknesses of the critique.

Critique of "Why we should lower the drinking age to 19" by Gene Ford

Margin Notes

PARA. 1

1 In "Why we should lower the drinking age to 19," Gene Ford gives insight to why the age-21 minimum drinking laws are counterproductive, claiming there is much evidence that reducing the drinking age to 19 would reduce the abuse of alcohol among young people. **2** In this paper I will critique Gene Ford's claims.

PARA. 2

3 His first claim is that the US has the strictest youth drinking laws in western civilization and yet has the most drinking-related problems among its young. **4** He says there is a connection between these two facts by stating that in his teen years, his peers drank to physical and mental oblivion on weekends to demonstrate their "manhood" and that alcohol prohibition encouraged alcohol abuse. **5** On the other hand, the US could have the most drinking-related problems among its youth because it has the biggest youth population, therefore, entitling it to have the most youth problems in numbers. **6** His claim has no clear reason whether these facts are connected and he uses a metaphor instead of providing evidence. **7** In my opinion, merely stating that in the 1930s, teens drank for their manhood isn't a conclusive argument for these connections.

PARA. 3

8 In his next claim, he states there is irrefutable scientific evidence that supports the fact that early introduction of drinking is the safest way to reduce juvenile alcohol abuse and continues to list countries with lowered drinking age limits. **9** Ford does not provide the irrefutable evidence but rather bases his claims on reasons without much evidence. **10** Furthermore, he tends to steer away from his claim by stating that Portugal and New Zealand have no minimum drinking age requirements. **11** This does not expand to how early introduction is the safest way to reduce juvenile alcohol. **12** Even though he does mention that Canada, Italy, and Spain allow young people of 16 years to consume in restaurants when with parents or another adult, it fails to explain the effects or effectiveness of it, such as by how much it would reduce the abuse of alcohol among young people. **13** When one country has a lower minimum drinking age law, another country does not necessarily have to.

PARA. 4

14 Additionally, he claims that only social and cultural constraints have enjoyed any success over past centuries. **15** His reasons are that prior to minimum drinking age laws (MDAL), adolescent alcohol consumption was regulated by the informal controls of family, community, peers, and self-restraint. **16** This assertion isn't conclusive to proving that social and cultural constraints enjoyed success. **17** Why would the MDAL be introduced in the first place if social and cultural constraints were so successful? **18** The MDAL of 21 has indeed, actually enjoyed some success. **19** For instance, a study found that high school seniors who could not legally drink until age 21 drank less before age 21 and between ages 21–25 than did seniors in states with lower drinking ages (HALL, n.d.). **20** Furthermore, alcohol-related fatal crashes involving teen drivers have dropped by more than half—from 22 per 100 000 licensed drivers 15 to 20 years old in 1982 to fewer than 10 per 100 000 in 2003. **21** The minimum drinking age has prevented an estimated 22 000 alcohol-related driving deaths—about 900 lives a year ("21 is the . . .").

PARA. 5

22 Ford goes on to describe young people as having the capacity to be truly adult in their behaviour, when given the chance. **23** He goes on to say that the MDAL disrespects them, and drives alcohol consumption "underground" instead of actually lowering consumption among young people. **24** In these claims, no evidence is provided, leaving these claims to be general assertions. **25** MDAL may deny young people their right to drink but it also protects them from themselves. **26** In addition to the statistics in the last paragraph, the Arizona Department of Public Safety report found that fatal accidents increased over

25 percent while traffic fatalities increased more than 35 percent after the state MDAL was lowered from 21 to 19 (HALL, n.d.). **27** Moreover, a lowered MDAL in fact has been shown to lower consumption. **28** Congress passed the National Minimum Drinking Age Act in 1984 that established 21 as the minimum legal drinking age and since then teen drinking is down; 26 percent fewer high school seniors drink today than did in 1983 and 17 percent fewer high school seniors engage in binge drinking today than did in 1983 ("21 is the . . ."). **29** Therefore, Ford's claims don't hold true because he fails to provide evidence and there is strong evidence against his claims.

PARA. 6

30 In his last claim, Ford says that a combination of reasonable laws backed by strong social sanctions has proven to work best around the world, whereas the US treats their emerging adults as infants resulting in infantile behaviour. **31** Again, Ford fails to support this with reasons or evidence. **32** In addition, he doesn't explain why the age 19 would be reasonable nor does he describe this infantile behaviour. **33** On the other hand, the behaviour of 19-year-olds is particularly influential on youth ages 15–18, as young people typically imitate the practices of those who are slightly older, rather than the practices of those who are significantly older. **34** If 19-year-olds can legally drink, their immediate, younger peers will drink too (HALL, n.d.). **35** In conclusion, Ford bases his claims on general assertions and weak premises because they lack strong support and evidence.

References

(Hall, n.d.)
HALL, J. (n.d.). Fact sheet: lowering the minimum drinking age is a bad idea. Retrieved from www.cspinet.org/booze/mlpafact.htm.
("21 is the . . . ")
"21 is the legal drinking age." (n.d.). Retrieved from www.dontserveteens.gov/legal.html.

CRITIQUE PEER REVIEW WORKSHEET

Name of reviewer: ______________________________

1. **Introductory paragraph**
   Does the introductory paragraph include any of the following?
   - The title of the article ______________________
   - The name of the author/organization ______________________
   - The date of publication—if there is one ______________________
   - The general topic—or argument ______________________
   - A statement of the main idea or argument of the author/article ______________________
   - A thesis, or the main reaction to the article of the writer of the critique ______________________

2. **Main paragraphs**

- Does each paragraph focus on one topic to be critiqued? Comment on the following in Lee's critique:
  - Presentation of Ford's main arguments
  - The reasons/examples/evidence that Ford supports arguments with
  - How Lee critiques the arguments/reasons/examples/evidence: Is his critique convincing? Does he expand upon and support his own arguments with reasons, examples, and evidence from other reliable sources? Is Lee's position clearly stated?

- Does the critique end with a brief paragraph summarizing or giving a final statement of the writer's position?

3. **Style**
Is the critique written with an appropriate balance of objective and subjective styles? Is the level of formality appropriate? Is there a good range of vocabulary, grammar, and a variety of sentence structures?

4. **Accuracy**
Comment on the accuracy of the grammar, spelling, vocabulary, and punctuation.

____

____

____

____

5. **Strengths and weaknesses**
First describe what you feel to be the overall strengths of the writing. Then mention any areas that you feel could be improved to make the summary better for you as a reader.

____

____

____

____

____

____

____

____

TASK 10

Now write a two-page, double-spaced critique of an article that presents a strong argument either for or against an important topic of debate in your subject area. Follow the stages below.

STAGE 1: EXPLORATORY WRITING

Take **three to five minutes** to write down any opinions or ideas that came to your mind as you were reading the article. This is freestyle writing: you can write in any style that you choose. The main thing is to get as many feelings and ideas as possible down on paper.

Exploratory Writing

____

____

____

____

____

____

____

____

____

____

____

____

STAGE 2: WRITE AN INTRODUCTORY SUMMARY

Write an introductory summary of the article of around 3 or 4 lines double-spaced. Include the following in the introductory summary:

- The title of the article
- The name of the author/organization
- The date of publication—if there is one
- The general topic
- A statement of the main argument of the author/article

End the introductory paragraph with your thesis, or main reaction to the article. Your thesis should guide the reader by indicating (either directly or indirectly) where you stand on the issue. You will study thesis statements in more detail in Chapter 4.

STAGE 3: WRITE THE REMAINING PARAGRAPHS OF THE CRITIQUE

Choose one of the article's themes or arguments for each paragraph. In each paragraph, include the following:

- Argument: what the argument or claim of the author/article is
- Reason: the reasons stated by the author in support of the argument
- Examples/evidence: examples/evidence stated by the author in support of the argument
- Critique: your critique of the claim, and the author's reasons, examples, and evidence

- Counter-argument: any counter-arguments that would be used by those opposing the argument (use your own ideas as well as ideas that you find in academic articles)
- Expand: a discussion around the counter-arguments
- Your position: a statement of whether you agree with the argument and why or why not

End with a brief paragraph in which you present a final statement of your position.

STAGE 4: SELF- AND PEER REVIEW

After you have written your two-page critique, read it through carefully and do a self-review of your work using the Critique Peer Review Worksheet. After you have done a self-review, ask a classmate or friend to review your work for you with the same worksheet. Compare the responses from both peer review worksheets.

CHAPTER 2 **SUMMARY**

In this chapter, you have studied some of the defining features of critical thinking in academic writing and have put the ideas into practice through writing.

UNDERSTANDING CRITICAL THINKING

Critical thinking involves developing three key learning skills:

- The ability to think about arguments and ideas in new ways
- The ability to look at problems and issues from many different angles
- The ability to recognize the limitations of your own arguments and consider counter-arguments and opposing views

Putting these three skills together will take you out of your comfort zone as a thinker and will not only help you with your academic writing but also help you deal with issues and problems in your everyday life.

STATING YOUR ARGUMENTS

Critical thinking requires you to back up arguments and look at counter-arguments as part of your analysis and evaluation of information. A common way to do this in academic writing is as follows:

- State the argument.
- Give reasons.
- Provide examples.
- Support with evidence.
- Recognize and consider the limitations of your own arguments.
- Recognize and consider counter-arguments.
- Expand on your counter-arguments.
- State your position.

By following this process, you can effectively position yourself in debates that are going on within communities of scholars and within society as a whole.

AVOIDING LOGICAL FALLACIES

Logical fallacies are forms of illogical or uncritical thinking. First, you need to recognize the different fallacies and break though their confusing Latin names. Then you need to avoid them in your academic writing. While some are very common in everyday life, for example, different forms of inaccurate generalization, others are less common twists of logical thinking that may be employed intentionally or used accidentally. Part of your critical engagement with information and ideas involves being on your guard for logical fallacies in what you read and what you write.

CHAPTER 3

Writing Paragraphs

In this chapter, you will study the following aspects of writing paragraphs:

- ✓ Topic sentences
- ✓ Paragraph coherence
- ✓ Keeping to one topic
- ✓ Supporting your ideas
- ✓ Concluding sentences

What Are Paragraphs?

A paragraph is one or more sentences that are grouped together to focus on one particular topic. In academic writing, most paragraphs have a topic sentence that tells the reader what the topic of the paragraph is. Normally, a paragraph will focus only on this one topic. Paragraphs should also be coherent and cohesive. To be coherent, the writer should present ideas in some kind of logical order. To be cohesive, the writer should use appropriate sentence structures and linking words to join the ideas together. It is also very important to support your ideas when you are writing paragraphs. If you state an opinion or argument, for example, you should provide reasons, examples, and evidence to back it up. Finally, some, but not all, paragraphs end with a concluding sentence, that is, a sentence that rounds off the paragraph smoothly, perhaps by summarizing or synthesizing the content.

Different Paragraphs

There is no single way to write a paragraph. The structure, style, and focus that you need to use in your paragraphs in academic writing will change according to the genre (type of text that you are writing), the audience (for whom you are writing), and the context (your task or purpose for writing). In this chapter, you will learn some general principles that will help you to write academic paragraphs. You will need to carefully consider genre, audience, and context when you come to apply these general principles in your academic writing.

TOPIC SENTENCES

A topic sentence can be found in most paragraphs in written academic English. The purpose of a topic sentence is to clarify the main topic and the focus of the paragraph as well as guide the reader through your argument. When writing a topic sentence, consider both its position in the paragraph and its content.

The Position of a Topic Sentence in a Paragraph

Traditionally, paragraphs in written academic English have followed a *deductive* approach to writing. In deductive writing, the writer starts with a specific point or topic and then presents related examples and discussion in the following sentences of the paragraph. Consequently, in many paragraphs in written academic English, the topic sentence is positioned in the first line of the paragraph. This tells the reader from the outset what the topic and focus of the paragraph are. The topic sentence is then followed by description, discussion, and examples in the remainder of the paragraph.

Students coming from other learning cultures may be less familiar with a deductive approach to paragraph writing. In many East Asian contexts, paragraphs are written following a more *inductive* approach. An inductive paragraph typically begins with the presentation of more general examples and discussion, followed by a specific topic sentence toward the end of the paragraph. Writing in this way can cause problems in so-called western universities, where readers may be expecting a more direct, deductive approach. Inductive writers may receive comments such as "What point are you trying to make?" or "Be specific, get to the point!" from their instructors. This is because the readers are expecting things to be spelled out clearly to them from the outset. However, this does not mean that the deductive style of writing paragraphs is better. It depends where you are writing and for whom. As a student from China who was studying in Canada once said of deductive writing: "If I wrote in this style for my professor at my university in China, I would be insulting his intelligence!" This is because in some other learning cultures, the writer is not expected to make things so easy for the reader.

What to Include in a Topic Sentence

A topic sentence should tell readers the general topic and the specific focus of the paragraph. The general topic is the broader topic that is being discussed, while the specific focus refers to what the writer wants readers to know about that topic.

TASK 1

Look at the following examples of topic sentences and identify the general topic and specific focus in each one. Underline the general topic and put brackets around the specific focus. The first one is an example.

EXAMPLE

1. Another important factor to consider in the climate change debate is the [evidence on what are reported to be several natural causes of climate change.]
2. The effectiveness of patient care is indeed another factor to consider when weighing the pros and cons of universal health care.
3. Another area where both English and Mandarin are having a significant impact in the world today is on other languages.
4. Another major problem that comes with attempting to solve homelessness is dealing with the addictions that so many of the homeless in London, including the mentally ill, suffer from.
5. Pro-legalization groups argue in favour of the legalization, or at least decriminalization, of all drugs; however, opponents suggest that such a path will only lead to an increase in addiction rates.
6. Many novels written by Colombian author Gabriel García Márquez are characterized by magic realism.

Paragraph Topic Sentences

Usually, topic sentences appear at the beginning of a paragraph to guide the reader. This type of topic sentence is called a *paragraph topic sentence*.

Section Topic Sentences

A *section topic sentence* can also come at the beginning of an essay section that looks at a topic from several perspectives, with each perspective forming a short paragraph of its own.

TASK 2

Read the following essay paragraph on homelessness in London and the essay section on universal health care. Add a paragraph topic sentence to Example 1 and section topic sentences to Example 2.

EXAMPLE 1: Add a paragraph topic sentence

Homelessness in London

____

____

____

____

One problem that would come to many people's minds when thinking about homelessness is poverty. Few would argue that homelessness and poverty are closely interrelated. When people lose their jobs and income, some can no longer afford to pay the rent or mortgage on the home that they live in, or the weekly bills, and they end up homeless. However, not all of London's homeless have gone from being in the workforce to being on the streets. A large number of homeless people have instead moved from government institutions to the streets: from psychiatric hospitals and children's homes to the streets or homeless hostels of London. As part of the well-intentioned but misguided policy of "care in community," it was felt that large psychiatric hospitals were not the place where many mentally ill people should be kept. Consequently, many hospitals were closed and patients moved to smaller care centres or sheltered housing, resulting in many of the former patients becoming homeless, unable to cope with controlling their own medicine and the wider demands of living in society. Mental illness is, therefore, clearly a significant cause of homelessness. Others gain their first experience of being homeless when they leave, or run away from, children's homes, heading for the "bright lights of London." And finally, a significant number of homeless people in London are veterans who, having served in the armed forces for several years, are unable to find secure accommodation and employment after leaving the services.

EXAMPLE 2: Add one or more section topic sentences

Universal health care

____

____

____

____

Those in favour of universal health care quite rightly argue that free health care is a right of citizenship, and that responsibility for a nation's health lies with the state, not the individual. Supporters would argue that the state has a duty to protect the health of the people, especially the poor and needy who cannot afford private health insurance. For example, if people become unemployed or unable to support themselves financially, their only option is to use a free health care system as they will have problems paying medical bills. Only the state can and should be the universal provider.

Nonetheless, opponents of universal health care may counter that no one should have a right to free health care, and that instead responsibility for one's health lies with the individual rather than the state. According to their position, it is individuals, not the state, who need to make decisions about how they are going to pay for their health care. Those arguing for individual responsibility also often cite individual freedom of choice: the freedom to choose private care and the freedom not to pay for the health care of others. In this sense, private systems, they argue, give greater choice to the individual than universal ones. A case in point would be a working father with private health insurance provided by his employer. Why should social responsibility mean that his taxes go toward paying for the health care of others? And, should he not, in his position, also be able to choose when and where he and his family get medical treatment?

Looking at the arguments related to individual versus state responsibility, I would argue that the state has an undisputable duty to provide a universal free system. Choice and individual responsibility are not an option for the poor and needy in—society. This does not mean, however, that a parallel private system should not exist. For those in a financial position to choose private care, a parallel private system will serve their needs, and free up space in the public system. This is an effective compromise in many countries, and one which I am familiar with.

PARAGRAPH COHERENCE

Paragraphs in academic writing need to be *coherent*. If a paragraph is coherent to the reader, this means that the reader is able to find some kind of logical ordering and sense in the ideas and information presented. Paragraphs also need to be cohesive, with the ideas held together effectively with appropriate linking words and sentence structures. (See Appendix 3: Common Linking Words in Academic Writing and Appendices 6, 7, and 8: Sentence Structure 1, 2, and 3 for examples of how to make paragraphs more cohesive.)

There are many different ways to order ideas logically in an essay paragraph or section. The choices you make will depend on the type of academic writing you are doing: expository (explaining a process), argumentative (arguing in favour of or against a proposition), comparative (comparing one or more things or situations), narrative (telling a story), etcetera.

Five Ordering Principles

As already mentioned, it is usual in academic written English for writers to introduce a paragraph or essay section with a topic sentence. Thereafter, the ideas and information in the paragraph may be ordered according to several principles. Here are five common ordering principles (there are many more):

a) Broad to narrow: starting off with some examples or information of a broad scope and shifting to those with a narrower scope

b) Expanding understanding of a given concept: presenting a common definition or understanding of a concept, then expanding upon it according to other contexts

c) Three sides of the ongoing debate: presenting arguments in favour, against, and the writer's opinion (in any order)

d) Chronological: following a time sequence

e) A combination of different ordering principles

TASK 3

Look again at Examples 1 and 2 from Task 2 above. Identify which of the first four ordering principles (a–d) above is structuring the information and ideas presented. Write the letter in the space provided.

Example 1: ______________________________

Example 2: ______________________________

TASK 4

Identify which of the five ordering principles above is being used in each of the following examples. Write the corresponding letter in the margin.

Margin Notes

EXAMPLE 1

Osmotic wave power plants

The production of wave energy involves placing electricity generators on the surface of the ocean. The power produced by the generators has several common uses: desalination plants, power plants, and water pumps. The four main factors that determine the rate of energy generated are wave height, wave speed, wavelength, and water density. In the world today, there are only a limited number of experimental wave generator plants that are operating. One such plant is in the world's first osmotic power plant, which opened in Norway in 2009.

Source: Adapted from "Wave Power: News and Information about Wave Energy and Ocean Power Technologies." www.alternative-energy-news.info/technology/hydro/wave-power/.

EXAMPLE 2

Ethanol cars in Brazil

In 1896, the first automobile to run solely on ethanol, the quadricycle, was built by Henry Ford. In the 1920s, the Standard Oil company started to add ethanol to gasoline. Interest in ethanol as an alternative fuel source only really took off in the early 1970s, when oil supplies were cut by many of the major producers. The country where ethanol fuel is used most widely in automobiles is Brazil, where a National Alcohol Program was set up in 1975. Thereafter, Brazil began the large-scale production of ethanol from sugar cane. By the mid-1980s, around 90 percent of all new cars sold in Brazil ran exclusively on ethanol.

Source: Adapted from "energy4me: Essential Energy Education." http://www.energy4me.org/energy-facts/energy-sources/biofuels/.

EXAMPLE 3

Codeswitching

Although the term "codeswitching" is widely used in the literature when referring to conversations in which speakers mix languages, there are several competing definitions to be found in the literature on the subject. Codeswitching is described in different ways in the literature: *codeswitching* (Gumperz, 1982; Heller, 1988, 1992, 1995; Romaine, 1989); *code alternation* (Auer, 1995); *code-crossing* (Rampton, 1995); and *code mixing* (Haugen, 1972; Heller, 1992). In Romaine's work on bilingualism, she defines *codeswitching* as "the juxtaposition within the same speech exchange of passages of speech belonging to two different grammatical systems or subsystems" (Romaine, 1989, p. 111). Put simply, this means using two different languages in a conversation. An example would be a family in which one parent speaks Spanish and another English as first languages, and where conversations frequently involve changes from Spanish to English and vice versa. Heller uses the term *codeswitching* in a more extended sense: not only with reference to switches between languages that take place between sentences, but also to "less structurally integrated instances of language alternation or language choice" (Heller, 1995, p. 59). Following this definition, visually identifying someone as a speaker of a particular language, for example a Spanish-speaker in California, and choosing to speak Spanish as a result, is part of codeswitching.

Source: Marshall, S. (2005). *Spanish-speaking Latin Americans in Catalonia: Constructions of Catalan*. Unpublished Ph.D. thesis, Institute of Education, University of London.

EXAMPLE 4

The cost of universal health care

Money is often a central factor in social and cultural debates, and health care is no exception. Money and profit are what drive all free enterprises, and again, private health care is no exception: access to private care is based on the ability to pay. Where this is the only option that people have, I argue that it is unethical as it excludes the poor and allows the rich to gain preferential and faster treatment. In fact, in US states without a health safety net for the poor, many people who declared bankruptcy in recent years did so as a result of the cost of serious illness. This is something that cannot happen where universal health care is available and paid for by taxes. Furthermore, as stated in the section above, universal health care can actually be a money-saver for individuals and states if we take into account how much individuals have to pay for private health insurance as well as the wider economic benefits that a healthy population can bring.

But is free health care really free? Of course, the answer is no; we pay for it in our taxes. This leads many opponents of free health care to question why they as taxpayers are obliged to pay for the health of the wider population, especially what they see as irresponsible people who lead unhealthy lives, or unemployed people who are not paying taxes for the health care that they may receive. Moreover, in terms of cost and a healthy workforce, supporters of private health care often bring another argument into the discussion: that of fast care for essential workers. For example, if a small business owner has key employees with serious health problems, and a free public system means long wait times (and months off work), then private health care is seen as the best option. It allows employers to invest in the health and continued care of key employees by buying faster access to care when in need.

Based on the arguments presented around the theme of cost, in my opinion, a mixed public-private system is the only solution. In a mixed system, users of private care normally still pay into the public system via their taxes, and when they use private care for the convenience that it offers, this creates a double windfall for the public sector: they are still paying into a free system but freeing up space in the system by not using it. A mixed system can also offer another benefit for the public system when public hospitals are allowed to buy treatment in private hospitals when public waiting lists are too long, as is the case in the UK.

EXAMPLE 5

Magic realism as postcolonial discourse

The concept of magic realism is a troubled one for literary theory.[1] Since Franz Roh first coined the term in 1925 in connection with postexpressionist art, it has been most closely associated, at least in terms of literary practice, with two major periods in Latin-American and Caribbean culture: the 1940s and 1950s, in which the concept was closely aligned with that of the "marvelous" as something ontologically necessary to the regional population's "vision of everyday reality,"[2] and the "boom" period of the Latin-American novel in the late 1950s and 1960s, where the term was applied to works varying widely in genre and discursive strategy. In none of its applications to literature has the concept of magic realism ever successfully differentiated between itself and neighboring genres such as fabulation, metafiction, the baroque, the fantastic, the uncanny, or the marvelous,[3] and consequently it is not surprising that some critics have chosen to abandon the term altogether.

Source: Dr. Stephen Slemon. "Magic Realism as Post Colonial Discourse." *Canadian Literature* 116 (1988):9–24. Footnotes omitted. Reprinted by permission of the author.

KEEPING TO ONE TOPIC

Paragraphs in written academic English should normally keep to one topic. This should be the topic that is introduced in the topic sentence. When a writer comes to a new topic, a new paragraph is required. In Examples 1, 2, 3, and 5 in Task 4, each paragraph focuses on one topic only: osmotic wave power plants, ethanol cars in Brazil, codeswitching, and magic realism.

The focus on one topic is presented differently in Example 4, which is an essay section made up of three paragraphs. Here, the topic is the cost of universal health care. This is the specific topic of the section, while each paragraph within the section looks at the issue from a different angle: *arguments that supporters would use*, *arguments that opponents would use*, and *the writer's opinion*.

TASK 5

The two paragraphs below fail to keep to one topic. Read each paragraph and underline the sentences that do not keep to the topic and focus presented in the topic sentence.

EXAMPLE 1

Human cloning

1 There is one main ethical issue that supporters and opponents argue over in the debate on human cloning, namely, the "playing God" argument. **2** Opponents argue that the natural process of creating human life should not be messed with: human cloning would mean humans playing at being God. **3** For such opponents, the fact that the process of cloning involves scientists radically altering and engineering the human cells that are central to reproduction is one step too far. **4** A small, but growing, number of scientists are arguing, however, on philosophical grounds, that human cloning does not represent "playing God." **5** They suggest that if humans are designed by God, and that if they are able to carry out such cloning procedures, then this must have been part of God's plan. **6** Accordingly, the whole playing God argument is seen to have no value. **7** What, then, are the benefits that human cloning may bring to humanity? **8** Supporters of human cloning believe that cloning will bring many benefits to society, most notably, children for parents who are recently bereaved or who are unable to have children naturally or through in vitro fertilization (IVF). **9** Considering the ethical issues discussed, I remain unconvinced that there is currently a need or ethical justification for human cloning. **10** Put simply, the cons outweigh the pros.

EXAMPLE 2

State funding for stem cell therapy

1 The next issue to consider in assessing the acceptability of stem cell therapy is whether government funding for research and treatment can be justified. **2** Currently, government funding is available for stem cell therapy in several jurisdictions around the world: European Union countries, Canada, and some US states, for example. **3** Where funding is provided, policy-makers argue that the medical and economic benefits that come with being at the forefront of this technology outweigh any concerns that opponents may have. **4** In the search for cures for neurological diseases such as multiple sclerosis and Parkinson's, and for the treatment of patients with organ failure, governments have given funding to stem cell researchers for the "greater good" of humanity. **5** Nonetheless, opponents base their opposition to government funding on the grounds that stem cell therapy often involves the creation of a human embryo, the extraction of stem cells, and then the destruction of the embryo. **6** For opponents, governments should not fund the destruction of a living embryo; for supporters, funding is justified because the embryo is merely a cluster of cells. **7** What, then, is the future of stem cell therapy? **8** Perhaps in the future, more cancer patients, patients with neurological diseases, and those who currently require plastic surgery will benefit from emerging medical therapies.

SUPPORTING YOUR IDEAS

Whatever the focus of your paragraphs may be, it is essential to support your ideas and arguments. In Chapter 2, you studied the importance of backing up arguments with reasons, examples, and evidence, and to recognize the limitations of your own arguments and consider counter-arguments. This level of support is required in most types of academic writing. For example, if you are describing a mechanical process in a paragraph, you need to illustrate the process, and provide specific details as necessary so that your reader can understand the complexities involved in the process. If you are critiquing a novel, the same need to support your ideas applies.

TASK 6

Read the following essay section, which you studied in Task 2 above. Underline any supporting evidence or examples that you find. For now, ignore the letters in brackets inserted after some of the sentences.

Universal health care

1 An important question to consider when discussing the arguments in favour of and against universal health care is the following: Who should be responsible for a nation's health care—the state or the individuals who make up the state?

2 Those in favour of universal health care quite rightly argue that free health care is a right of citizenship, and that responsibility for a nation's health lies with the state, not the individual. **3** Supporters would argue that the state has a duty to protect the health of the people, especially the poor and needy who cannot afford private health insurance. [**A**] **4** For example, if people become unemployed or unable to support themselves financially, their only option is to use a free health care system as they will have problems paying medical bills. [**B**] **5** Only the state can and should be the universal provider.

6 Nonetheless, opponents of universal free care may counter that no one should have a right to free health care, and that instead responsibility for one's health lies with the individual rather than the state. **7** According to their position, it is individuals, not the state, who need to make decisions about how they are going to pay for their health care. [**C**] **8** Those arguing for individual responsibility also often cite individual freedom of choice: the freedom to choose private care and the freedom not to pay for the health care of others. **9** In this sense, private systems, they argue, give greater choice to the individual than universal ones.

10 A case in point would be a working father with private health insurance provided by his employer. **11** Why should social responsibility mean that his taxes go toward paying for the health care of others? **12** And, should he not, in his position, also be able to choose when and where he and his family get medical treatment?

13 Looking at the arguments related to individual versus state responsibility, I would argue that the state has an undisputable duty to provide a universal free system. **14** Choice and individual responsibility are not an option for the poor and needy in society. **15** This does not mean, however, that a parallel private system should not exist. **[D]** **16** For those in a financial position to choose private care, a parallel private system will serve their needs, and free up space in the public system. **17** This is an effective compromise in many countries, and one which I am familiar with. **[E]**

Incorporating Supporting Examples, Statistics, and Evidence from Reliable Academic Sources

The paragraphs in Task 6 are taken from an in-class writing task that did not involve any research. As a result, the supporting evidence and examples are limited. To be more convincing, the writer needs to bring in some supporting examples, statistics, and evidence from reliable academic sources. Also, the writer should make the examples specific by referring to specific countries or medical systems.

TASK 7

Below, List 1 presents five types of supporting evidence, and List 2 presents examples that were added to a later draft of the essay section on state and individual responsibility in universal health care. First, read the types of supporting evidence in List 1 and match them to the examples in List 2. There is one type of supporting evidence for each example. Then decide where each example of supporting evidence would best fit in the essay section in Task 6. Match the example to one of the letters in brackets at the end of a sentence.

LIST 1: FIVE TYPES OF SUPPORTING EVIDENCE

1. Statistics cited from a magazine
2. A supporting opinion cited from a non-governmental organization (NGO)
3. A supporting opinion cited from an online news media source
4. A perspective cited from an academic journal article
5. Personal life experience

LIST 2: FIVE EXAMPLES OF SUPPORTING EVIDENCE TO ADD

1. This view has supporters in high places in the US medical profession. News agency CNN states that the influential American Medical Association opposes a public health insurance option, advocating instead for an expansion of private health insurance coverage (CNN, 2009).

   Type of supporting evidence: ______________________________

   Insert at letter ______________________________

2. According to a report in the *New Yorker* magazine (*New Yorker,* 2009), in 2003, 44 million Americans had difficulty paying their medical bills, a figure that rose to 57 million in 2007. The average medical debt incurred was $2000, and, on average, those in debt had been contacted by a debt collector on at least one occasion.

   Type of supporting evidence: ______________________
   Insert at letter ______________________

3. Admittedly, parallel private systems such as the one in the UK can arise as a result of an erosion of entitlement to free state-provided health care, as stated in Propper's (2009) article on the demand for private health care in the UK. However, at the same time, parallel private systems serve the needs of those who are unhappy with public health care and who are able to pay to go private.

   Type of supporting evidence: ______________________
   Insert at letter ______________________

4. It is with regard to such poor and needy people that the NGO Oxfam UK states the following: "No one should have to check their wallet before seeing a doctor" (Oxfam UK, 2010).

   Type of supporting evidence: ______________________
   Insert at letter ______________________

5. Writing as someone who has used parallel private health care to beat long waiting lists, despite being barely able to afford it, I believe that this compromise does work in practice.

   Type of supporting evidence: ______________________
   Insert at letter ______________________

CONCLUDING SENTENCES

When you reach the end of your paragraph, you need to consider whether to end the paragraph with a concluding sentence or concluding sentences. Concluding sentences allow you to end your paragraph smoothly rather than abruptly. There are many strategies for writing concluding sentences. Here are three common ones:

1. **The end of a list**

   If the paragraph or section presents a list, for example, of steps in a process or procedure, causes, effects, or defining features of something, you can conclude by presenting the final item of the list.

2. **A final opinion**

   If the paragraph or section is argumentative, you can conclude with a final opinion on the topic being discussed.

3. **A synthesis of ideas**

   If the paragraph or section is made up of several related ideas, you can conclude by briefly synthesizing them into one overall idea to close with.

TASK 8

Look at the underlined concluding sentences in the three example paragraphs below. Identify which of the three types of concluding sentence is being used.

EXAMPLE 1

Homelessness in London

There are many reasons why people in London, and elsewhere, become homeless. One problem that would come to many people's minds when thinking about homelessness is poverty. Few would argue that homelessness and poverty are closely interrelated. When people lose their jobs and income, some can no longer afford to pay the rent or mortgage on the home that they live in, or the weekly bills, and they end up homeless. However, not all of London's homeless have gone from being in the workforce to being on the streets. A large number of homeless people have instead moved from government institutions to the streets: from psychiatric hospitals and children's homes to the streets or homeless hostels of London. As part of the well-intentioned but misguided policy of "care in community," it was felt that large psychiatric hospitals were not the place where many mentally ill people should be kept. Consequently, many hospitals were closed and patients moved to smaller care centres or sheltered housing, resulting in many of the former patients becoming homeless, unable to cope with controlling their own medicine and the wider demands of living in society. Mental illness is, therefore, clearly a significant cause of homelessness. Others gain their first experience of being homeless when they leave, or run away from, children's homes, heading for the "bright lights of London." <u>And finally, a significant number of homeless people in London are veterans who, having served in the armed forces for several years, are unable to find secure accommodation and employment after leaving the services.</u>

Type of concluding sentence:____________________________________

EXAMPLE 2

Human cloning

There is one main ethical issue that supporters and opponents argue over in the debate on human cloning, namely, the "playing God" argument. Opponents argue that the natural process of creating human life should not be messed with: human cloning would mean humans playing at being God. For such opponents, the fact that the process of cloning involves scientists radically altering and engineering the human cells that are central to reproduction is one step too far. A small, but growing, number of scientists are arguing, however, on philosophical grounds, that human cloning does not represent "playing God." They suggest that if humans are designed by God, and that if they are able to carry out such cloning procedures, then this must have been part of God's plan. Accordingly, the whole playing God argument is seen to have no value. <u>Considering the ethical issues discussed, I remain unconvinced that there is currently a need or ethical justification for human cloning. Put simply, the cons outweigh the pros.</u>

Type of concluding sentences:____________________________________

EXAMPLE 3

State funding for stem cell therapy

The next issue to consider in assessing the acceptability of stem cell therapy is whether government funding for research and treatment can be justified. Currently, government funding is available for stem cell therapy in several jurisdictions around the world: European Union countries, Canada, and some US states, for example. Where funding is provided, policy-makers argue that the medical and economic benefits that come with being at the forefront of this technology outweigh any concerns that opponents may have.

In the search for cures for neurological diseases such as multiple sclerosis and Parkinson's, and for the treatment of patients with organ failure, governments have given funding to stem cell researchers for the "greater good" of humanity. Nonetheless, opponents base their opposition to government funding on the grounds that stem cell therapy often involves the creation of a human embryo, the extraction of stem cells, and then the destruction of the embryo. For opponents, governments should not fund the destruction of a living embryo; for supporters, funding is justified as the embryo is merely a cluster of cells. The division between supporters and opponents centres on an unbridgeable dichotomy: the greater good of humanity versus the sanctity of human life from conception.

Type of concluding sentence: ______________________________

TASK 9

The two paragraphs below end rather abruptly and would benefit from having concluding sentences. Read the paragraphs, focusing on the content of the paragraph, and write an appropriate concluding sentence for each one.

EXAMPLE 1: Write a synthesis of ideas

Euthanasia: The right to choose when to die

Supporters of euthanasia argue that just as we have the right to life as a human right, so too should we have the right to choose when to end our lives. Accordingly, this right should be given to individuals with incurable illness and with such physical and emotional suffering that their quality of life is reduced to nil, for example, someone in the final stages of terminal cancer or motor neuron disease. In this regard, Humphry (2002) argues that the right to know how to die, or to choose how to die, should only be extended to a terminally ill person with unbearable suffering, or one with an advanced degenerative condition. Most advocates of euthanasia would insist that, as part of exercising this right, that is, ending one's life, individuals must pass through several medical and psychological steps before taking any action.

____

____

____

____

____

EXAMPLE 2: Write a final opinion

Second-hand smoke in restaurants

Perhaps the strongest reason why smoking should be banned in public places such as restaurants is the danger that comes with second-hand smoking. When smokers smoke in a public place with other people around them, the surrounding people are forced to breathe in the unfiltered smoke from the burning cigarette as well as the filtered smoke that the smoker exhales. In this way, non-smokers become second-hand smokers. In a study of 152 restaurant staff in European cities where smoking was allowed in public places, García (2001) found that those non-smoking staff who had worked for more than 20 years in smoke-filled workplaces were 30 percent more likely to suffer from respiratory illness than those working in smoke-free environments. Many smokers, nonetheless, still insist that smoking zones should be allowed in public places such as restaurants in the form of closed-off separate rooms in which they could freely enjoy a cigarette with their meal. To do otherwise, they would argue, represents an erosion of the already dwindling human rights of smokers. While a separate room may indeed protect the general public from second-hand smoke, employees would still have to serve the smokers and breathe in the smoke. Is it justifiable, therefore, to restrict the rights of one group in society to protect those of another group?

Coherence and Attribution

The essay section below is on euthanasia, focusing on whether individuals should have the right to end their own lives. It illustrates most of the aspects of paragraph writing you have studied in this chapter. First, read the paragraphs through without stopping. Then answer the questions that follow.

Euthanasia: The right to choose when to die

1 The most important factor to consider when discussing euthanasia is human rights: the rights of individuals to end their own lives when they choose to. **2** Supporters of euthanasia argue that, just as we have the right to life as a human right, so too should we have the right to choose when to end our lives. **3** Accordingly, this right should be given to individuals with incurable illness and with such physical and emotional suffering that their quality of life is reduced to nil, for example, someone in the final stages of terminal cancer or motor neuron disease. **4** In this regard, Humphry (2002) argues that the right to know how to die, or to choose how to die, should only be extended to a terminally ill person with unbearable suffering, or one with an advanced degenerative condition. **5** Most advocates of euthanasia would insist that, as part of exercising this right, that is, ending one's life, individuals must pass through several medical and psychological steps before taking any action. **6** Thus, they will exercise their right to live in dignity and to die in dignity.

7 Opponents of euthanasia do not accept this view of human rights. **8** First, many health care professionals are opposed to euthanasia. **9** As stated by Andersen and Caddell (1993, p. 105), the Hippocratic Oath, which all doctors are bound by, is clear in its opposition to euthanasia by stating, "*I will neither give a deadly drug to anybody if asked for it, nor will I make a suggestion to this effect.*" **10** Other points of opposition are based on religious belief, according to which the right to life and death is a God-given right, not something that humans have the right to exercise. **11** Many secularists would even challenge the view of the pro-euthanasia lobby that individuals should be given the legal right to be able to choose when to end their lives. **12** Rather than citing religion, they tend to focus on the societal contexts of exercising this right; for example, they argue that with advances in medicine and palliative care, there is no validity to the argument that euthanasia is justifiable on the grounds of individuals exercising the right to end suffering (see Materstvedt et al. 2003, for a balanced discussion on palliative care and euthanasia). **13** In sum, opponents see the right to choose when to die as something that should be left to the morals of the church and/or the apparatus of the state.

14 Based on the arguments in this section on whether an individual should have the right to choose when to end their own life, I strongly believe that this is a human right that should be accorded to all, but based on very strict rules around how the right is exercised. **15** I believe that euthanasia is an individual human right, but that the state should enforce rigorous conditions of medical and psychological assessment when individuals want to exercise their right.

TASK 10

Locate the following types of sentences in the essay section above.

1. Topic sentence for the essay section:

   Sentence ______________________________
2. Sentences presenting arguments that supporters of euthanasia would use:

   Sentences ______________________________
3. Sentences presenting arguments that opponents of euthanasia would use:

   Sentences ______________________________
4. Sentences presenting the writer's opinion:

   Sentences ______________________________
5. Sentences that refer to academic sources:

   Sentences ______________________________
6. Concluding sentences:

   Sentences ______________________________

TASK 11

In Sentence 2 in the essay section on euthanasia, the writer states, "Supporters of euthanasia argue that . . . " This is an example of *language of attribution*. Language of attribution is language that guides the reader by indicating who different ideas belong to. Read the essay section again and underline any language of attribution that you find. Look for language that attributes opinions to the following: supporters of euthanasia, opponents of euthanasia, and the writer.

CHAPTER 3 SUMMARY

In this chapter, you have studied five important aspects of writing paragraphs: topic sentences, paragraph coherence, keeping to one topic, supporting your ideas, and concluding sentences.

TOPIC SENTENCES

Most topic sentences in written academic English come at the beginning of the paragraph or section, and refer to the general topic as well as the specific focus of the paragraph or section.

PARAGRAPH COHERENCE

Coherence means that your ideas, arguments, and other information are logically ordered. There are many different ordering principles, five of which you studied:

1. Broad to narrow: starting off with some examples or information of a broad scope and shifting to those with a narrower scope
2. Expanding understanding of a given concept: presenting a common definition or understanding of a concept, then expanding upon it according to other contexts
3. Three sides of the ongoing debate: presenting arguments in favour, against, and the writer's opinion (in any order)
4. Chronological: following a time sequence
5. A combination of different ordering principles

KEEPING TO ONE TOPIC

You should always keep to one topic in each paragraph or section, namely, the topic and focus that you state in your topic sentence. When you come to a new topic, it is time to begin a new paragraph or section.

SUPPORTING YOUR IDEAS

In Chapter 2, you studied the importance of supporting your ideas with reasons, examples, and evidence. You also learned the importance of recognizing your own limitations and considering counter-arguments. Remember the ways to support ideas in paragraphs.

CONCLUDING SENTENCES

It is not always necessary to end a paragraph or section with a concluding sentence. However, concluding sentences allow you to round off your paragraphs or sections smoothly. You studied three common strategies for writing concluding sentences:

1. The end of a list
2. A final opinion
3. A synthesis of ideas

CHAPTER 4

Introductions and Conclusions

In this chapter, you will study the following aspects of writing introductions and conclusions:

- ✓ Common features of introductions
- ✓ Thesis-guided writing
- ✓ Different introductions in academic writing
- ✓ Common features of conclusions
- ✓ Different conclusions in academic writing

In this chapter, you will study some of the general features of introductions and conclusions.

Introductions give readers a first impression of you as a writer. Writers often use their introduction to provide general background information about their topic, give their reader an indication of their views on the issue being studied, and guide their reader as to how they are going to write the essay.

Conclusions give readers a final impression of you as a writer and of your knowledge on the topic being studied. Writers often use the conclusion to summarize and synthesize the issues that have been covered in the essay, give a final opinion on any question or problem being discussed, and leave readers with food for thought. In academic writing, conclusions are especially important because the reader who is forming a final impression is often the person who grades your work.

There are many different ways to introduce and conclude in academic writing. Moreover, certain forms of academic writing do not require introductions or conclusions, for example, some forms of personal and reflective academic writing and short response essays to questions or problems.

COMMON FEATURES OF INTRODUCTIONS

Introductions are written in many different formats in academic writing. The most predominant of these is a format that shifts from general to specific.

Shifting from General to Specific

In introductions, the shift from general to specific can be accomplished in many different ways. The following is a common format for shifting from general to specific. It involves starting the introduction with one or more sentences that provide general background information. This is followed by sentences that make a shift to the specific focus of the essay. In many introductions, the shift from general to specific is completed with some form of thesis statement and/or by referring to the structure of the essay.

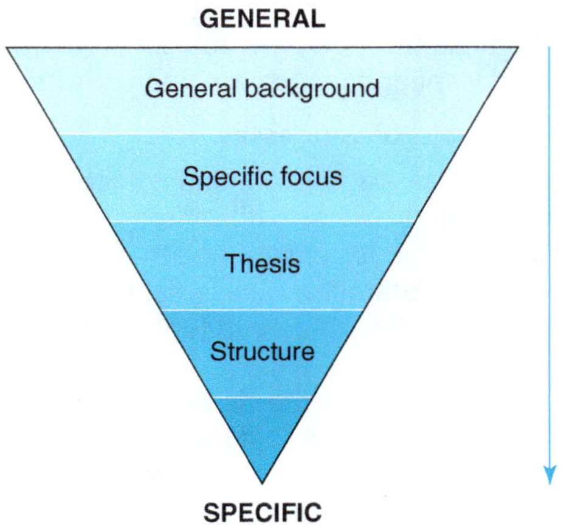

When writing an introduction that shifts from general to specific, the following steps are usually followed, although not always in the same order:

1. Provide general background information.
2. Shift to the specific focus of your essay.
3. State a thesis that will guide your writing.
4. Refer to the structure of the essay.

Read the following example of an introductory paragraph to an argument essay on the pros and cons of universal health care. As stated above, there are many ways to write introductions; this is because different writers arrange ideas differently.

Universal health care: Introductory paragraph

1 The pros and cons of universal health care and private health care have been the subject of lengthy and heated debate in many countries around the world. **2** In countries such as Canada, the UK, and France, universal health care systems are available to all citizens, with different sources of funding in each country, and different roles for private health care. **3** In many other countries, for example, the United States, no universal health care system exists at a national level, and private health care is funded through private insurance or on a pay-as-you-use basis. **4** The arguments in favour of and against universal health care will be discussed in this essay, focusing on three key themes: individual versus state responsibility, effectiveness, and cost. **5** Central to the arguments presented is a relationship between public and private that is often presented in terms of either one or the other. **6** I will argue that the discussion needs to rise above this level and accept that each system has its strengths and weaknesses, and that each system should have a place in societies.

The following steps for writing an introduction were taken in the example above:

1. **Provide general background information.**

   "The pros and cons of universal health care and private health care have been the subject of lengthy and heated debate in many countries around the world."

   This is a very general introductory statement about the topic of the essay. By stating that the topic has been the subject of lengthy and heated debate, the writer is also attempting to catch the interest of the reader.

2. **Shift to the specific focus of your essay.**

   "In countries such as Canada, the UK, and France, universal health care systems are available to all citizens, with different sources of funding in each country, and different roles for private health care. In many other countries, for example, the United States, no universal health care system exists at a national level, and private health care is funded through private insurance or on a pay-as-you-use basis."

   In the first sentence, the writer is beginning a gradual shift from general to specific, and by referring to different systems in countries around the world, the writer is also showing that the topic is interesting and has broad scope. In the second sentence, the writer mentions the private system in the US to give balance to the essay from the outset.

3. **Refer to the structure of the essay.**

   "The arguments in favour of and against universal health care will be discussed in this essay, focusing on three key themes: individual versus state responsibility, effectiveness, and cost."

   In this sentence, the shift from general to specific is completed. It tells the reader the structure of the essay by first restating key words from the title, and then telling the reader the three analytic perspectives around which the issues will be organized.

4. **State a thesis that will guide your writing.**

   "Central to the arguments presented is a relationship between public and private that is often presented in terms of either one or the other. I will argue that the discussion needs to rise above this level and accept that each system has its strengths and weaknesses, and that each system should have a place in societies."

The two sentences above form a kind of thesis statement. In the first sentence, the writer mentions an important relationship that will run through the debate in the essay as the first part of a thesis statement. And in the second part, the writer gives an opinion.

Notice that the order of steps is different from the order presented on page 63 (the thesis is stated *after* the structure). The example illustrates an important point that you should remember: there is no single formula to follow when writing an introduction.

THESIS-GUIDED WRITING

In many types of academic writing, a thesis statement is included in the introduction. The purpose of a thesis statement is to give important information about your essay to your readers before they start reading the main body sections. In this sense, a thesis statement can be understood as a guiding idea that should run through the essay like a thread, holding the various sections together conceptually.

There are five common strategies for writing thesis statements. Two of them (4 and 5) are not accepted as common practice in all disciplines, so it is important to find out what normal practice is in your area of study.

1. Explain a central idea that will run through the essay.
2. Present an argument or your opinion.
3. State your purpose for writing.
4. Ask questions.
5. State the focus of the essay.

Here are some example sentences that illustrate how thesis statements can follow these five strategies for an argument essay on universal health care.

1. Explain a central idea that will run through the essay.

"The main theme that runs through the essay is patient choice: the extent to which patients should be able to choose when and where to obtain medical treatment."

This type of thesis statement gives a central thematic focus, or thread, to your essay. It tells the reader that a main idea to consider in the coming discussion is patient choice. This is the idea around which the writer is centring the argument.

2a. Present an argument or your opinion (explicit).

"I will argue that universal health care should be provided in all countries, with parallel private health care for those willing to pay for it."

This thesis statement gives the essay a direct, argumentative focus from the outset. The writer is presenting an opinion to the reader at the beginning. Some readers do not like this approach, as they feel it is too direct for an introduction and takes away the need to read on: why read on if I already know the writer's opinion on the issues? An alternative is to state the opinion in a more indirect, implicit way.

2b. Present an argument or your opinion (implicit).

"The pros and cons of universal health care cannot be studied without considering what many see as the important roles that private health care can play, either as an alternative or parallel system."

This thesis statement is less direct. It states a similar argument to Sentence 2a above but in a more implicit way. The reader now has a hint of the writer's opinion (i.e., that private health care can play an important role). However, the opinion is stated in a way that requires the reader to read on to find out the writer's definitive view on the matter.

3a. State your purpose for writing (opinion).

"By analyzing the advantages and disadvantages of universal health care, I aim to lay bare the arguments that proponents of private health care put forward in public debates."

In this thesis statement, the writer's purpose is to put forward a strong opinion or argument. Again, this example is very direct.

3b. State your purpose for writing (goal).

"My purpose is to search for a reasonable way forward in the heated debate on health care, one that will best meet the health care needs of all Canadians."

In this thesis statement, the writer's stated purpose is a broader goal for society rather than a personal opinion. Because the writer is stating this in the introduction to the essay, the reader will form a view of the writer as someone who is basing his or her discussion on the needs of society.

4. Ask questions.

"Two questions will be addressed in an analysis of the benefits and drawbacks of universal health care: Is universal health care a feasible option for developed and developing countries? And, can private and public health care function effectively side by side?"

In this thesis statement, the writer is setting out questions that will be addressed in the essay. The writer can then return to the same questions in the conclusion of the essay and answer them. This strategy is controversial. Some instructors do not like questions as thesis statements, arguing that questions fail to give any indication of the writer's stance on the subject and lack details about the scope of the coming discussion.

5. State the focus of the essay.

"The arguments used by supporters and opponents of universal health care will be analyzed from three perspectives: equity and the right to care, cost to the taxpayer, and effectiveness of each system."

This strategy is also controversial. It tends to lead to the most neutral and bland form of thesis statement, in which the writer avoids presenting any central theme, opinion (implicit or explicit), or purpose; instead, the thesis statement sets out the structure of the essay, telling the reader what will be discussed in each of the coming sections. As is the case with the "Ask questions" strategy, some instructors dislike it when students merely state the focus of the essay. Stating the focus results in more of a statement of intent rather than a position or stance to be followed on a subject.

Compound Thesis Statements

A *compound thesis statement* is a thesis statement that combines more than one of the strategies above. It can be one or more sentences.

TASK 1

Look again at the compound thesis statement from the introductory paragraph on page 64.

> **5** Central to the arguments presented is a relationship between public and private that is often presented in terms of either one or the other. **6** I will argue that the discussion needs to rise above this level and accept that each system has its strengths and weaknesses, and that each system should have a place in societies.

Which of the strategies for writing thesis statements do you find in Sentences 5 and 6?

____

____

____

Academic Writing with No Thesis Statement

Not all essays or forms of academic writing require a thesis statement. In some scientific academic writing, such as lab reports and essays that describe complex processes, the thesis statement is redundant. In a lab report, for example, the guiding concept in the report is usually the process that the student went through in doing the experiment. In such cases, an explicit thesis statement may be stating the obvious. If, however, the lab report is based on an experiment, the writer may employ a thesis statement that introduces a hypothesis.

DIFFERENT INTRODUCTIONS IN ACADEMIC WRITING

Introductions are written differently in different subject areas, in different genres of writing, and for different audiences. Depending on the genre and audience, there may be different ordering principles (e.g., general to specific, specific to general), different types of thesis statements, and different ways of telling the reader about the content of the essay.

TASK 2

The following are examples of different types of introductions in academic writing. Read each example and complete the corresponding information.

a) **Academic journal article**

SCIENCE FOR FEMINISTS: MARGARET ATWOOD'S BODY OF KNOWLEDGE

1 Many powerful ideas of modern science have fallen on artistic deaf ears. **2** Except for writers of science fiction, relatively few contemporary fiction writers have made natural science a central preoccupation. **3** In fact, most authors ignore scientific developments altogether. **4** An interesting exception is Margaret Atwood, who not only refers to science but also does so from a woman's perspective, something comparatively rare in literary evocations of science. **5** Science is not Atwood's central concern, but she does suggest, albeit in a light and at times even whimsical fashion, that modern physics is suited to describing women's experiences. **6** In so doing she produces a striking adaptation of a predominantly male discourse (natural science).

Source: Deery, J. (1997). Science for feminists: Margaret Atwood's body of knowledge. *Twentieth Century Literature, 43.*

Which sentence(s) carries out the following functions of an introduction? Write the sentence number(s) in the blank.

a) Sentence _______ is the most general and makes no reference to literature.

b) Sentences _______ begin the shift from general to specific by highlighting the lack of reference to science in literature.

c) Sentences _______ refer specifically to the work of Margaret Atwood, linking her treatment of science to women and feminism.

b) **Academic journal article**

NOVELS AND NEWSPAPERS IN THE AMERICAS

1 In this essay, I will be discussing the interaction of novelistic and journalistic subjects and narrative strategies in a number of works by Latin American and US writers. **2** I will pay particular attention to *Gringo viejo (The Old Gringo,* 1985), by Carlos Fuentes—first to Fuentes' fictionalization of Ambrose Bierce, and then to his narrative and thematic uses of Agustin Victor Casasola's famous photographs of the Mexican Revolution. **3** But my intention is also more general. **4** Fuentes' text centers on a US journalist and fiction writer in Mexico, and I too will be crossing territorial borders to entertain some broad historical comparisons (and contrasts) between US and Latin American literary attitudes toward journalism. **5** My comparative discussion is based on the hypothesis that the explicit integration of journalistic discourse into literary narration tends to foreground the truth claims of the work and raise pointed questions about narrative referentiality. **6** We are, of course, well accustomed to the current critical conflation of "factual" and "fictional" narrative: this conflation is the theme of the literary works I will be discussing, and a primary source of their narrative energy. **7** It is also the basis for their critique of narrative as such. **8** By establishing an explicit dialectic between the journalistic and novelistic discursive modes, they acknowledge and often embody multiple versions of the world, and ask their readers to make distinctions among those versions. **9** We will see that these distinctions, like attitudes toward journalism, vary considerably in the Americas from North to South. **10** Let's begin with Latin America.

Source: Lois Parkinson Zamora, "Novels and Newspapers in the Americas," in *Novel* 23.1, pp. 44–62.

Which sentence(s) carries out the following functions of an introduction? Write the sentence number(s) in the blank.

a) Sentences _______ introduce the specific focus of the article.

b) Sentence _______ introduces the writer's general intention before listing specific examples.

c) Sentence _______ is a kind of thesis statement because it introduces a hypothesis.

c) Academic journal article

ANALYSIS OF A SIMULATED SPRINT COMPETITION IN CLASSICAL CROSS COUNTRY SKIING

1 Sprint competitions in cross country (XC) skiing were first established in the middle of the 1990s. **2** In brief, a sprint competition in XC skiing is separated into two parts: first, a qualification heat, in the form of a time trial, and second, after a break of 1–3 h, the final event containing three heats with breaks of about 20–25 min in between. **3** The 16 or 30 fastest skiers qualify for the final event, where, in each heat, groups of four to six athletes (depending on the mode) compete together, while only the two fastest will qualify for the next heat. **4** Regarding classical WC-sprint races in XC skiing over the past few years, a single sprint run had a mean distance of 1350 m and a mean finishing time in the qualification run of 2 min 50 s. **5** In order to reach place one to eight in a sprint competition, an athlete has to pass through four heats, with a total competition time of about 3–4 h. **6** With sprint events becoming more popular, different approaches in the field of special sprint training, testing and skiing techniques are beginning to emerge. **7** To date, published investigations in the literature regarding physiological stress, and biomechanical aspects measured during an XC skiing sprint competition are lacking. **8** Only a few studies regarding predictors of XC skiing sprint performance can be found (Rusko, 2003; Stöggl et al., 2006). **9** Stöggl et al. (2006) developed test concepts for the XC skiing sprint, roller skiing on a treadmill using the double poling (DP) technique. **10** Maximal DP speed tests and a 1000m DP test were shown to be reliable and valid tests for the prediction of DP sprint performance on roller skis. **11** Maximal DP speed together with a high strength endurance level was found to be strongly related to DP sprint performance. **12** Rusko (2003) measured maximal anaerobic skiing power with an incremental sprint ski test on an indoor 200 m track using the skating technique. **13** He suggested that sprint skiing requires high anaerobic capacity and high maximal oxygen uptake (VO2max), even though neuromuscular force–velocity characteristics, good skiing technique and skiing economy are probably the most important characteristics for a good sprint skier.

Which sentence(s) carries out the following functions of an introduction? Write the sentence number(s) in the blank.

a) Sentence _______ gives a brief history of sprint competitions in cross country skiing.

b) Sentences _______ describe the process and features of the topic.

c) Sentence _______ signals a shift from general background to specific analysis in the study.

d) Academic journal article

LIFE HISTORY OF COHO SALMON

1 Coho salmon were first described by Walbaum in 1792 as *salmo kisutch*, the specific name being the vernacular for salmon in Kamchatka, USSR (Mcphail and Lindsey 1970). **2** Coho (*Oncorhynchus kisutch*), one of the seven recognized species of Pacific salmon belonging to the genus *Oncorhynchus*, are widely distributed in commercially harvestable quantities throughout their natural range, from the Soviet Far East around the Bering Sea, to Alaska, and south along the North American coast to California (Hart 1973). **3** During the 1970s the world catch of all Pacific salmon averaged just over 400 million kg annually and of this total, approximately 9% consisted of coho, with the North American catch about double the Asian catch (Fredin 1980).

4 The basic life history pattern for this species begins as adult salmon migrate from the sea into streams to deposit their eggs in gravel. **5** Each female produces several thousand eggs, which are reduced in number by a high mortality during the coho's early life history (Salo and Bayliff 1958). **6** After spawning, the adults die. **7** The eggs incubate during winter in the gravel, and in the spring free-swimming fry emerge. **8** The fry take up residency in the stream for a year or more, migrate to sea as smolts, and then begin their rapid growth phase (Davidson and Hutchinson 1938). **9** After eighteen months or so at sea, the now maturing adults travel hundreds of kilometers across ocean waters, up streams, and through lakes to return to their place of origin (Hoar 1958). **10** Within this basic pattern there are a great many variations that have evolved in response to opportunity and selective pressures.

Which sentence(s) carries out the following functions of an introduction? Write the sentence number(s) in the blank.

a) Sentences _______ give technical definitions of the term *coho salmon.*

b) Sentence _______ shifts to the specific focus of the article by mentioning key words from the title.

c) Sentence _______ opens up the focus to differences in the coho's life cycle to be discussed in the article.

e) Student's comparative essay

A COMPARISON OF TWO CITIES' PUBLIC TRANSIT SYSTEMS

1 It is a human trait to compare things and to make judgments about whether one thing or place is better than the other. **2** It is, therefore, no surprise that, as I wait twenty-five minutes for my bus in the Vancouver rain on my hour-long journey home, I think back to my student days in Toronto when I covered a similar distance by subway in a mere twenty-five minutes. **3** Toronto transit, or the TTC, is the backbone of the largest city in Canada. **4** Vancouver transit, or TransLink as it is more affectionately called, is little more than an alternative mode of transportation. **5** To compare the transit of Toronto and that of Vancouver would be like comparing a small and nimble sports car to a slow awkward tank. **6** To make an accurate comparison between the two, the cost, efficiency, and accessibility are just a few factors to take into consideration.

Which sentence carries out the following functions of an introduction? Write the sentence number in the blank.

a) Sentence _______ gives the most general statement of the introduction.

b) Sentence _______ shifts from general to specific by making a first mention of the two cities being compared.

c) Sentence _______ is a kind of thesis statement in which an opinion is stated implicitly in metaphorical style.

Abstracts

It is common for academic journal articles to open with an abstract, which is often a paragraph of 100 to 150 words. An abstract precedes the introduction and serves as an overall summary of the article. It includes information such as an introductory statement, the research question or problem being addressed, methodology, and a brief summary of the findings of the article.

TASK 3

Read the following abstracts and complete the corresponding information.

a) Academic journal article

PORTRAIT OF THE ARTIST AS A YOUNG COLONIAL GIRL: EMILY CARR AND JUDITH WRIGHT

1 In their autobiographical writing, painter Emily Carr and poet Judith Wright record a remarkably similar experience of how growing up in colonial/postcolonial Canada and Australia shaped them as artists. **2** Although each identified strongly with the region of her birth, and felt a deep love of its landscape, issues of belonging preoccupied both women from childhood on as they negotiated their place within the family, the immediate society and the nation. **3** Neither could fully conform to family expectations, nor comply with the restrictions society sought to impose on them as artists and each actively sought, or else found herself cast in, an outsider role. **4** Carr and Wright's self portraits each have something in common with James Joyce's representation of Stephen Dedalus in *A Portrait of the Artist as a Young Man* as an insider/outsider figure who seeks to escape the confining networks of nation and society, only to find himself thoroughly entangled in them.

Source: Anne Collett and Dorothy Jones. "Portrait of the Artist as a Young Colonial Girl: Emily Carr and Judith Wright." From *The Journal of Commonwealth Literature* 44.3 (September 2009), 51–67. Copyright © 2009, Sage Publications.

Which sentence(s) carries out the following functions of an abstract? Write the sentence number(s) in the blank.

a) Sentence _______ introduces the similarities in the life experiences of the two authors.

b) Sentences _______ start a shift from general to specific.

c) Sentence _______ marks the shift to the specific focus of the article by using key words from the title.

b) Academic journal article

TOTAL QUALITY MANAGEMENT AS COMPETITIVE ADVANTAGE: A REVIEW AND EMPIRICAL STUDY

1 Total Quality Management (TQM) has become, according to one source, "as pervasive a part of business thinking as quarterly financial results," and yet TQM's role as a strategic resource remains virtually unexamined in strategic management research. **2** Drawing on the resource approach and other theoretical perspectives, this article examines TQM as a potential source of sustainable competitive advantage, reviews existing empirical evidence, and reports findings from a new empirical study of TQM's performance consequences. **3** The findings suggest that most features generally associated with TQM—such as quality training, process improvement, and benchmarking—do not generally produce advantage, but that certain tacit, behavioral, imperfectly imitable features—such as open culture, employee empowerment, and executive commitment—can produce advantage. **4** The author concludes that these tacit resources, and not TQM tools and techniques, drive TQM success, and that organizations that acquire them can outperform competitors with or without the accompanying TQM ideology.

Source: Thomas C. Powell. "Total quality management as competitive advantage: A review and empirical study." From *Strategic Management Journal* 16.1 (1995), 15–37. Copyright © 2006, John Wiley and Sons.

Which sentence carries out the following functions of an abstract? Write the sentence number in the blank.

a) Sentence _______ highlights a gap in the existing literature.

b) Sentence _______ introduces the approach and theoretical perspectives of the article.

c) Sentence _______ summarizes the findings of the article.

d) Sentence _______ gives the author's opinion.

c) Academic journal article

SELF-REPORTS VERSUS SLEEP LABORATORY FINDINGS IN 122 DRUG-FREE SUBJECTS WITH COMPLAINTS OF CHRONIC INSOMNIA

1 The authors compared the sleep laboratory recordings of 122 drug-free subjects who complained of chronic insomnia with the subjects' estimates of their habitual sleep characteristics and their estimated sleep time on the morning after sleeping in the laboratory. **2** Most subjects consistently underestimated the amount of time they slept and overestimated the amount of time it took them to get to sleep in comparison with laboratory data. **3** All subjects consistently underestimated the number of arousals they experienced. **4** The authors discuss the implications of these findings for the treatment and definition of insomnia and for further research.

Source: Carskadon, M.A, Dement, W.C., Mitler, M.M., Guilleminault, C., Zarcone, V.P., and Spiegel, R. (1976). Self-reports versus sleep laboratory findings in 122 drug-free subjects with complaints of chronic insomnia. *American Journal of Psychiatry, 133,* 1382–1388.

Which sentence(s) carries out the following functions of an abstract? Write the sentence number(s) in the blank.

a) Sentence _______ describes the research method.

b) Sentences _______ summarize the findings of the article.

c) Sentence _______ mentions that the implications of the findings will be discussed.

COMMON FEATURES OF CONCLUSIONS

As is the case with introductions, there are also many different ways to write academic conclusions. How you choose to write a conclusion will depend on the genre, audience, and context. Writing conclusions, however, typically involves the following strategies:

1. Summarize the main content and/or perspectives analyzed in the essay.
2. Synthesize the main content and/or perspectives analyzed in the essay.
3. Answer the essay question definitively.
4. Finish with an end statement.

A Mirror Image

One way to think of a conclusion in academic writing is as a mirror image of the introduction. Academic conclusions often shift from *specific to general*, whereas introductions tend to shift from *general to specific*. This idea is illustrated below.

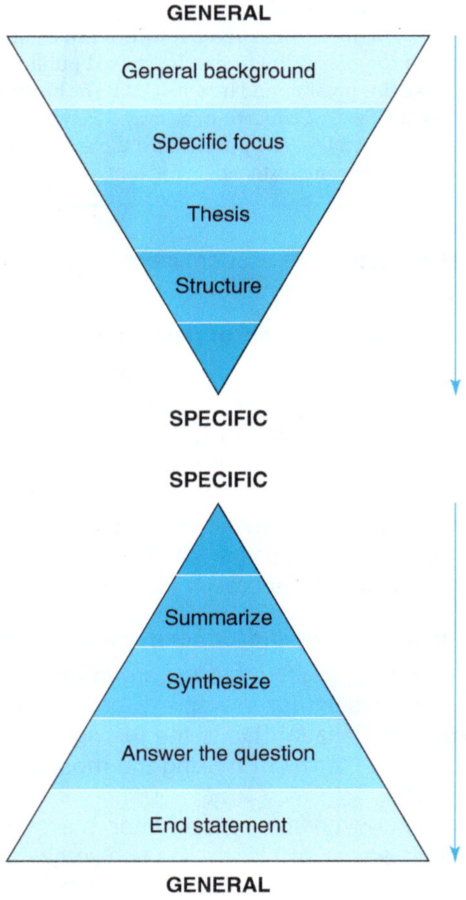

Read the following example of a concluding paragraph, which comes from the argument essay on the pros and cons of universal health care. In the conclusion, you will notice a shift from specific to general.

Universal health care: Concluding paragraph

1 In focusing my discussion on the pros and cons of universal health care systems around three key themes—individual versus state responsibility, effectiveness, and cost—I have suggested that both systems offer benefits as well as problems for individuals and society. **2** In each case, I have suggested that the arguments in question do not warrant an either-or conclusion: for example, a private system as in the US, or a public system as in Canada. **3** This is the wrong focus. **4** Instead, we should be practical and think in terms of making the most of the benefits that both systems can bring. **5** Granted, universal health care systems alone are often inadequate at meeting demand, but exclusively private systems are also inadequate at reaching the needs of all people. **6** A complementary mixed public-private system, as can be found in the UK and France, represents a realistic and pragmatic way forward. **7** When the public system cannot cope, individuals should have the right to seek private alternatives paid for by the public system, at no individual cost; when those who can afford it require fast private care, or when employers want fast treatment for key workers, they should have the right to exercise this choice. **8** In doing so, they free up space in the public sector. **9** Such a complementary relationship would clearly bring benefits to both systems and to their patients. **10** In conclusion, therefore, I argue for universal health care as a must in all societies, but not ruling out the possibility to develop mixed public-private systems where resources and demand make this possible and beneficial. **11** The health of current and future generations depends on many factors: education, healthy lifestyle, and speedy and efficient access to health care, to name but a few. **12** I put forward the argument that these factors are best addressed in mixed public-private systems.

The following strategies used to write academic conclusions are present in the concluding paragraph above.

1. **Summarize the main content and/or perspectives analyzed in the essay.**

   "In focusing my discussion on the pros and cons of universal health care systems around three key themes—individual versus state responsibility, effectiveness, and cost—I have suggested that both systems offer benefits as well as problems for individuals and society."

   In the sentence above, the writer signals the shift from the main body sections of the essay to the conclusion by summarizing the three analytic perspectives on which the discussion has been centred. The writer also summarizes the balanced analytic approach that has been employed.

2. **Synthesize the main content and/or perspectives analyzed in the essay.**

   "In each case, I have suggested that the arguments in question do not warrant an either-or conclusion: for example, a private system as in the US, or a public system as in Canada. This is the wrong focus. Instead, we should be practical and think in terms of making the most of the benefits that both systems can bring."

   In the three sentences above, the writer is synthesizing the main content and perspectives analyzed in the essay. Synthesis here means bringing together all of the ideas and arguments put forward in the essay into an overall, all-encompassing, closing idea. By doing this, the writer avoids repeating too much old information and makes it easier for the reader by concluding with one overall idea. Writers often synthesize in conclusions by highlighting one common theme that has run through the essay. In this regard, the synthesis can be understood as a kind of restating of the thesis statement of the essay, albeit in a more developed way.

3. **Answer the essay question definitively.**

"Granted, universal health care systems alone are often inadequate at meeting demand, but exclusively private systems are also inadequate at reaching the needs of all people. A complementary mixed public-private system, as can be found in the UK and France, represents a realistic and pragmatic way forward. When the public system cannot cope, individuals should have the right to seek private alternatives paid for by the public system, at no individual cost; when those who can afford it require fast private care, or when employers want fast treatment for key workers, they should have the right to exercise this choice. In doing so, they free up space in the public sector. Such a complementary relationship would clearly bring benefits to both systems and to their patients. In conclusion, therefore, I argue for universal health care as a must in all societies, but not ruling out the possibility to develop mixed public-private systems where resources and demand make this possible and beneficial."

A very important function of conclusions is to answer any questions definitively, or address the key problem that was set out in the essay question or in the introduction. In the sentences above, the writer starts by giving some context for the final answer, stating an opinion, and developing it in a way that corresponds to earlier discussion. This part of the conclusion would normally include several sentences.

4. **Finish with an end statement.**

"The health of current and future generations depends on many factors: education, healthy lifestyle, and speedy and efficient access to health care, to name but a few. I put forward the argument that these factors are best addressed in mixed public-private systems."

End statements round off the essay generally and smoothly, and give the reader food for thought. Often, end statements refer to the issue that has been discussed in terms of a hypothetical future. In the example above, the first sentence refers to the future and is followed by a more emphatic sentence that reiterates the writer's opinion.

DIFFERENT CONCLUSIONS IN ACADEMIC WRITING

Writers put together conclusions in academic writing in different ways, depending on the genre, audience, and context.

TASK 4

The following are examples of concluding paragraphs in different forms of academic writing. Read each example and complete the corresponding information.

a) Academic journal article

"A CHOICE OF NIGHTMARES": THE ECOLOGY OF *HEART OF DARKNESS*

1 *Heart of Darkness* emerges from a moment when differing constructions of nature jostled for precedence, and the intellectual world was moved to consider the consequences of ecology's insights. **2** That is why *Heart of Darkness* is a novel balanced across the troubling distance between people and nature, and the fearful implications of closing that gap. **3** This is an environmental novel for three reasons. **4** First, *Heart of Darkness* is set in a place and time of ecological disaster, and it is part of the text's acute sensitivity that it manages to connect the logic of imperialism with the practice that generates crushing ecological exploitation. **5** Next, *Heart of Darkness* engages competing definitions of humanity in nature, and in these definitions explores the possibility of a man empowered by identification with his wild context. **6** The novel thus figures an escape from the discursive feedback loop by which a modern society defines itself against a false image of nature, and by which that false image of nature is enforced by the power of society. **7** Finally, Marlow's and Kurtz's journeys through ecological extinction in the Congo occasion "that supreme moment of complete knowledge" wherein civilization is known as just one of many possible outcomes for a humanity shaped by goalless nature. **8** To read *Heart of Darkness* we should think not just about culture, but also about nature because the text enacts, examines, and anticipates modernity's conflicted attitudes toward itself on this earth.

Which sentence carries out the following functions of a conclusion? Write the sentence number in the blank.

a) Sentence _______ summarizes the historical moment around which the novel was set.

b) Sentence _______ synthesizes by highlighting the interrelationship between people and nature.

c) Sentence _______ rounds off by introducing a broader theme (modernity) as food for thought.

Does the conclusion shift from general to specific, from specific to general, or in another way?

---

b) Academic book chapter

THE ARTICULATE MAMMAL: AN INTRODUCTION TO PSYCHOLINGUISTICS

1 Although we have now completed our discussion of language acquisition, there is one point which remains quite open. **2** What kind of internal grammar does someone who has completed the acquisition of language have? **3** In other words, what does the internalized grammar of an adult look like? **4** This is the next question to be considered. **5** But before that, we have a brief excursus in which we discuss the following topic: how did Chomsky conceive the idea of a transformational grammar in the first place? **6** And why has he changed his mind so much in recent years?

Source: Aitchison, J. (1998). *The Articulate Mammal: An Introduction to Psycholinguistics.* Florence, KY: Routledge. p. 174.

Which sentence(s) carries out the following functions of a conclusion? Write the sentence number(s) in the blank.

a) Sentence ________ signals the end of the chapter and states that there is an issue that still requires study.

b) Sentences ________ discuss a remaining issue.

c) Sentences ________ serve as transitions by asking questions that will be addressed in the next chapter.

Does the conclusion shift from general to specific, from specific to general, or in another way?

___

c) Professional journal article

MOBILE PHONES IN THE CLASSROOM: IF YOU CAN'T BEAT THEM, JOIN THEM

1 The use of mobile phones in the classroom has the potential to increase some negative outcomes or distractions such as phones ringing during class or students engaging in off-task activities (e.g., sending messages to their friends). **2** However during the TXT-2-LRN trial these issues were not experienced or perceived by the instructor. **3** Nowadays, the reality of the large classroom is that most students have their mobile phones switched on (usually on silent mode) and that occasionally they exchange messages with their social network during class (usually trying to hide the device under the table). **4** Our experience has shown that positive results can be achieved by encouraging students to bring their mobile phones out in the open and to use them to contribute to the class, and to their own learning—that is, by joining them instead of trying to beat them.

Source: Eusebio Scornavacca, et al. "Mobile phones in the classroom: If you can't beat them, join them." From *Communications of the ACM* 52.4 (April 2009), 142–146. Copyright © 2009, Association for Computing Machinery, Inc.

Which sentence carries out the following functions of a conclusion? Write the sentence number in the blank.

a) Sentence ________ summarizes potential outcomes of mobile-phone use by students in class.

b) Sentence ________ shifts from potential to actual outcome seen in the study.

c) Sentence ________ restates the opinion of the writers as first introduced in the title of the article.

Does the conclusion shift from general to specific, from specific to general, or in another way?

___

d) Book review in an academic journal

ENGAGING THE MIDDLE EAST: NAPOLEON'S INVASION OF EGYPT

1 All three of these books make valuable contributions to this ongoing debate by discussing the interplay of power politics, cultural interaction, and the search for knowledge. **2** Cole's *Napoleon's Egypt* is the most academic of the three, adding to our knowledge of the subject both through new sources and new scholarship. **3** Its primary flaw is only that it does not cover the entire expedition. **4** The strongest recommendation for Strathern's *Napoleon in Egypt* is that it is an easy and enjoyable narrative and, at the same time, well-researched and comprehensive. **5** If the book has a flaw, it lies in its attempt to explain many of the controversial issues that surrounded the expedition only in terms of Napoleon Bonaparte and his personality, with insufficient consideration of the social and cultural factors involved. **6** Burleigh's *Mirage* is an excellent account of an important and too-often-neglected aspect of the expedition in terms of its greater historical and cultural impact. **7** Detailed but never tedious, *Mirage* is a pleasure to read, although a broader portrait of the expedition would be useful to the reader, and serious students will be frustrated by the imperfect citations. **8** Together, these three books make significant contributions to the study of both Egypt and the Napoleonic period, and they would be a valuable addition to the library of anyone interested in these subjects.

Which sentence(s) carries out the following functions of a conclusion? Write the sentence number(s) in the blank.

a) Sentence _______ synthesizes by introducing an interplay between three factors in the ongoing debate.

b) Sentences _______ briefly summarize the main strengths and weaknesses of each book.

c) Sentence _______ rounds off by recommending all three books.

Does the conclusion shift from general to specific, from specific to general, or in another way?

____

e) Comparative university essay

A COMPARISON OF ENGLISH AND MANDARIN IN THE WORLD TODAY

1 The effects, impacts, and influences of English and Mandarin have been discussed, focusing on how they are affecting culture, languages, and media and communications around the world today. **2** One important factor underpins each of the points discussed, that is, that languages reflect the economic, political, and cultural power of the nation states with which they are associated. **3** Today, it is the English language which has greater overall influence. **4** This is due to the economic, political, and cultural power of, historically, the British Empire, and currently of the United States. **5** Nonetheless, as China's power and influence in these areas grows, so too will the world presence of Mandarin and its effects on other languages and cultures. **6** In the future, the growth of China will mean the status of English as the world's lingua franca and international language of communication will be challenged by Mandarin.

Which sentence(s) carries out the following functions of a conclusion? Write the sentence number(s) in the blank.

a) Sentence ________ summarizes the content and perspectives that have been the specific focus of the essay.

b) Sentence ________ introduces a concept that synthesizes the main content and perspectives of the essay.

c) Sentences ________ refer to the future, which contextualizes the overall answer and rounds off the essay by giving food for thought.

Does the conclusion shift from general to specific, from specific to general, or in another way?

____

CHAPTER 4 SUMMARY

Introductions and conclusions are very important in academic writing, as they give your reader a first and last impression of you as a writer. It is common to shift from general to specific in introductions and from specific to general in conclusions. In this way, the introduction and conclusion are like mirror images. However, there are probably as many differences as similarities in how writers introduce and conclude when writing different types of academic texts for different audiences. Your role is to consider the different ways of introducing and concluding that you have studied in this chapter and apply them in appropriate ways according to different genres, audiences, and contexts. The focus and structures will change; however, whatever the differences may be, remember to write your ideas and arguments clearly and convincingly.

COMMON FEATURES OF INTRODUCTIONS

You studied four common steps for writing a general-to-specific introduction (which can be followed in a different order):

1. Provide general background information.
2. Shift to the specific focus of your essay.
3. State a thesis that will guide your writing.
4. Refer to the structure of the essay.

You also saw that in different genres of academic writing, introductions are written in very different ways. An introduction for an academic journal article on literary analysis will differ significantly from one that describes the life cycle of a fish. In the abstract to a journal article, a writer will summarize the article as a whole.

THESIS-GUIDED WRITING

Thesis-guided writing means that your thesis statement acts like a thread that runs through your work, holding everything together conceptually. Five common strategies for writing thesis statements were introduced:

1. Explain a central idea that will run through the essay.
2. Present an argument or your opinion.
3. State your purpose for writing.
4. Ask questions.
5. State the focus of the essay.

Keep in mind that different instructors have different views on what makes a good thesis statement. Merely raising questions to be addressed or stating the focus of the essay does not present the stance that you intend to take in the essay—these two strategies are controversial. Always check with your instructor if you are not sure about what is appropriate.

COMMON FEATURES OF CONCLUSIONS

Four common strategies for writing a specific-to-general conclusion were highlighted:

1. Summarize the main content and/or perspectives analyzed in the essay.
2. Synthesize the main content and/or perspectives analyzed in the essay.
3. Answer the essay question definitively.
4. Finish with an end statement.

Again, the examples from different genres of writing and different subject areas illustrated considerable variety in how writers conclude. Find out what is best for you as a writer in the forms of academic writing that you will be doing.

CHAPTER 5

Writing Research Essays

In this chapter, you will study the following aspects of writing research essays:

- ✓ What is a research essay?
- ✓ What is plagiarism?
- ✓ Avoiding plagiarism
- ✓ Paraphrasing
- ✓ Using reporting verbs and citation phrases

The focus of this chapter is on understanding the processes that are involved in writing research essays, from defining your research problem or question to writing in-text citations and a reference list.

An important issue in writing research essays is plagiarism. You will look at a definition of *plagiarism* and study several ways to avoid committing plagiarism when bringing others' ideas into your own work. You will also study two referencing systems that are commonly used in the arts and humanities, and in the social sciences: MLA and APA. Both systems involve learning how to write in-text citations (which appear in the main body of the essay) and corresponding references (which appear at the end of the essay).

Appendices 1 and 2 provide a more detailed explanation of the MLA and APA citation styles that you will study in this chapter.

WHAT IS A RESEARCH ESSAY?

Research essays are based on research that you have carried out. Most research can be defined as either *primary* or *secondary research*. Primary research for an essay includes finding a problem, location, and/or group of participants, and collecting original data. Typically, the data for primary research would be gathered via surveys, interviews, observation, and/or experiment. Secondary research, on the other hand, is research that is already published in academic journals and books, and which you incorporate into your own work.

Writing a research essay involves a multi-stage process. Nine of the most important stages in this process are listed below.

Nine Stages of the Research Essay Process

1. **Find a research problem, issue, or question to analyze.**

   As you begin the planning stage of your research essay, it is important to find a central research problem, issue, or question to focus on. Once you define your research problem, you can then break the problem down into a number of sub-questions that you will attempt to answer. Then you can think about the type of research that will allow you to answer these questions.

   Sometimes your instructor will assign a question for you to answer. On other occasions, you may be required to select your own topic and question.

   EXAMPLE 1

   Question:
   Is climate change an exclusively human-made phenomenon?

   Sub-questions:
   What human-made activities cause climate change?

   Are there any natural causes of climate change?

   What evidence is available in studies to prove either case?

   Type of research:
   Secondary: critical reading of studies in journals; looking at environmentalist, government, and corporate websites; determining who is funding the studies; giving your opinion on the evidence

   EXAMPLE 2

   Question:
   What particular problems do English-language learners have on campus?

   Sub-questions:
   What additional languages do students speak?

   How do we define languages as opposed to dialects?

   How can we be sure that the cause of problems is only language?

   Type of research:
   Primary: interview six students about their own languages and the problems that they have faced as students

   Secondary: literature review of studies in journals and books

2. **Search online and in libraries for materials.**

   Once you have identified the problem(s) and/or question(s) that you will be analyzing, you should begin to search for materials using library catalogues, databases for academic journals, and other research tools such as search engines. By trying different combinations of key words, you will be able to find a broad range of related materials.

At this stage, it is very important to be selective. First, you should try to focus as much as possible on materials that relate closely to your problem(s) and/or question(s). Second, you need to evaluate the reliability of the materials that you may be considering using—this is particularly important if you are using online sources that may not have gone through the rigorous editing processes that articles in academic journals and published books go through. At this stage, you can refer back to the criteria for assessing the reliability of online sources that you studied in Chapter 1.

3. **Keep the essay in focus and on task from the outset.**

   Your essay should have a general background topic and a central focus in the form of a thesis statement, question, or problem that you are addressing and aiming to answer. It is important to have a clear idea of your topic and focus early on as you read and take notes. This will save you spending many hours reading and taking notes that you will not need in your final essay. It is also important to keep to your focus and task throughout the essay—avoid going off on tangents and writing about things that are not related and which will not appear in the final essay.

4. **Take effective notes while reading.**

   Once you have found relevant and reliable materials for your topic and focus, the next key stage is to read actively: skimming for gist and scanning for specific information, highlighting and annotating as you read, and taking note of the information required for accurate citation and referencing: author's name(s), title, place of publication, publisher, and page numbers. (See Chapter 1 for active and critical reading skills.)

5. **Draw up an outline for the essay.**

   After you have found materials and begun reading and taking notes, you should draw up a firm outline for your research essay. Your outline should include notes on the following: introduction and thesis statement, the thematic focus of the main body paragraphs and sections, and possible ideas for the conclusion. It is common for writers to change and adapt their outlines as new themes emerge during the writing process; however, it is still important to structure your ideas before you start writing the essay itself.

6. **Develop a suitable method for collecting data (if doing primary research).**

   If your research essay involves primary research, you will need to write about the method used for collecting data in your essay.

Data Collection Method: Points to Consider

- Why did you select one method (e.g., interviews), over another (e.g., surveys)?
- How did your data-gathering method provide answers to your research questions?

- How did you contact participants?
- Why did you choose these participants?
- How did your relationship with participants affect the data they provided?
- What ethical issues did you face?

7. **Write with a good balance of summarizing, paraphrasing, and quoting.**

   One of the challenges of writing research essays is being able to incorporate others' ideas, arguments, and statistics in your writing. You cannot include everything. Which notes should you build into your essay and which should you discard? Which information should be summarized or paraphrased (written in your own words) and which should be quoted directly from your source materials?

8. **Avoid plagiarism by using in-text citations and a list of works cited or reference list.**

   Because research essays involve bringing others' ideas, arguments, and statistics into your work, it is essential that you acknowledge others' work with in-text citations (in the main body of the essay) and with a matching list of works cited or reference list (at the end of the essay). Failure to do so accurately may result in accusations of plagiarism, which can lead to varying degrees of academic sanction. (See Appendices 1 and 2 for detailed explanations of how to use MLA and APA citation styles.)

9. **Make it clear to readers who thinks what.**

   Good critical writing in research essays usually includes arguments, counter-arguments, and the writer's own opinions and perspectives. This kind of three-way analysis requires good writing skills. It is especially important that you provide accurate *language of attribution* to avoid contradicting yourself when presenting different sides of arguments and to make it clear to your reader *who thinks what*: which ideas are yours and which belong to others.

WHAT IS PLAGIARISM?

In Latin, the term *plagiarius* was used to refer to a kidnapper. Although plagiarism cannot be equated with kidnapping people, it does relate to stealing others' ideas and can have serious consequences. When writers present an original idea or argument, data, statistics, or image in academic work, it becomes their intellectual property. If you use someone else's idea and pass it off as your own, you are committing plagiarism.

- **A definition**

  Plagiarism is the use of others' ideas, arguments, creative works, or statistics in your work without acknowledgement. Put simply, it means that you use others' ideas, arguments, creative works, or statistics as if they were your own.

- **Consequences of plagiarism**

  Colleges and universities have written policies regarding plagiarism that instructors are required to adhere to when they come across possible cases. If a case of plagiarism seems unintentional, the student may lose some grades and/or be given the opportunity to resubmit the work with adequate citations and references. If, however, a case of plagiarism is judged to be intentional, then the consequences can be more severe, including failing a course and even suspension from a course of study.

- **Degrees of plagiarism and intention**

  There are varying degrees of plagiarism. Sometimes, plagiarism is clear and obvious, and sometimes it is not. One factor that determines whether or not cases of plagiarism are considered to be serious or less serious is *intention*. Students might commit plagiarism unintentionally, perhaps if they forget to add a citation to a piece of information they have taken from another source, or if they misunderstand what needs to be cited and what can be included without a citation. At the other end of the spectrum is intentional plagiarism, whereby students in a panic may download an essay, or parts of one, from the internet and submit the work as their own. This type of plagiarism is very serious.

TASK 1

Test your understanding of plagiarism.

Below are 10 situations in which a writer is using another's ideas. Look at each situation and decide whether you think it constitutes plagiarism. Give a reason for your answer in the space below each situation.

1. You downloaded an essay from the internet and submitted it as your own work with no changes.

____

____

____

____

2. You downloaded an essay from the internet and submitted it as your own work with a few changes to grammar and vocabulary.

____

____

____

____

3. You resubmitted an essay that you already submitted in a previous course.

____

____

____

____

4. You got help from a private tutor or friend who corrected the grammar and vocabulary in your essay.

5. You got help from a private tutor or friend who rewrote sections of the essay to express your arguments more effectively.

6. You forgot to include an in-text citation when you brought in someone else's idea.

7. You included an in-text citation in your essay when you brought in someone else's idea, but forgot to match it with a corresponding entry in your references at the end of the essay.

8. You forgot to include quotation marks in a direct quotation (i.e., when using the exact words of a writer).

9. You used a direct quotation and didn't include a page number in the in-text citation.

10. You didn't include a citation for information in your essay that could be described as a common fact or common knowledge.

____

____

____

____

AVOIDING PLAGIARISM

There are many effective strategies for incorporating the ideas of others into your academic work in ways that avoid plagiarism.

1. Take Effective Notes

In Chapter 1, you studied how to take notes by annotating a text as a form of active reading. The origin of many problems associated with plagiarism can be found in poor note-taking strategies. Two note-taking problems that can lead to plagiarism are (1) forgetting to write down the source and page number for each set of notes and (2) not being sure if your notes are direct quotations or paraphrases of the original text.

Every time you take notes from a text, remember to take a note of the author, title, publication date, place of publication, and publisher. As you take notes, record the corresponding page numbers in the margin. And finally, make sure that you use quotation marks in your notes when you copy the exact words from a text.

EXAMPLE

Richards, S. (2005). *How to take effective notes.* London: Academic Press.

p. 2 taking notes = important – 1st engage w/ others' ideas
bad notes = bad essay (disorg, not coherent, etc.)
req's patience, focus, understanding; pays off long term

p. 4 study at UofA: 50 undergrads, 33% = no note of author/page no.

p. 12 "taking effective notes is the key to effective research essays"

Giggs, G. (2006). Note-taking and student engagement. *Journal of Note-taking Studies, Volume 2, Issue 1,* pp. 28–39.

p. 28 says Richards is wrong; first engagement = earlier in process, when searching for sources, reading round a text, etc.

2. Write Appropriate In-Text Citations

Every time you incorporate into your essay an idea, argument, creative work, or statistic that you found in someone else's work, you need to include an in-text citation in the corresponding paragraph of the essay. The following example illustrates three ways to write in-text citations using APA style.

Example of in-text citations

1 Taking effective notes in academic reading and writing is very important and requires considerable patience, focus, and understanding (Richards, 2005). **2** According to Richards, note-taking represents a student's first active engagement with the writer whose work is being read. **3** In contrast, Giggs (2006) argues that a student's first active engagement with another writer comes before the note-taking stage, when the student begins the search for literature on a particular subject.

In Sentence 1 in the example above, the writer includes the following in-text citation using APA style: "(Richards, 2005)." Following APA style, the writer places the author's surname, a comma, and the year of publication in parentheses immediately after the information. The in-text citation tells the reader where the writer got the information from; it also points the reader to the full reference in the reference list at the end of the essay. Placing this type of in-text citation in parentheses after information is a rather neutral style in which the citation performs the sole function of acknowledging where the information was taken from.

In Sentence 2, the writer uses the citation phrase "According to Richards" to add more information to the previous sentence. It is not necessary to add the author's name and date in parentheses to this sentence, as it is implicitly understood that the writer is referring to the same source.

In Sentence 3, the writer introduces the ideas of another writer as follows: "Giggs (2006) argues that." This type of in-text citation uses the author's name as the subject of the sentence and a corresponding reporting verb (such as *argues*, *states*, *suggests*, etc.) Because the author's name is included in the citation phrase, only the year of publication is needed in parentheses. This type of citation gives more emphasis to the author and his or her ideas.

Other referencing systems do not include a comma between the author and the year in in-text citations, but they may include a page number rather than a year of publication or place citation information in the footnotes of the text. Whatever citation style you use, follow it consistently.

3. Write an Appropriate List of Works Cited or Reference List

Every in-text citation should include a corresponding full reference in the list of *works cited* or *reference list* at the end of the essay. This full reference will include more information than the in-text citation. Although some may use the terms *list of works cited, reference list,* and *bibliography* interchangeably, each term is associated with a distinct referencing style. A list of works cited (MLA) or reference list (APA) should only include full references for works cited in the text. (See Appendices 1 and 2 for more information on MLA and APA styles, respectively.) A bibliography, on the other hand, can also include full references for sources that the writer read, and which informed his or her thinking, but which are not cited in the essay. If in doubt about which referencing style to follow, ask your instructor.

In the example of in-text citations above, two sources were cited: Richards (2005) and Giggs (2006). Each in-text citation should refer to a full, matching reference at the end of the essay in the list of works cited or reference list.

EXAMPLE: MLA style
Works cited

Giggs, George. "Note-taking and Student Engagement." *Journal of Note-taking Studies* 2.1 (2006): 28-39. Print.

Richards, Steve. *How to Take Effective Notes.* London: Academic Press, 2005. Print.

EXAMPLE: APA style
References

Giggs, G. (2006). Note-taking and student engagement. *Journal of Note-taking Studies, 2*(1), 28–39.

Richards, S. (2005). *How to take effective notes.* London: Academic Press.

In MLA and APA styles, references are arranged in alphabetical order according to author surname, or organization name or work title for sources that do not have a stated author. Note that the format of the first reference, a journal article, is different from that of the second reference, a single-author book. You can find out more about different formats in Appendices 1 and 2.

Six Common Problems with Writing References

Here are six common problems to look out for when you are writing in-text citations and a list of works cited or reference list in academic writing:

1. **In-text citation but no corresponding full reference in the reference list**

   This is a common mistake. Remember to review each in-text citation after finishing the essay to ensure there is a corresponding full reference in the reference list.

2. **Full reference in the reference list without a corresponding in-text citation**

   This is a less common mistake. Review each full reference in the reference list to make sure that it corresponds with an in-text citation.

3. **Mismatch between the in-text citation and the full reference in the reference list**

   This mistake makes it difficult for the reader to find a full reference in the reference list. Below is an example where a writer has cited an internet source in the text by the author's name, but listed the full reference by the webpage:

   In-text citation: (Walsh, 2002)
   Full reference: [incorrect]
   How to write a reference list by B. Walsh. Retrieved from www.onlinerefideas.net/apa/refs/html

   Full reference: [correct]
   Walsh, B. (2002). *How to write a reference list.* Retrieved from http://www.onlinerefideas.net/apa/refs/html

   Note: The name of the author, article, or organization that appears in the in-text citation must also appear at the beginning of the full reference in the reference list.

4. **Formatting inconsistencies**

   It is important to format in-text citations and full references consistently. For example, if you are following APA style, it is necessary to separate the author name and year of publication with a comma in in-text citations. Avoid including commas in some in-text citations and not in others. Similarly, make sure that your reference list consistently follows the required APA, MLA, or other citation style guidelines. Avoid mixing referencing systems. There are several websites and software packages you can use to keep your formatting consistent.

5. **Reference list in non-alphabetical order**

   This is another common mistake. Most referencing systems require the full references in the reference list to be ordered alphabetically rather than numbered or in the order they appeared in the essay. Make sure you find out what is required and follow the appropriate guidelines.

6. **Incorrect formatting of online sources**

   Online references can be tricky in terms of formatting the in-text citations and full references in the reference list, especially if the information being cited is unauthored or undated. If this is the case, it is necessary to check carefully the citation style guidelines you are required to use. You will find that nearly all possible types of online sources are covered.

4. Use Direct Quotations

One effective way to bring others' ideas into your work is to use direct quotations, in which you copy an author's exact words from a text. Direct quotations have pros and cons. One pro is that they allow readers to get directly to the essence of an author's ideas and arguments by reading his or her exact words. Direct quotations can be very effective if you want to create a strong impact. However, some writers use too many direct quotations in college and university essays. A common comment from instructors is something like the following: "Why have you used a direct quotation here? A paraphrase would be much better."

So, when should you use direct quotations instead of paraphrases? Here are two guidelines:

1. You should directly quote the key words that sum up an idea or argument concisely, effectively, and/or in words that you could not paraphrase without losing the essence of the quotation—you should just quote the key words, not the whole sentence or paragraph.
2. You should directly quote a word or phrase that is commonly associated with a certain author. For example, "Cultural and economic globalization has been linked to 'McDonaldization' (Ritzer, 1993)."

If the information you are incorporating into your research essay does not meet either of these guidelines, you should probably paraphrase the information instead.

When you use direct quotations, it is important to follow the citation style guidelines of the referencing system you are using.

MLA

MLA citation style requires inclusion of the author's surname and page number(s) for direct quotations. If the author's surname is included in the citation phrase, only the page number(s) is required in parentheses. If not, then both are placed in parentheses without a comma.

> **EXAMPLES**
> Miller argues that there is "a critical period up until the age of 13 during which language acquisition is more likely" (15).
>
> I question the view, however, that there exists "a critical period up until the age of 13 during which language acquisition is more likely" (Miller 15).

MLA guidelines stipulate that quotations of longer than four lines should start on a new line, be indented from the left margin by one inch, and have no quotation marks.

APA

APA citation style requires inclusion of the author's surname, year of publication, and page number for direct quotations. Again, the information included in the citation phrase will determine how much information should be included in parentheses.

> **EXAMPLES**
> Miller (1999) argues that there is "a critical period up until the age of 13 during which language acquisition is more likely" (p. 15).
>
> I question the view, however, that there exists "a critical period up until the age of 13 during which language acquisition is more likely" (Miller, 1999, p. 15).

APA guidelines stipulate that quotations of longer than 40 words should start on a new line, be indented from the left margin five spaces, and have no quotation marks.

PARAPHRASING

The majority of researched information that you bring into your essay should be summarized or paraphrased rather than quoted directly.

Summarizing

In Chapter 1, you studied how to read actively by highlighting and annotating a text, and how to convert the annotations into a summary.

What should you summarize in a research essay?

- The information that you summarize for your research essay will often be general background information, perhaps historical background, statistical information, or information that is not related to your main focus.
- When summarizing, you still need to use in-text citations for any ideas, information, creative works, or statistics you have found in others' work.

Paraphrasing

Paraphrasing is the main alternative to using direct quotations when bringing others' ideas into research essays. Paraphrasing involves rewriting the original text in your own words, and changing the vocabulary, grammar, and order of information. Paraphrasing is commonly used to incorporate ideas that are more closely related to the specific focus of your essay. This is information that has to be included in your essay, but which does not merit a direct quotation.

Several challenges come with paraphrasing:

- What should I paraphrase and what should I quote directly?
- How different from the original should my paraphrase be? Can I just change a few words and add a citation?

Effective paraphrasing requires not only good judgment about what to and what not to paraphrase but also good writing technique to change vocabulary and grammar enough to make the writing your own but not so much that the original meaning is changed. When paraphrasing others' work, you are required to use in-text citations to acknowledge the original source.

TASK 2

Write paraphrases of the following sentences. Change the vocabulary, grammatical structure, and/or order of ideas in order to make the writing your own. At the same time, make sure you do not change the meaning of the original sentence. If necessary, break a long sentence into two shorter ones.

1. The Vancouver 2010 Winter Olympics faced a number of serious problems before the Games even started.

____

____

____

____

____

2. Protesters in Metro Vancouver criticized the Vancouver Organizing Committee for the 2010 Olympic and Paralympic Winter Games (VANOC) for spending so much money on new venues and security for the Games, money which could have been directed to solving the city's chronic homelessness problem.

____

____

____

____

____

3. Others opposed the decision to allow Coca-Cola and McDonald's to be major sponsors for the Games, on the grounds that sponsors associated with healthier eating should have been given preference.

4. Another serious problem was the warm weather, which meant that snow had to be trucked in to one of the local ski hills, Cypress Mountain, at great cost, in the run-up to the Games.

5. In Whistler, the government-sponsored "Own the Podium" campaign (supporting athletes to win gold for Canada), which was seen to favour access to race sites for Canadian athletes, and the blaming of the death of a luge athlete on technical error rather than the lack of protective barriers on a very fast track caused even more controversy.

6. In the end, however, a record 14 gold medals, including an overtime defeat of Team USA in the men's ice hockey final, and the party atmosphere in Vancouver and Whistler left many Canadians jubilant with national pride.

TASK 3

Read the following excerpt from page 1 of David Fetterman's book, *Ethnography: Step by Step*, 2nd edition (1990). Then read the two example paraphrases that follow. One of the example paraphrases represents effective paraphrasing: it has appropriate changes in vocabulary, grammar, sentence structure, and ordering of ideas. The other example represents patchwriting, in which a few changes have been made but in a way that is too close to the original, and constitutes plagiarism. Which is which?

EXCERPT

Ethnography
Ethnography is the art and science of describing a group or culture. The description may be of a small tribal group in an exotic land or a classroom in middle-class suburbia. The task is much like the one taken on by an investigative reporter, who interviews relevant people, reviews records, weighs the credibility of one person's opinions against another's, looks for ties to special interests and organizations, and writes the story for a concerned public and for professional colleagues.

PARAPHRASE EXAMPLE 1

Ethnography
Ethnography can be defined as the art and science of describing a group or culture. The description could be of a small tribal group in a far-off land or a classroom in a middle-class suburb. The task is similar to the one taken on by an investigative journalist, who interviews relevant people, looks at records, weighs the credibility of people's opinions, searches for links to special interests and organizations, and writes the story for the public and other journalists (Fetterman, 1990, p. 1).

PARAPHRASE EXAMPLE 2

Ethnography
Fetterman (1990) defines ethnography as "the art and science of describing a group or culture" (p. 1), whether it be in a local urban setting or a far-off country. Fetterman likens the role of an ethnographer to that of a journalist who writes reports for colleagues and the public based on data collected from selected people and official records.

USING REPORTING VERBS AND CITATION PHRASES

When you cite an author's work, you can introduce that work with a variety of reporting verbs beyond *said*. Your choice of reporting verb and citation phrase can add a subjective angle to what you are citing: it can indicate the opinion of the author that you are citing as well as your own opinion of the author and information.

- **Reporting verbs to cite another's opinion: general ideas**
  - argues
  - claims
  - maintains
  - supports the view that
  - puts forward the view that

Either the past simple or present simple tense can be used for most reporting verbs and citation phrases, with little or no difference in meaning.

> **EXAMPLE: Past simple tense**
> Smith (2002) argued that language and identity are closely related. She also claimed that the link between the two is sometimes understated.
>
> **EXAMPLE: Present simple tense**
> Smith (2002) argues that language and identity are closely related. She also claims that the link between the two is sometimes understated.

In the two examples above, the writer is citing some general ideas/opinions that can be associated with the 2002 work of Smith. In the first example, the reporting verbs "argued" and "claimed" are in the past simple tense, while the reporting verbs in the second example are in the present simple tense. In this case, the decision on which tense to use for the reporting verb is more a matter of style and does not affect meaning. The choice of which tense to use may also reflect a writer's personal preference or what may seem appropriate in a specific subject area. The use of the present simple tense for "are" and "is" in both examples adds an idea of general time to Smith's opinion. In this sense, Smith's view can be seen as one that can be applied in wider contexts.

- **Reporting verbs to cite another's opinion: primary research**

  If you are citing the findings of a study (for example, experimental research), the use of either the past simple or present simple tense in your citation phrase and any following phrase can give your reader an indication of your opinion about the research.

> **EXAMPLE: Past simple tense**
> In her study of 15 adult immigrants, Smith (2002) found that language and identity were closely related. She also claimed that the link between the two was sometimes understated.
>
> **EXAMPLE: Present simple tense**
> In her study of 15 adult immigrants, Smith (2002) finds that language and identity are closely related. She also claims that the link between the two is sometimes understated.

In the first example, the writer is citing Smith's 2002 study by using citation phrases that include the reporting verb and following phrase in the past simple tense. This can be interpreted in two possible ways by readers. First, the use of the past tense can be interpreted as suggesting that the reader believes that Smith's findings are limited within the parameters of that particular study in 2002; that is, they cannot be generalized to a wider population or to broader contexts. Second, the use of the past tense can also imply a distance between the writer and the author of the work cited. For example, a reader might interpret the use of the past tense in the first example as a way for the writer to create distance from the findings of Smith's study.

In the second example, all of the verbs are in the present simple tense. This can be interpreted as suggesting that the writer feels that Smith's findings can be generalized outside the parameters of the study, to broader contexts or to other populations. Equally, a reader may interpret the tense usage as implying that the writer agrees with or has similar ideas to the ideas being cited.

- **Reporting verbs that challenge an opinion**
  - questions
  - challenges

> **EXAMPLES**
> Xiang (2005) <u>challenges</u> the methodology employed by Smith (2002) in her study, noting that . . .
>
> Xiang (2005) <u>questioned</u> whether the interrelationship between language and identity can be understood without considering culture.

The use of the reporting verbs "challenges" and "questioned" show the reader that Xiang disagrees with Smith. The choice of tense does not change the meaning.

- **Reporting verbs that are more neutral**
  - states
  - suggests
  - implies

> **EXAMPLES**
> Xiang (2005) <u>states</u> that language can be better defined through its interrelationship with culture rather than identity.
>
> Xiang (2005) <u>suggests</u> that the interrelationship between language and identity <u>may be</u> understood without considering culture.

The use of the reporting verb "states" gives a neutral and less opinionated tone to the citation. The use of the reporting verb "suggests" tells the reader that the view being expressed is tentative. The addition of the modal auxiliary "may" adds to the tentativeness.

- **Using the present perfect tense in citations**

> **EXAMPLES**
> There <u>has been</u> little research on the relationship between language and socio-economic status in western countries.
>
> The relationship between culture, identity, and ethnicity <u>has been</u> the subject of several qualitative studies (Jackson, 1999; Martinez & Shaw, 2006; Singh et al., 2003).

The present perfect tense is commonly used in two ways to refer to another's work. In the first sentence, the present perfect form "has been" is used to refer to general research activity (in this case, the lack of it) in a sentence that does not mention any specific authors or studies. In the second, the present perfect tense is used to refer to several studies together.

- **Adding opinion with adverbs**

The above reporting verbs/citation phrases can give readers an indication of the opinion of the author you are citing. The writer of the text may, however, want to indicate more directly his or her opinion of the author and information. One easy and effective way for the writer to add his or her opinion to the citation phrase is through an adverb of opinion.

Expressing agreement

- rightly
- quite rightly
- correctly

> **EXAMPLE**
> Xiang (2005) <u>quite rightly</u> states that language can be better defined through its interrelationship with culture rather than identity.

Expressing disagreement

- wrongly
- mistakenly

EXAMPLE

In her study of 15 adult immigrants, Smith (2002) found that language and identity were closely related. However, she mistakenly claimed that the link between the two was irrelevant when immigrants move to a new country where their mother tongue is spoken.

Adding your voice with other adverbs

- interestingly
- apparently
- seemingly
- somewhat optimistically

EXAMPLES

Xiang (2005) interestingly states that language can be better defined through its interrelationship with culture rather than identity.

In her study of 15 adult immigrants, Smith (2002) somewhat optimistically suggests that immigrants might learn languages more effectively through immersion education; however, many immigrants do not live in areas where such programs are available.

TASK 4

In this task, you will put into practice the aspects of writing research essays you have learned in this chapter. Follow the instructions below.

1. Read the following two texts straight through without stopping.

Text 1
Author: David M. Fetterman
Book: *Ethnography: Step by Step* (2nd edition)
Place of publication: Thousand Oaks, California
Publisher: Sage Publications Ltd.
Year of publication: 1990

Margin Notes

Ethnography
Page 1

Ethnography is the art and science of describing a group or culture. The description may be of a small tribal group in an exotic land or a classroom in middle-class suburbia. The task is much like the one taken on by an investigative reporter, who interviews relevant people, reviews records, weighs the credibility of one person's opinions against another's, looks for ties to special interests and organizations, and writes the story for a concerned public and for professional colleagues. A key difference between the investigative journalist and the ethnographer, however, is that whereas the journalist seeks out the unusual—the murder, the plane crash, or the bank robbery—the ethnographer writes about the routine, daily lives of people. The more predictable patterns of human thought and behaviour are the focus of inquiry.

Ethnographers are noted for their ability to keep an open mind about the group or culture they are studying. This quality, however, does not imply any lack of rigor. The ethnographer enters the field with an open mind, not an empty head. Before asking the first question in the field, the ethnographer begins with a problem, a theory or model, a research design, specific data collection techniques, tools for analysis, and a specific writing style.

The ethnographer also begins with biases and preconceived notions about how people behave and what they think—as do researchers in every field. Indeed, the choice of what problem, geographic area, or people to study is in itself biased. Biases serve both positive and negative functions. When controlled, biases can focus and limit the research effort. When uncontrolled, they can undermine the quality of the ethnographic research. To mitigate the negative effects of bias, the ethnographer must first make specific biases explicit.

Page 2

An open mind also allows the ethnographer to explore rich, untapped sources of data not mapped out in the research design. The ethnographic study allows multiple interpretations of reality and alternative interpretations of data throughout the study. The ethnographer is interested in understanding and describing a social and cultural scene from the emic, or insider's, perspective. The ethnographer is both storyteller and scientist.

Source: David M. Fetterman. *Ethnography: Step by Step,* 2nd edition. Copyright © 1998 Sage Publications Inc. Reprinted by permission of Sage Publications Inc.

Text 2
Authors: Martyn Hammersley and Paul Atkinson
Book: *Ethnography: Principles in Practice*
Place of publication: London
Publisher: Routledge
Year of publication: 1998

Margin Notes

Ethnography
Page 1
What is ethnography?

Over the last few years there has been a growth of interest in ethnography among researchers in many different fields, both theoretical and practical.

Page 2

As will become clear later, for us ethnography (or participant observation, a cognate term) is simply one social research method, albeit a somewhat unusual one, drawing as it does on a wide range of sources of information. The ethnographer participates, overtly or covertly, in people's daily lives for an extended period of time, watching what happens, listening to what is said, asking questions; in fact collecting whatever data are available to throw light on the issues with which he or she is concerned.

In many respects, ethnography is the most basic form of social research. Not only does it have a very long history (Wax 1971), but it also bears a close resemblance to the routine ways in which people make sense of the world in everyday life. Some commentators regard this as its basic strength, others see it as a fundamental weakness. Ethnography has sometimes been dismissed as quite inappropriate to social science, on the grounds that the data and findings that it produces are 'subjective', mere idiosyncratic impressions that cannot provide a solid foundation for rigorous scientific analysis. Others argue that only through ethnography can the meanings that give form and content to social processes be understood. 'Artificial' methods such as experiments and survey interviews are rejected on the grounds that these are incapable of capturing the meaning of everyday human activities.

Source: Martyn Hammersley and Paul Atkinson. *Ethnography: Principles in Practice.* London: Routledge, 1983. pp. 1–2. Reprinted by permission of Taylor & Francis Books (UK).

2. Now read each text for a second time and, as you read, highlight key points and make annotations in the margin.

3. Now use your annotations to write a 200-word summary of the two texts. Refer back to the information on summary writing in Chapter 1. Follow the stages below:

   a) Start the summary with a general sentence that summarizes the content of both excerpts.

   b) Paraphrase the main ideas that will go into the summary.

   c) Choose one or more ideas from the text that are suitable for direct quotations.

   d) Use MLA or APA style, and write a list of works cited (MLA) or a reference list (APA) that includes both books excerpted above.

e) Now write the summary in 200 words.

In your summary, remember to include citation phrases that clearly indicate which ideas belong to Fetterman and which to Hammersley and Atkinson.

Refer to the MLA or APA citation style guidelines in Appendices 1 and 2 for different ways to write in-text citations and for the appropriate format for the list of works cited or reference list.

Ethnography: A 200-word summary

CHAPTER 5 SUMMARY

This chapter has focused on several important aspects of writing research essays.

WHAT IS A RESEARCH ESSAY?

Research essays involve either primary and/or secondary research. Nine stages of writing research essays have been highlighted in this chapter:

1. Find a research problem, issue, or question to analyze.
2. Search online and in libraries for materials.
3. Keep the essay in focus and on task from the outset.
4. Take effective notes while reading.
5. Draw up an outline for the essay.
6. Develop a suitable method for collecting data (if doing primary research).
7. Write with a good balance of summarizing, paraphrasing, and quoting.
8. Avoid plagiarism by using in-text citations and a list of works cited or reference list.
9. Make it clear to readers who thinks what.

Following these stages will keep your thinking, reading, and writing focused and connected.

WHAT IS PLAGIARISM?

Plagiarism was defined as follows: "The use of others' ideas, arguments, creative works, or statistics in your work without acknowledgement. Put simply, it means that you use others' ideas, arguments, creative works, or statistics as if they were your own."

The consequences of plagiarism were discussed, as were the varying degrees and grey areas of plagiarism.

AVOIDING PLAGIARISM

You can avoid committing plagiarism by using the following strategies when writing research essays:

1. Take effective notes.
2. Write appropriate in-text citations.
3. Write an appropriate list of works cited or reference list.
4. Use direct quotations.

Even if you are paraphrasing, and have changed the language and structure considerably from the original, you still need to include citations and references if you use others' ideas, arguments, creative works, or statistics.

USING REPORTING VERBS AND CITATION PHRASES

When you choose your reporting verbs and tenses for citation phrases, the choices that you make can give your reader an indication of what you think of the information you are bringing into your essay.

Writing Modes across the Disciplines

PART 2

CHAPTER 6

Expository Writing

In this chapter, you will study the following aspects of expository writing:

- ✓ What is expository writing?
- ✓ Expository writing: Organizing your information
- ✓ Review: Writing the introduction
- ✓ Review: Writing main body paragraphs
- ✓ Review: Writing the conclusion
- ✓ Features of expository writing in academic journal articles
- ✓ Language focus: Personal reflective language
- ✓ Language focus: The passive voice

In this chapter, you will learn about some of the defining features of expository writing and see how different writers employ these features in different forms of academic writing. This chapter also takes you through the preparation stages of writing an expository essay. Two specific forms of expository writing—writing about problems and solutions, and writing about causes and effects—will be studied in more detail in Chapters 9 and 10.

You will also review the following from Chapters 3 and 4: writing introductions, main body paragraphs, and conclusions.

WHAT IS EXPOSITORY WRITING?

In its broadest sense, the term *expository writing* refers to any form of writing that involves exposition, that is, providing information on, describing, or explaining a subject to your reader. Expository writing tends to be more descriptive than argumentative writing, and is present in most forms of academic writing. It can also be an essay type in its own right if an instructor sets an expository essay as an assignment.

Academic expository writing can involve providing information on, describing, or explaining any of the following:

- **Specific topics:** a detailed explanation of a specific topic to inform your reader about what you consider to be the most important information
- **Processes or procedures:** a detailed description, for example, of how something works, how an experiment was carried out, the procedure for a policy, or the stages in a sequence of events
- **Definitions of key terms:** a general definition of each term, sometimes followed by a more specific definition that matches the focus of your study
- **Comparisons:** a description of the similarities and differences between two theories, situations, or important people, for example
- **Causes and effects:** a description of a situation or problem and an analysis of the possible causes and effects
- **Problems and solutions:** a description of a problem and suggested solutions to that problem

Effective expository writing involves focused investigation of a subject and careful organization of information and notes. It also requires detailed and clear description and explanation, with supporting examples and evidence where necessary.

EXPOSITORY WRITING: ORGANIZING YOUR INFORMATION

Expository writing is an integral part of all types of academic writing, whether in published academic journal articles or in written assignments for university courses. Whether an article or essay is argumentative, comparative, or reflective, it cannot be written successfully without clear and detailed explanation and description of key information.

It is also common for instructors to assign expository essays to test and assess understanding of important concepts, theories, or processes (to name but a few). In this case, the whole essay requires an expository focus.

When you are presented with an essay question, as a course assignment or in an examination, you should first take some time to understand the question and organize your thoughts. You need to figure out what the question is asking you to do.

Here is the question for an expository essay that you will be analyzing in this chapter, and the guidelines for writing it:

> **Question:** What is bilingualism and how do people communicate bilingually?
>
> **Guidelines:** You should explain the different ways that bilingualism can be understood and the different ways that people communicate bilingually. Refer to key definitions and examples in the literature. Try also to give your own examples from different settings around the world as you work through the essay.

Genre, Audience, and Context

As a starting point, you can think about the genre, audience, and context of the essay, as studied in Chapter 1.

The *genre* in this case is an expository essay. The essay question clearly requires an expository focus. It asks the writer to *define* bilingualism with support from the literature and to *describe* how people communicate bilingually. In this essay, the focus is on describing what something is and how it works (expository) rather than on why it works in that way and whether it is a good thing (argumentative).

The *audience* is a university instructor who is teaching a course on multilingualism in the world today.

The essay is written in the *context* of a formal graded writing assessment to test and assess theoretical knowledge as part of a course on multilingualism in the world today.

Understanding Essay Questions: Topic, Focus, and Task

In Chapter 5, you studied the importance of keeping *in focus* and *on task* as part of the process of writing research essays. A good first step in organizing your information for an expository essay question, as well as for other types of essay questions, is to break the question down according to topic, focus, and task:

- The *topic* is the general topic of the question, in its broadest sense. You should not write too much about the general topic. Writers often choose to write a limited amount about the general topic early on in the essay to provide readers with some background information.
- The *focus* refers to the specific aspect(s) of the topic that you will be concentrating on in your essay. Most of what you write in the essay should relate to the *focus*.
- The *task* is what you have to do. This is often stated with a word such as "describe" or "explain" in expository essays or "discuss" or "analyze" in argument essays. Make sure that most of your writing is related to your *task*.

TASK 1

Break down the essay question on bilingualism according to *topic*, *focus*, and *task*:

Topic: ______________________________

Focus: ______________________________

Task: ______________________________

Creating an Outline

Creating the outline for an essay involves gathering and organizing ideas from existing knowledge, and investigating the topic by reading relevant literature and taking notes. Some writers begin by brainstorming ideas from their existing knowledge and then moving on to the literature. Others use notes from the literature to form the outline, then add their own ideas. In many cases, the two processes take place concurrently. In Boxes A to D on page 107, you can see a basic outline for the essay on bilingualism.

Outline for essay on bilingualism

BOX A

1. **Background:** statement about bilingualism around the world and contexts in which languages are learned
2. **Specifics:** ideas related to definitions and ways of communicating bilingually
3. **Structure:** different definitions of "bilingual" and different forms of bilingual communication
4. **Thesis statement:** e.g., bilingualism is complex, multifaceted, and depends on local contexts and individuals' perceptions

BOX B

1. What does *bilingual* mean? = speak 2 languages fully or just a few words? (Edwards, 1994) e.g., tourist Spanish versus fluent Spanish = being bilingual? traditional definitions (Bloomfield, 1933; Haugen, 1953; Weinreich, 1953)
2. Sometimes skills stronger in one area than another (Romaine, 1989) e.g., speaking versus writing (Spolsky, 1998)

BOX C

1. How do bilinguals communicate? Do speakers know each other?
2. People can use one language only in a conversation—Montreal example of bilinguals selecting one language only for communication
3. Or, people can use two different languages together in a conversation
4. Codeswitching: mixing languages, different definitions—*codeswitching* (Gumperz, 1982; Heller, 1988, 1992, 1995; Romaine, 1989); *code alternation* (Auer, 1995); *code-crossing* (Rampton, 1995); and *code mixing* (Haugen, 1972; Heller, 1992)
5. What is a code? e.g., you can change accent but not language?
6. Language choice, e.g., Barcelona (Marshall, 2007; Pujolar, 2001; Woolard, 1989)

BOX D

1. **Summarize:** bilingualism and bilingual communication = multifaceted and complex
2. **Synthesize:** multilingualism adds to the complexity: globalization
3. **Answer the question:** no clear answers
4. **End statement:** lots of debate and argument to continue

Boxes A to D above illustrate the coming together of two processes: gathering ideas from existing knowledge and investigating the literature to find information. They also show the importance of supporting your own ideas with examples and evidence from reliable academic sources. Even if you are sure of your own ideas, you still need to look for support from academic sources.

Sample Expository Essay on Bilingualism

Now read the following sample expository essay on bilingualism. After you read the essay, you will analyze the introduction, a main body section, and the conclusion.

Question: What is bilingualism and how do people communicate bilingually?

Guidelines: You should explain the different ways that bilingualism can be understood and the different ways that people communicate bilingually. Refer to key definitions and examples in the literature. Try also to give your own examples from different settings around the world as you work through the essay.

What is bilingualism and how do people communicate bilingually?

1 Most of the world's population speak a first language and understand or speak at least a few words of another language. **2** They may have learned the additional language at school, at home, in their local community, doing business, or through travel. **3** They may speak more than one language, but are they bilingual? **4** Whether an individual can be described as bilingual depends on how the term *bilingual* is defined and understood. **5** There are also many different ways in which people can communicate bilingually. **6** Often, when two bilingual people communicate, they do so in one language that both have chosen to use instead of another; alternatively, bilingual people may use or mix more than one language in their conversations with other bilinguals. **7** Bilingualism is a complex and multifaceted linguistic phenomenon which changes not only according to individuals' abilities and perceptions, but also according to local contexts.

8 In everyday conversations, the term *bilingual* is used when referring to people who can speak two languages, and usually with reference to people who can speak two languages very well. **9** However, scholars disagree on what it means to be bilingual. **10** Perhaps the most open definition of bilingualism was offered by Edwards (1994), who originally suggested that virtually everyone could be considered bilingual, even a speaker with a passive understanding of a number of terms in another language. **11** That would mean that someone who goes on holiday to Mexico and understands and speaks limited Spanish such as *por favor* (please) and *gracias* (thanks) could be considered bilingual. **12** This academic definition is far from the "everyday" understanding of the term that most people have, which is associated with having a high degree of competence in more than one language. **13** This more traditional view of bilingualism is more in line with historical definitions such as those given by linguists Bloomfield, Weinreich, and Haugen. **14** According to Bloomfield (1933, p. 56), being bilingual requires "native-like control of two languages," while Weinreich describes bilingualism as "the practice of alternately using two [or more] languages" (1953, p. 1). **15** Haugen (1953, p. 7) suggests that bilingualism begins when the speaker of one language can produce "complete meaningful utterances in the other language" (in Romaine, 1989, p. 10). **16** An example of these more traditional definitions of bilingualism would be the children of immigrants in North America who speak a family language and the national language (English, French, or Spanish) equally well.

17 In many cases, however, bilinguals do not have equal abilities in both languages. **18** Part of being bilingual can also involve having varying degrees of competence in the different language skills; bilinguals may have passive or receptive bilingualism if they understand a language but do not speak it (Romaine, 1989). **19** For example, second- and third-generation Chinese immigrants in Canada and the US may understand the language of their parents and grandparents, which they hear at home, but they do not always have the "productive skills" (Romaine, 1989) necessary to speak it. **20** Bilinguals sometimes also have what has been a described as a "functional division of speech repertoire" (Spolsky, 1998, p. 26); this means that they are bilingual, but they speak one language and write in another. **21** This phenomenon was common in Catalonia, Spain, during the Franco dictatorship, when many Catalans spoke Catalan but wrote in Spanish due to Catalan being banned from schools.

22 How, then, do bilingual speakers communicate bilingually if bilingualism can be taken to mean different things? **23** As in all situations of communication between people, an important factor is whether the interlocutors (the people talking to each other) know each other. **24** In many contexts, bilinguals communicate monolingually, that is, using one language rather than two. **25** Monolingual communication may be through habit if the bilinguals know each other. **26** If they do not, they would normally go through a stage of negotiation before deciding which language to use; then they will continue by using one of their available languages only. **27** The reasons why they may choose one language rather than the other are complex. **28** The social context may make one language more common or appropriate than the other; one speaker may detect a weakness in the other speaker and continue, as a courtesy, in what he or she thinks is the other speaker's stronger language; or the physical appearance or sound of voice of one of the speakers may trigger the other speaker's use of one language rather than another. **29** In Montreal, Quebec, for example, where French, English, and a wide range of immigrant languages are spoken, a bilingual businessman visiting from an English-speaking part of Canada may want to use French rather than English. **30** If his French is strongly accented from English, or lacking in grammar and vocabulary, this may result in bilingual French speakers switching to English, choosing the language that appears to be more comfortable for both speakers. **31** When the same two meet again, they may automatically use English, having already established it as their language of communication.

32 Many conversations, however, involve the use of more than one language between two bilingual speakers. **33** Such communication often involves "codeswitching," that is, changing from one language to another at various stages of a conversation. **34** Codeswitching is described in different ways in the literature: *codeswitching* (Gumperz, 1982; Heller 1988, 1992, 1995; Romaine, 1989); *code alternation* (Auer, 1995); *code-crossing* (Rampton, 1995); and *code mixing* (Haugen, 1972; Heller, 1992). **35** In Romaine's work on bilingualism, she defines *codeswitching* as "the juxtaposition within the same speech exchange of passages of speech belonging to two different grammatical systems or subsystems" (Romaine, 1989, p. 111). **36** Put simply, this means using two different languages in a conversation. **37** An example would be a family in which one parent speaks Spanish and another English as first languages, and where conversations frequently involve changes from Spanish to English and vice versa. **38** Heller uses the term *codeswitching* in a more extended sense: not only with reference to switches between languages that take place between sentences, but also to "less structurally integrated instances of language alternation or language choice" (Heller, 1995, p. 59). **39** Following this definition, visually identifying someone as a speaker of a particular language, for example, a Spanish speaker in California, and choosing to speak Spanish as a result, could be understood as a part of codeswitching.

40 In understanding what codeswitching is, it is necessary to consider what a code is. **41** Does codeswitching occur only when the interaction involves different languages, or does it continue when two varieties of the same language take over? **42** Romaine's definition of the term *code* is of particular relevance in this respect. **43** In Romaine's view, a code also refers to "varieties of the same language as well as styles within a language" (1989, p. 111). **44** This would imply that codeswitching can involve changes of variety and style in the same language as part of either a monolingual or bilingual conversation. **45** This could be exemplified by a working class student from Newcastle, England, switching between accented Geordie English (a dialect form of English spoken in and around Newcastle) and more standard middle-class English in conversations with fellow students in the UK.

46 Deciding which language to speak, or to switch to, often relates to the social and cultural contexts of the conversation. **47** There is often a more common or economically powerful language that speakers select or switch to in conversations. **48** Often speakers of minority languages are forced to accommodate to speakers of majority languages. **49** In her study of Catalan and Spanish speakers in Barcelona, Woolard (1989) described an "accommodation norm," by which Catalan speakers would frequently switch to Spanish with other speakers who looked or sounded like they were not Catalans. **50** An alternative is also highlighted by Woolard, a *bilingual norm*, in which neither speaker switches; instead, speakers continue in their own language. **51** This form of bilingual communication is called "passive bilingualism" in Pujolar (2001) and "reciprocal bilingualism" in Marshall (2007). **52** An example of this reciprocal bilingualism would be a conversation between a French speaker and an English speaker in Canada in which both speakers understand the other's language.

53 However, rather than selecting French or English as the sole language for a monolingual conversation, the speakers would use their own language: the French speaker speaks in French and the English speaker speaks in English without switches on either side.

54 The different definitions of *bilingualism* explained above and the descriptions of how bilinguals use their languages in a variety of ways in bilingual communication illustrate the complex and multifaceted nature of languages and their use. **55** A further complexity that has not been discussed in this paper is *multilingualism*, that is, when more than two languages are spoken, understood, and used in conversations. **56** Multilingualism is an extension of bilingualism, and increasingly common as globalization results in new migration and new forms of digital media in many languages. **57** In conclusion, there are no clear answers to the questions "What is bilingualism?" and "How do people communicate bilingually?" **58** It has been suggested above that, behind the common understanding that *bilingualism* means the ability to speak two languages, there is considerable debate and disagreement. **59** This debate will no doubt continue.

References

Auer, P. (1995). The pragmatics of code-switching: A sequential approach. In L. Milroy & P. Muysken (Eds.), *One speaker, two languages: Cross-disciplinary perspectives on code-switching* (pp. 115–135). Cambridge, UK: Cambridge University Press.

Bloomfield, L. (1933). *Language.* New York, NY: Holt.

Edwards, J. (1994). *Multilingualism.* London and New York: Routledge.

Gumperz, J. J. (1982). *Discourse strategies.* Cambridge, UK: Cambridge University Press.

Haugen, E. (1953). *The Norwegian language in America: A study in bilingual behavior.* Philadelphia, PA: University of Pennsylvania Press. (Reprinted in 1969, Bloomington, IN: Indiana University Press).

Haugen, E. (1972). The stigmata of bilingualism. In A. Dil (Ed.), *The ecology of language. Essays by Einar Haugen* (pp. 307–324). Stanford, CA: Stanford University Press.

Heller, M. (Ed.). (1988). *Codeswitching: Anthropological and sociolinguistic perspectives.* The Hague, Netherlands: Mouton de Gruyter.

Heller, M. (1992). The politics of code-switching and language choice. *Journal of Multilingual and Multicultural Development, 13*(1), 123–142.

Heller, M. (1995). Code-switching and the politics of language. In L. Milroy & P. Muysken (Eds.), *One speaker, two languages: Cross-disciplinary perspectives on code-switching* (pp. 158–174). Cambridge, UK: Cambridge University Press.

Marshall, S. (2007). New Latino diaspora and new zones of language contact: A social constructionist analysis of Spanish-speaking Latin Americans in Catalonia. In J. Holmquist, A. Lorenzino, & L. Sayahi (Eds.), *Selected proceedings of the third workshop on Spanish sociolinguistics* (pp. 150–161). Somerville, MA: Cascadilla Proceedings Project.

Pujolar, J. (2001). *Gender, heteroglossia and power: A sociolinguistic study of youth culture.* Berlin, Germany: Mouton de Gruyter.

Rampton, B. (1995). *Crossing: language and ethnicity among adolescents.* Harlow Essex, UK: Longman.

Romaine, S. (1989). *Bilingualism.* Oxford, UK: Basil Blackwell.

Spolsky, B. (1998). *Sociolinguistics.* Oxford, UK: Oxford University Press.

Weinreich, U. (1953). *Languages in contact.* The Hague, Netherlands: Mouton de Gruyter.

Woolard, K. A. (1989). *Double talk: Bilingualism and the politics of ethnicity in Catalonia.* Stanford, CA: Stanford University Press.

REVIEW: WRITING THE INTRODUCTION

In Chapter 4, four steps for writing introductions that shift from general to specific were introduced:

1. Provide general background information.
2. Shift to the specific focus of your essay.

3. State a thesis that will guide your writing.
4. Refer to the structure of the essay.

In Chapter 4, you also analyzed several different introductions written in different subject areas, in different genres, and for different audiences. The examples illustrated that these four aspects do not always appear in introductions, nor do they always appear in the order listed above. Depending on the genre, audience, and context, you may follow different ordering principles (e.g., general to specific, specific to general, or other), different types of thesis statements, and different ways of telling the reader about the content of the essay.

Read the introductory paragraph below from the expository essay on bilingualism and answer the questions that follow.

1 Most of the world's population speak a first language and understand or speak at least a few words of another language. **2** They may have learned the additional language at school, at home, in their local community, doing business, or through travel. **3** They may speak more than one language, but are they bilingual? **4** Whether an individual can be described as bilingual depends on how the term *bilingual* is defined and understood. **5** There are also many different ways in which people can communicate bilingually. **6** Often, when two bilingual people communicate, they do so in one language that both have chosen to use instead of another; alternatively, bilingual people may use or mix more than one language in their conversations with other bilinguals. **7** Bilingualism is a complex and multifaceted linguistic phenomenon which changes not only according to individuals' abilities and perceptions, but also according to local contexts.

TASK 2

Look at each sentence in the introductory paragraph above and complete the corresponding information below.

Which sentence carries out the following functions of an introduction? Write the sentence number in the blank.

a) Sentence _______ marks a shift from general to specific by asking a question that relates to the essay question.

b) Sentence _______ introduces the second main issue that the writer will focus on: bilingual communication.

c) Sentence _______ is a kind of thesis statement as it states the writer's stance on the question.

REVIEW: WRITING MAIN BODY PARAGRAPHS

In Chapter 3, the following five aspects of paragraph writing were introduced:

1. Topic sentences
2. Paragraph coherence

3. Keeping to one topic
4. Supporting your ideas
5. Concluding sentences

In the examples of paragraphs from different subject areas that you analyzed, you saw how these five aspects can be given different emphasis in paragraphs.

Read the paragraph below from the expository essay on bilingualism and answer the questions that follow.

> **8** In everyday conversations, the term *bilingual* is used when referring to people who can speak two languages, and usually with reference to people who can speak two languages very well. **9** However, scholars disagree on what it means to be bilingual. **10** Perhaps the most open definition of bilingualism was offered by Edwards (1994), who originally suggested that virtually everyone could be considered bilingual, even a speaker with a passive understanding of a number of terms in another language. **11** That would mean that someone who goes on holiday to Mexico and understands and speaks limited Spanish such as *por favor* (please) and *gracias* (thanks) could be considered bilingual. **12** This academic definition is far from the "everyday" understanding of the term that most people have, which is associated with having a high degree of competence in more than one language. **13** This more traditional view of bilingualism is more in line with historical definitions such as those given by linguists Bloomfield, Weinreich, and Haugen. **14** According to Bloomfield (1933, p. 56), being bilingual requires "native-like control of two languages," while Weinreich describes bilingualism as "the practice of alternately using two [or more] languages" (1953, p. 1). **15** Haugen (1953, p. 7) suggests that bilingualism begins when the speaker of one language can produce "complete meaningful utterances in the other language" (in Romaine, 1989, p. 10). **16** An example of these more traditional definitions of bilingualism would be the children of immigrants in North America who speak a family language and the national language (English, French, or Spanish) equally well.

TASK 3

Look at each sentence in the paragraph above and complete the corresponding information below.

Which sentence(s) carries out the following functions of a paragraph? Write the sentence number(s) in the blank.

a) Sentences ________ are both topic sentences.
b) Sentence ________ presents the broadest definition of bilingualism.
c) Sentence ________ gives a supporting example for the broad definition.
d) Sentences ________ form a link between broad and traditional definitions.
e) Sentences ________ cite authors who give more traditional definitions.
f) Sentence ________ gives a supporting example of a more traditional definition.

The paragraph above is an example of an expository paragraph that describes different definitions of bilingualism. The paragraph has a strong descriptive focus and the writer's opinion is not explicitly stated. The paragraph follows a structure that is common in this type of expository paragraph:

- Topic sentence(s)
- Definition A
- Supporting citations from the literature
- Supporting example for definition A
- Transition sentence(s)
- Definition B
- Supporting citations from the literature
- Supporting example for definition B

Notice as well that the supporting example for definition B serves as a concluding sentence. The author has not added a concluding sentence that summarizes and/or synthesizes, perhaps because it would be too repetitive or because the paragraph is written clearly enough as it is.

REVIEW: WRITING THE CONCLUSION

In Chapter 4, you studied the following strategies for writing academic conclusions:

1. Summarize the main content and/or perspectives analyzed in the essay.
2. Synthesize the main content and/or perspectives analyzed in the essay.
3. Answer the essay question definitively.
4. Finish with an end statement.

The examples that you studied in Chapter 4 also showed how conclusions are written very differently in different subject areas, depending on genre, audience, and context.

Read the concluding paragraph below from the expository essay on bilingualism and answer the questions that follow.

> **54** The different definitions of *bilingualism* explained above and the descriptions of how bilinguals use their languages in a variety of ways in bilingual communication illustrate the complex and multifaceted nature of languages and their use. **55** A further complexity that has not been discussed in this paper is *multilingualism*, that is, when more than two languages are spoken, understood, and used in conversations. **56** Multilingualism is an extension of bilingualism, and increasingly common as globalization results in new migration and new forms of digital media in many languages. **57** In conclusion, there are no clear answers to the questions "What is bilingualism?" and "How do people communicate bilingually?" **58** It has been suggested above that, behind the common understanding that *bilingualism* means the ability to speak two languages, there is considerable debate and disagreement. **59** This debate will no doubt continue.

TASK 4

Look at each sentence in the conclusion above and complete the corresponding information below.

Which sentence(s) carries out the following functions of a conclusion? Write the sentence number(s) in the blank.

a) Sentence _______ summarizes the main points covered in the essay.

b) Sentences _______ synthesize by introducing a new closing idea.

c) Sentences _______ give a final answer to the two questions.

d) Sentence _______ serves as a general end statement to round off the essay and leaves food for thought.

The concluding paragraph uses the four strategies for writing conclusions set out on page 113. First, the writer summarizes the main content of the essay and then synthesizes by introducing a new concept to the discussion: multilingualism. The two questions "What is bilingualism and how do people communicate bilingually?" are then answered, albeit in a somewhat inconclusive manner. The essay would have been stronger if the writer had ended with more definitive answers to the question by formulating his or her own definition for the first part of the question at least. The rather abrupt end statement leaves food for thought.

Overall, the expository nature of the essay as a whole is evident through its detailed and clear description of a specific topic—bilingualism—and a discussion that ranges from broad to narrow definitions. The descriptions and definitions are written clearly, with examples and supporting evidence in the form of citations from the work of experts in the field. The essay does contain a lot of technical vocabulary and terminology from linguistics, but it is written in a way that non-experts should be able to understand.

FEATURES OF EXPOSITORY WRITING IN ACADEMIC JOURNAL ARTICLES

As already mentioned, academic writing changes according to genre, audience, and context. As a result, expository writing comes in many different forms across the disciplines.

The following two examples of expository writing are excerpts from academic journal articles. By reading both articles, you will learn more features of effective expository writing, as well as the different styles of expository writing in different subject areas.

TASK 5

Excerpt 1 is the first two introductory paragraphs to an article that appeared in the academic journal *Canadian Literature* (genre). It is written for academics and students with considerable expert knowledge of the topic (audience). In the article, the author is defining a literary concept, magic realism, as "postcolonial discourse." The title tells the reader from the outset that the writer is presenting a clear stance, or position, on the topic. The excerpt is a mainly expository section of an article that is presenting a clear argument.

Read Excerpt 1 and answer the questions that follow.

EXCERPT 1

1 The concept of magic realism is a troubled one for literary theory. **2** Since Franz Roh first coined the term in 1925 in connection with postexpressionist art, it has been most closely associated, at least in terms of literary practice, with two major periods in Latin-American and Caribbean culture: the 1940s and 1950s, in which the concept was closely aligned with that of the "marvelous" as something ontologically necessary to the regional population's "vision of everyday reality," and the "boom" period of the Latin-American novel in the late 1950s and 1960s, where the term was applied to works varying widely in genre and discursive strategy. **3** In none of its applications to literature has the concept of magic realism ever successfully differentiated between itself and neighboring genres such as fabulation, metafiction, the baroque, the fantastic, the uncanny, or the marvelous, and consequently it is not surprising that some critics have chosen to abandon the term altogether.

4 But the term retains enough of what Fredric Jameson calls a "strange seductiveness" to keep it in critical currency, despite the "theoretical vacuum" in which it lies. **5** In Latin America, the badge of magical realism has signified a kind of uniqueness or difference from mainstream culture—what in another context Alejo Carpentier has called *lo real maravilloso Americano* or "marvellous American reality"—and this gives the concept the stamp of cultural authority, if not theoretical soundness. **6** And recently, the locus for critical studies on magic realism has been broadened from Latin America and the Caribbean to include speculations on its place in the literatures of India, Nigeria, and English Canada, this last being perhaps the most startling development for magic realism in recent years, since Canada, unlike these other regions, is not part of the Third World, a condition long thought necessary to the currency of the term in literary practice and to offer to centralizing genre systems a single locus upon which the massive problem of *difference* in literary expression can be managed into recognizable meaning in one swift pass.

Source: Dr. Stephen Slemon. "Magic Realism as Post Colonial Discourse." *Canadian Literature* 116 (1988): 9–24. Reprinted by permission of the author. Footnotes omitted.

1. What do you notice about the vocabulary? (Support your answer with examples from the text.)

____

____

____

____

____

____

2. What do you notice about the length of the sentences? (Support your answer with examples from the text.)

____

____

____

____

____

____

3. Where can you detect the author's opinion in Sentences 3 and 4? (Support your answer with examples from the text.)

4. What is the general style of the excerpt?

TASK 6

Excerpt 2 is also an academic journal article, but it is written in a different expository style. The excerpt is from an article on laser dentistry that appeared in the *Journal of the American Dental Association*. It is an experimental research report (genre), written for professional and academic readers with specialist knowledge (audience). In the article, the author describes a laser treatment for dentistry and refers to data from an experiment that tested the effectiveness of the new technology. The excerpt is from two sections of the article: the methodology section (which describes the two phases of the experiment) and the clinical procedure section (which describes how the treatment was carried out).

Read Excerpt 2 and answer the questions that follow.

EXCERPT 2

Phase I

1 To be included in Phase I of this study, the patients had to be between the ages of 12 and 60 years and have a tooth scheduled for extraction. **2** Exclusion criteria included decay closer than 1 millimeter to the pulp, a history of local anesthetic allergy, existing gum disease in the area of the tooth scheduled for extraction, any extenuating health or medical conditions and direct pulpal pathology. **3** The criteria were established to limit patient risk and to avoid the complicating effects of other disease states; investigators took a standard patient dental history and radiographs as part of the preoperative examination. **4** A total of 60 patients participated in Phase I of this study. **5** The laser group had 24 patients and the control group had 36 patients. **6** From these 60 patients

350 procedures were performed on 62 teeth in the laser group and 63 teeth in the control group. **7** Approximately one-third of the teeth were extracted immediately after treatment, another third 48 hours after treatment and the final third approximately 1 month after treatment. **8** The majority of extracted teeth were molars (see Table 1). **9** Both the laser and control groups were subjected to a standard histologic evaluation to determine the laser's effects on the underlying dental tissue. **10** All patients received postoperative care and were seen 1 month after their teeth were extracted. **11** The investigators monitored and treated the patients according to standard dental practice until the symptoms disappeared.

Phase II

12 In Phase II, the procedures were handled as they were in Phase I, except that the teeth were not extracted. **13** The patients' age range was expanded in Phase II to include all ages because process safety was demonstrated in Phase I. **14** Phase II patients ranged in age from 2 to 84 years. **15** A total of 107 patients participated in Phase II of this study. **16** The laser group had 53 patients and the control group had 54 patients. **17** From these 107 patients, 512 laser procedures and 357 control procedures (not including the procedures in Phase IIA and Phase IIB) were performed on 168 teeth in the laser group and 146 teeth in the control group.

Clinical procedure

18 The clinical procedure for the Er:YAG laser is similar to the clinical procedure for the high-speed drill. **19** However, because previous studies of the Er:YAG laser had shown that anesthetic was not needed, patients were not routinely offered anesthetic at the beginning of the laser procedure. **20** Anesthetic was available on request. **21** The Er:YAG laser has a sterile, removable tip that is used with a handpiece attached to a fiber-optic delivery system. **22** Because the Er:YAG laser is invisible, a helium neon laser beam is used as an aiming beam. **23** The laser parameters are selected on the control panel according to the procedure to be accomplished. **24** Low dosimetries are used to remove caries, and high dosimetries are used to cut dentin and enamel. **25** This lets operators remove the carious dentin without removing the sound dentin, until they decide to increase the dosimetries and cut dentin or enamel. **26** The laser was used for amalgam or composite cavity preparations and restorations. **27** The investigators prepared the cavity for amalgam following the procedure outlined by G.V. Black. **28** However, the surface of the floor was not as smooth as that achieved with the high-speed drill. **29** For composite cavity preparations, the investigators completed the preparation, used the laser (with focus/defocus mode) to etch the enamel surface and then acid etched the tooth. **30** After the teeth were prepared, the investigators restored them with their choice of materials. **31** In this study, the majority of composites were polymerized with an argon laser. **32** When using the laser, as when using the high-speed drill, practitioners need to apply air or water spray to the tooth for efficient cutting and cooling. **33** The laser is equipped with either straight or angled handpieces, and the air or water spray can be delivered through the handpiece or applied externally by an assistant. **34** The millijoule and hertz parameters shown in Table 3 were cleared by the FDA, based on previous animal and human research data. **35** The investigators used standard dental procedures to prepare or remove caries from the teeth in the control group.

Source: Cozean, C., Arcoria, C.J., and colleagues. "Dentistry for the 21st century? Erbium: YAG laser for teeth." *JADA* 1997; 128(8): 1080–87. Tables omitted.

1. What do you notice about the vocabulary? (Support your answer with examples from the text.)

2. What do you notice about the length of the sentences? (Support your answer with examples from the text.)

3. Where can you detect the author's opinion? (Support your answer with examples from the text.)

4. What is the general style of the excerpt?

Text Analysis of a Student's Expository Writing

The following expository essay by Rika crosses the disciplines of political science and communications (genre). It is written for a reader who is not an expert on the subject, her academic writing instructor (audience). Rika wrote the essay as a graded task in an academic writing course; she was required to choose a topic of interest and of relevance to her ongoing university studies (context) and to write the essay as a take-home paper, following APA citation style.

TASK 7

Carefully read Rika's expository essay. As you read, think about the purpose of this essay, which is to explain the topic in detail and to present evidence and examples to support and expand upon the information presented.

As you read, take notes in the margin on what you feel to be the strengths and weaknesses of the essay.

Political mass media and its influence on people

Margin Notes

Section 1

1 "We are ready to lead once more," President Obama quotes in the front cover of my favourite magazine, *Newsweek* (Meacham, 2009). **2** For the past eight months, President Obama has been on the cover page of *Newsweek* at least eleven times. **3** Reading, listening, and watching president Obama on a daily basis has certainly created a deep impression of him in my mind. **4** Eventually, I find this advertisement in politics is known as political mass media (*Longman English Dictionary*, 2009). **5** Today, political media can be found in books, magazines, and journals, on television, on the radio and on the Internet. **6** Because it can be found in so many forms, its power is certainly significant and influential. **7** These facts attracted my curiosity. **8** I wanted to learn about and research "political mass media."

Section 2

9 The history of political mass media can be traced back to as many as eighty years ago. **10** Hitler's fanatic follower, Joseph Goebbels, was the puppet master of political mass media. **11** Unlike today, Hitler's political mass media was extremely biased. **12** *Propaganda*, which means political parties provide partly false information to make people agree with their way of thinking, is a word developed to name political mass media. **13** Along with the fanatic members of the Nazis, Hitler and Goebbels educated numerous teens with biased information and manipulated history. **14** These kids were named "Hitler Youth" and were completely brain-washed. **15** They would slaughter anyone who betrayed Hitler (Truman, 2000). **16** According to Tobbias Ebrecht, "media [has] effects on the audience's images of historical events, and participates in constructing a narrative of collective memory." (2007, p. 221). **17** Ebrecht wants to emphasize that media is influential in people's daily life. **18** Television political advertisements can influence our voting decisions. **19** Political magazine articles can change our view of certain things. **20** Though such massive biased education occurs less and less in today's society, the power of political mass media cannot be ignored since studies do show that mass media has a huge impact on us as citizens. **21** For instance, strong political speech can impact our way of behaving.

Section 3

22 All the politicians bring some level of impact to their citizens. **23** In fact, there are a number of politicians who have used their leadership wisely and influenced their citizens positively. **24** In Canada, Pierre Trudeau encouraged many young adults to gain interest in politics in the seventies. **25** Canada's seventies turned into a decade of green and political movements (Whitaker, 2001). **26** Franklin D. Roosevelt, who assumed the Presidency at the depth of the Great Depression in the thirties, helped the American citizens to gain fame and wealth. **27** His famous quote, "The only thing we have to fear is fear itself," is taught and remembered by people of all ages (the White House, 2009). **28** Sir Winston Churchill, another heroic figure during World War II, had not only given his British citizens courage to fight against their enemies but also impressed the whole world with great quotes and military strategies. **29** Churchill once told his citizens, "The Germans have received back again that measure of fire and steel which they have so often meted out to others. **30** Now this is not the end; it is not even the beginning of the end. **31** But it is, perhaps, the end of the beginning." (Churchill Center, 2009). **32** The word play of "end" and "beginning" is extremely insightful and inspirational. **33** Unfortunately, today's politicians seem to exercise their power to achieve only one goal: getting re-elected.

Section 4

34 During my research, I was shocked at how powerful today's politicians are in conducting political mass media. **35** The *New York Times*' former White House correspondent John Herber notes with regard to the White House:

> **36** No other institution can demand space and attention throughout the media when there is no news there. **37** The White House does every day. **38** The President can demand front-page coverage by holding a press conference in which he says nothing that has not been said before. **39** Newspapers feel compelled to write about it at length because millions saw it on television. (Jamieson, 2001, p. 251)

40 The president of the United States can call the media's attention without an obvious reason. **41** I am surprised to find that in a country like the United States, the president holds such power on the media. **42** The presidents or the prime ministers can use their political power along with the aid of the media to influence people's minds so easily. **43** As citizens, we do have influence on the fate of the political leaders because after all they depend on our votes. **44** For instance, the current Canadian prime minister Stephen Harper's promises during his political campaign in 2008 sounded so motivational that they led us to have further faith in him. **45** Harper told his citizens that he felt confident with the Canadian economy prior to his election. **46** However, a few weeks later, he announced nationally that Canada is having an "economic downturn." (Laghi, 2008). **47** Opponents have suggested that Prime Minister Harper lied to his citizens about the Canadian economy in order to get re-elected. **48** Perhaps there was also pressure from his party members, but this evidence proves that the citizens' fate is indeed in the hands of politicians. **49** We must understand who we are voting for and why. **50** We must not be deceived by promises that can be easily broken.

Section 5

51 In both Canada and the United States, each year there is a budget for political parties to spend on political campaigns. **52** There are laws and regulations that are developed to control excessive use of political mass media on citizens. **53** Though this financial limit in performing propaganda controls some level of the influence on citizens, it is not enough (Campbell, 2006, p. 200). **54** How do we know if the information is true? **55** How can we make sure we are making the right choices? **56** How much information is too much? **57** Each individual answers differently because we all have different standards and measures. **58** Thus, every citizen must be prepared to answer these questions by having his or her own priorities, values, and thoughts. **59** If we all gain more knowledge and understanding of the current political as well as world events, we are more prepared to make good decisions.

Section 6

60 The power of political mass media can be felt in today's society. **61** In fact, politicians are perhaps more powerful than ever to advertise themselves. **62** History has shown how too much political influence can distort our thoughts. **63** Media can take various forms such as television, radio, magazine, books, and the Internet. **64** These are the objects which citizens are always interacting with. **65** Therefore, people must be prepared to gain critical skills. **66** People must have their own values and standards to make the best decision. **67** We have to learn how to influence the media.

References

Campbell, K. K. (2006). *News, advertising, politics, and the Internet.* Belmont, CA: Wadsworth.
Churchill Center. (n.d.). *Quotation & stories.* Retrieved from http://www.winstonchurchill.org/
Ebrecht, T. (2007). History, public memory, and media event. *Media History, 13,* 221–234.
Jamieson, K. H. (2006). *The interplay of influence.* Belmont, CA: Wadsworth.
Laghi, B. (2009, March 11). Why Stephen Harper is suddenly an optimist. *Globe and Mail.*
Longman English dictionary. (2009). London, UK: Longman.
Meacham, J. (2009, January 20). That great gift of freedom. *Newsweek Commemorative Inaugural Edition,* 8–9.
Truman, C. (n.d.). Hitler & Nazis. *History Learning Site.* Retrieved from http://www.historylearningsite.co.uk/index.htm
Whitaker, A. (n.d.). Pierre Trudeau. *The Canadian Encyclopedia.* Retrieved from http://www.thecanadianencyclopedia.com/index.cfm?PgNmTCE&Params=A1ARTA0008141
The White House. (n.d.). Biography of Franklin D. Roosevelt. Retrieved from http://www.whitehouse.gov/about/presidents/franklindroosevelt/

TASK 8

Now read Rika's essay again and fill in each section of the Expository Essay Evaluation Form. Refer to your margin notes as you complete the form.

Expository Essay Evaluation Form	
Introduction	
Does the introduction shift from general to specific?	
Is there a clear thesis statement?	
Does the writer refer to the structure of the essay?	
Essay structure	
Is the essay organized logically?	
Main body sections/paragraphs	
Take notes below on the strengths and weaknesses of each section/paragraph, considering the following: • Topic sentences • Keeping to one topic • Detailed explanation with supporting evidence, examples, citations • Concluding sentence(s)	

Section 2	
Section 3	
Section 4	
Section 5	
Conclusion	
Does the writer clearly signal the beginning of the conclusion?	
Does the conclusion shift from specific to general?	
Does the writer summarize?	
Does the writer synthesize?	
Does the writer answer the question?	
Does the writer round off the essay with an end statement?	

LANGUAGE FOCUS: PERSONAL REFLECTIVE LANGUAGE

Rika expresses her personal voice in the essay on political mass media by using the following personal reflective language:

4 Eventually, I find this advertisement in politics is known as political mass media (*Longman English Dictionary,* 2009).

7 These facts attracted my curiosity.

8 I wanted to learn about and research "political mass media."

34 During my research, I was shocked at how powerful today's politicians are in conducting political mass media.

TASK 9

The four sentences above stand out as being more appropriate for writing a reflective essay (in which writers give their personal reflections on the learning process they have gone though on a course) than for an academic expository essay.

Read the list below of an instructor's comments about Rika's use of personal reflective language in an expository essay. Match each comment (a to d) to a corresponding sentence above (4, 7, 8, and 34). Note the sentence number in the margin.

Sentence Number

a) This sentence reads as a little too emotional for an essay on politics. Try to focus more on the wider social implications of the power of politicians rather than your own personal feelings here.

b) Try to use a more formal structure for defining, for example, "Such activities fall under the definition of . . ."

c) It is fine to describe your feelings with personal language in reflective writing tasks in which you are required to describe how your feelings developed during a process of learning. However, for this essay, you need to develop a more distant and objective tone. Rather than personalizing the interest as personal curiosity, you could give a broader, less personal scope (e.g., ". . . are of considerable interest to many people in society.").

d) Although the personal language "I wanted" does not make the writing informal, your tone seems more reflective and narrative than analytical.

LANGUAGE FOCUS: THE PASSIVE VOICE

The passive voice is commonly used in many forms of academic writing. Whether you choose to write in the passive voice will depend on the following: emphasis of the sentence, writing style, and personal preference. (You can find more practice exercises on the passive voice in Appendix 9.)

What to Emphasize in the Sentence

When you use the active or passive voice, you emphasize different parts of the sentence.

Active voice: The active voice can be formed as follows:

William Shakespeare	wrote	Romeo and Juliet.
[William Shakespeare]	[wrote]	[Romeo and Juliet].
subject	***main verb***	***object***

Passive voice: To form the passive voice, the object from the active voice moves to the subject position. The passive voice can be formed as follows:

1. **With stated agent:** that is, the person or thing that did something is mentioned and given emphasis in the sentence.

Romeo and Juliet	was written	by William Shakespeare.
[Romeo and Juliet]	[was written]	[by William Shakespeare].
subject	***to be + past participle***	***by + agent***

2. **Without stated agent:** The person or thing that did something is not mentioned or given emphasis in the sentence—the agent is unknown or not important to the meaning or purpose of the sentence. For example, in the sentence below the date is more important than the author.

Romeo and Juliet	was written	in the 1590s.
[Romeo and Juliet]	[was written]	[in the 1590s].
subject	***to be + past participle***	***complement***

An Objective Scholarly Style?

Some writers argue that the passive voice gives academic writing a less personal and more objective scholarly tone. This is seen as especially appropriate for expository writing, where the focus is less on the writer's personal opinions and powers of persuasion and more on detailed explanation and supporting ideas and examples.

EXAMPLE

Active voice with personal style: In the study, I interviewed nine participants.
Passive voice with impersonal style: Nine participants were interviewed in the study.

Others disagree. They argue that the passive voice can weaken your writing by limiting your voice as a writer and researcher.

Personal Preference vs. Genre and Audience

Your decision about whether to use the passive voice may also be a question of personal preference, that is, the way that you prefer to write. However, you also need to consider common practice associated with the specific genre of writing as well as your reader's expectations and preferences.

It is not always easy to make a choice, as the following scenarios illustrate:

SCENARIO 1

You are writing a physics lab report. You prefer to write in a more direct, personal way, which means that you prefer to use the active voice. However, you have noticed from reading lab reports in journals that most writers use the passive voice very often, and you assume that your instructor will expect a more impersonal style with the passive voice. What should you do?

SCENARIO 2

You are the kind of writer who enjoys expressing ideas with the passive voice, with and without a stated agent. You are studying English literature. Your friends tell you that in English, you are expected to avoid the passive voice wherever possible, and that your instructor always picks up on the passive voice. What should you do?

In both scenarios, you may not be in a position to write in your preferred style because this may have a negative effect on your grades. The best advice would be to get in touch with your instructor, find out what is expected of you, and weigh your preferences against your instructor's expectations.

TASK 10

Look at the two passive-voice sentences below and answer the question that follows.

1. My bag was stolen last night at the train station.
2. It was stolen by two teenagers who threatened me.

Why do you think that the writer states the agent in Sentence 2 but not in Sentence 1?

____

____

____

____

TASK 11

Read again the "clinical procedure" section from the journal article on laser dentistry (below). Underline any examples of the passive voice that you can find. Then in the margin, note whether the agent is stated or not stated: mark examples where the agent is stated **S** and where it is not stated **NS**.

Clinical procedure

Margin Notes

18 The clinical procedure for the Er:YAG laser is similar to the clinical procedure for the high-speed drill. **19** However, because previous studies of the Er:YAG laser had shown that anesthetic was not needed, patients were not routinely offered anesthetic at the beginning of the laser procedure. **20** Anesthetic was available on request. **21** The Er:YAG laser has a sterile, removable tip that is used with a handpiece attached to a fiber-optic delivery system. **22** Because the Er:YAG laser is invisible, a helium neon laser beam is used as an aiming beam. **23** The laser parameters are selected on the control panel according to the procedure to be accomplished. **24** Low dosimetries are used to remove caries, and high dosimetries are used to cut dentin and enamel. **25** This lets operators remove the carious dentin without removing the sound dentin, until they decide to increase the dosimetries and cut dentin or enamel. **26** The laser was used for amalgam or composite cavity preparations and restorations. **27** The investigators prepared the cavity for amalgam following the procedure outlined by G.V. Black. **28** However, the surface of the floor was not as smooth as that achieved with the high-speed drill. **29** For composite cavity preparations, the investigators completed the preparation, used the laser (with focus/defocus mode) to etch the enamel surface and then acid etched the tooth. **30** After the teeth were prepared, the investigators restored them with their choice of materials. **31** In this study, the majority of composites were polymerized with an argon laser. **32** When using the laser, as when using the high-speed drill, practitioners need to apply air or water spray to the tooth for efficient cutting and cooling. **33** The laser is equipped with either straight or angled handpieces, and the air or water spray can be delivered through the handpiece or applied externally by an assistant. **34** The millijoule and hertz parameters shown in Table 3 were cleared by the FDA, based on previous animal and human research data. **35** The investigators used standard dental procedures to prepare or remove caries from the teeth in the control group.

TASK 12

In the paragraph above, nearly all of the examples of the passive voice have no stated agent. Explain why you think the writer does not state the agent in most sentences.

CHAPTER 6 SUMMARY

In this chapter, you have studied several important aspects of expository writing. You have also reviewed material from Chapters 3 and 4 on writing introductions, main body paragraphs, and conclusions.

WHAT IS EXPOSITORY WRITING?

Expository writing involves providing information on, describing, or explaining a subject to your reader. It tends to be more descriptive than argumentative and can involve any of the following:

- A detailed explanation of a specific topic
- A detailed description of a process or procedure
- Definitions of key terms
- A description of the similarities and differences between two theories, situations, or key figures, for example
- A description of a situation or problem and an analysis of the possible causes and effects
- A description of a problem and suggested solutions to that problem

Expository writing requires focused investigation of a subject, careful organization of information and notes, detailed description, and supporting examples and evidence. Writing with an expository focus may be part of an essay in which other types of writing are involved (e.g., an argument essay), or it may be the main form of writing in an expository essay.

EXPOSITORY WRITING: ORGANIZING YOUR INFORMATION

When you begin to organize your information and ideas for an expository essay, or for any other type of essay, think of the genre, audience, and context of the writing, as well as the topic, focus, and task in the question.

FEATURES OF EXPOSITORY WRITING IN ACADEMIC JOURNAL ARTICLES

Academic journal articles from different subject areas apply the features of expository writing in many ways. In the excerpt from the article on magic realism in literature, many sentences were very long, with very detailed description. The description was combined with the author's stance and opinions on the subject. In the excerpt from the article on laser dentistry, the sentences were much shorter with many more passive-voice structures. The writer's stance and opinions were not evident.

LANGUAGE FOCUS: PERSONAL REFLECTIVE LANGUAGE

In Rika's essay on political mass media, she expressed her personal voice by using personal reflective language in several places. Be careful not to be too personal and reflective in essays where this is not required.

LANGUAGE FOCUS: THE PASSIVE VOICE

When deciding whether to use the passive voice in your academic writing, think about the emphasis of each sentence, the style of writing, and personal preference (yours and that of your reader). If in doubt, ask your instructor.

CHAPTER 7

Writing about Arguments

In this chapter, you will study the following aspects of writing about arguments:

- ✓ Gathering your ideas
- ✓ Organizing your ideas into an effective outline
- ✓ Adding supporting reasons, examples, and evidence
- ✓ Analyzing an argument essay

All academic writing involves writing about arguments. Whether you are writing an argument essay in which you argue for or against a topic, or a scientific lab report in which you describe an experiment and discuss your findings, you need to be able to present arguments effectively.

In this chapter, you will study how to write an argument essay. Argument essays are especially common in the arts, social sciences, and humanities, and come in many forms. You will also practise some of the aspects of active and critical reading, and critical thinking that you studied in Chapters 1 and 2.

GATHERING YOUR IDEAS

When you are presented with an essay question as a course assignment or in an examination, you first need to understand the question and organize your thoughts. You need to figure out what the question is asking you to do. In Chapter 6, you studied the following preparation stages of gathering information and ideas for an expository essay:

- Consider the genre, audience, and context.
- Break the question down according to topic, focus, and task.

The outline for the expository essay on bilingualism in Chapter 6 brought together the writer's existing knowledge and supporting examples and evidence from the literature on bilingualism. You were reminded that, even when you are sure of your own ideas, you should still find supporting examples and evidence from reliable academic sources.

Here is the essay question that you will be working on in this chapter, and the guidelines for writing about it:

Question: Should marijuana be legalized?

Guidelines: Your task is to present a balanced analysis. Include arguments that supporters and opponents of legalization would use, while at the same time making your own opinion clear to the reader.

TASK 1

Break down the essay question for this chapter according to *topic*, *focus*, and *task*:

Topic: ____________________

Focus: ____________________

Task: ____________________

Writers gather their ideas in many different ways, often depending on what kind of learners they are. Some writers prefer to spend some time gathering their own ideas before they begin to look for examples and evidence from reliable academic sources. They brainstorm ideas from their existing knowledge and create an outline for the essay before doing the research. In this section, you are going to try out three common methods for gathering your ideas in this way:

1. **Exploratory writing:** Exploratory writing involves writing down any ideas you have that are related to your essay question. You can write in any form—you don't need to use complete sentences, formal language, or standard punctuation. Just write! The purpose of exploratory writing is to get started by putting your existing ideas down on paper, and generating more ideas as you write.
2. **Concept mapping:** Some writers, especially those who are more visual learners, prefer to organize their ideas in concept maps. In a concept map, you literally map out your ideas by linking "areas" or circles on the map to each other. You can use arrows to link ideas depending on how they relate to each

other—for example, they may be advantages, disadvantages, causes, effects, problems, opinions, or solutions. Again, the idea is to generate more ideas about the topic, and create more areas (or circles) on the map as you write.

3. **Traditional notes:** Some writers prefer a more linear approach to getting ideas down on paper. One such way is to take notes in a traditional form, selecting headings and subheadings, and then writing a list of ideas in note form under each heading.

As you gather your ideas, remember the topic, focus, and task of the essay, and try to add reasons, examples, and supporting evidence for your ideas as you go along.

TASK 2

You are going to try out three methods for gathering ideas for the essay on whether marijuana should be legalized. As you write down your ideas, think about which of these methods works best for you, and why.

METHOD 1: EXPLORATORY WRITING

In the box below, take **three to five minutes** to write down as many ideas as you can about the legalization of marijuana. This is freestyle writing: you can write in any style that you choose. The main thing is to get as many ideas as possible down on paper.

Exploratory Writing: Just Write!

In my opinion, the legalization of marijuana is

____

____

____

____

____

____

____

____

____

____

____

____

____

____

____

METHOD 2: CONCEPT MAPPING

Complete the concept map below by adding some of your own ideas and ideas you think supporters and opponents would use.

Concept Map: Make the Connections

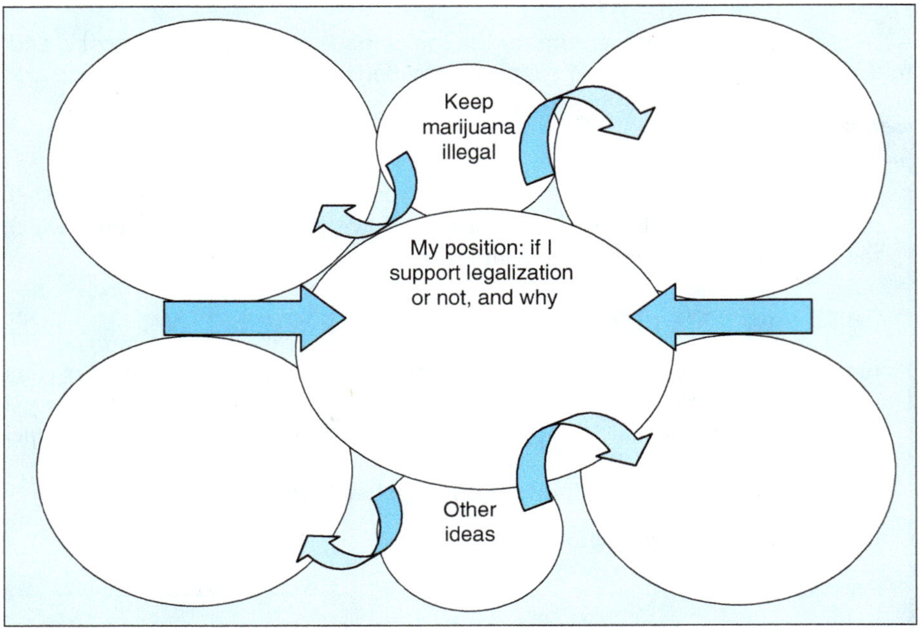

METHOD 3: TRADITIONAL NOTES

Write down your ideas under each heading below.

Traditional Notes: Linear Structure

Arguments supporters of legalization would use:

____

____

____

____

____

____

____

____

Arguments opponents of legalization would use:

Your position:

ORGANIZING YOUR IDEAS INTO AN EFFECTIVE OUTLINE

Now that you have gathered some ideas using the three methods above, you need to create an effective outline for the argument essay. You can do this by transferring your notes from above into either a *for-then-against outline* or a *thematic outline*.

A For-Then-Against Outline

In a for-then-against outline for the argument essay on the legalization of marijuana, you cover the three main aspects that are required for critical analysis:

A. Arguments in favour (ideas that would be used by those supporting legalization)

B. Arguments against (ideas that would be used by opponents of legalization)

C. Your position (what you think)

In this type of outline, the three aspects of critical analysis—A for, B against, and C your position—are organized and presented in separate sections of the essay.

Carefully read through Outline 1 on the next page, which is a for-then-against outline for the essay on the legalization of marijuana. As you read, take notes in the margin about the strengths and weaknesses of organizing ideas in this way for an argument essay.

Margin Notes

Outline 1: For-then-against outline

INTRODUCTION

1. **Background:** general information on marijuana—history and legislation
2. **Specifics:** shift to the specific focus and task: the pros and cons of legalization
3. **Structure:** will look at pros, then cons, then my opinion
4. **Thesis statement:** e.g., I oppose/support legalization

A. ARGUMENTS IN FAVOUR OF LEGALIZATION

1. **Social aspects:**
   - Makes users calm and relaxed, unlike alcohol, which can make people aggressive
   - Safer for users as they can buy it legally
   - Remove the black market and reduce crime; police will be able to focus on other crimes and more dangerous drugs
   - Fewer drug users will clog up the court system
2. **Health issues:**
   - Reduces stress for some people
   - Alcohol and tobacco are worse for your health and both are legal
   - Can prevent dealers from lacing marijuana with more dangerous drugs
   - Has medical benefits, e.g., for MS sufferers
3. **Financial implications:**
   - Regulation can stimulate the economy by collecting taxes from users and dispensaries
   - Hemp by-products can also stimulate the economy
   - Governments will save money because the police will spend less time arresting users who possess small amounts

B. ARGUMENTS AGAINST LEGALIZATION

1. **Social aspects:**
   - Strong marijuana can make people paranoid and dangerous
   - Dealers won't disappear, they'll still sell other drugs
   - Legal/tolerating zones, e.g., Amsterdam, attract many drug users and organized crime
   - Users may commit crimes to fund their habit
2. **Health issues:**
   - Makes people lazy and non-productive; can make users psychotic after prolonged use
   - THC levels are very high in modern marijuana, e.g., skunk
   - Studies suggest that tar from marijuana could be as harmful as tobacco tar
   - If the government sells marijuana, dealers will still try to mix it with other drugs
   - Data on medical use is not accepted by all scientists
3. **Financial implications:**
   - Creating and implementing new laws would cost a lot
   - Policing will still cost the same, even if attention is redirected
   - There may not be enough purchasers to bring in tax revenue—costs would outweigh benefits

C. YOUR POSITION

1. The drawbacks outweigh the advantages:
    - Social aspects: alcohol, cigarettes, recreational drugs—all should be discouraged rather than encouraged
    - Cost: would need a lot of new users to bring in enough taxes to make legalization worthwhile economically; does society want to encourage more people to use drugs?
    - Evidence suggests that marijuana is harmful to mental health, and to physical health in the long term
2. Legalization would legitimize marijuana and send the wrong signal to young people
3. In some countries, marijuana has been decriminalized—still officially illegal but possession of small amounts is tolerated. This was tried in Brixton, London, and created more problems than it solved—it increased crime in the local area

CONCLUSION

1. **Summarize:** arguments for and against
2. **Synthesize:** bring ideas together into one closing idea—weighing things from all perspectives, cons outweigh the pros
3. **Answer the question:** I am opposed to legalization because . . .
4. **End statement:** societies today and in the future need people healthy in body and mind; governments should actively discourage marijuana as a result

TASK 3

Answer the following three questions about the for-then-against outline above. Refer to your notes.

1. Does the writer clearly and convincingly list ideas in favour, ideas against, and her own opinion in the outline?

____

____

____

____

2. What do you think are the main strengths of the for-then-against outline above?

____

____

____

____

3. What do you think are the main weaknesses of the for-then-against outline above?

____

____

____

____

A Thematic Outline

An alternative, and many would say more effective, way of organizing the same ideas into a coherent essay outline is by making a thematic outline. With a thematic outline, arguments in favour (A), arguments against (B), and your position (C) are presented together in the same essay section under relevant themes or analytic perspectives. In this way, critical analysis is evident in each section of the essay.

Carefully read through Outline 2 below, which is a thematic outline for the same essay as above. As you read, take notes in the margin about the strengths and weaknesses of organizing ideas in this way for an argument essay.

Margin Notes

Outline 2: Thematic outline

INTRODUCTION

1. **Background:** general information on marijuana—history and legislation
2. **Specifics:** shift to the specific focus and task: the pros and cons of legalization
3. **Structure:** three perspectives—social aspects, health, financial implications
4. **Thesis statement:** e.g., I oppose/support legalization

SOCIAL ASPECTS

A. **Arguments in favour:**
- Makes users calm and relaxed, unlike alcohol, which can make people aggressive
- Safer for users as they can buy it legally
- Remove the black market and reduce crime; police will be able to focus on other crimes and more dangerous drugs
- Fewer drug users will clog up the court system

B. **Arguments against:**
- Strong marijuana can make people paranoid and dangerous
- Dealers won't disappear, they'll still sell other drugs
- Legal/tolerating zones, e.g., Amsterdam, attract many drug users and organized crime
- Users may commit crimes to fund their habit

C. **Your position:**
- Based on these arguments, I argue that . . .

HEALTH ISSUES

A. **Arguments in favour:**
- Reduces stress for some people
- Alcohol and tobacco are worse for your health and both are legal
- Can prevent dealers from lacing marijuana with more dangerous drugs
- Has medical benefits for MS sufferers

B. Arguments against:
- Makes people lazy and non-productive; can make users psychotic after prolonged use
- THC levels are very high in modern marijuana, e.g., skunk
- Studies suggest that tar from marijuana could be as harmful as tobacco tar
- If the government sells marijuana, dealers will still try to mix it with other drugs
- Data on medical use is not accepted by all scientists

C. Your position:
- Having considered these arguments, I support/oppose . . .

FINANCIAL IMPLICATIONS

A. Arguments in favour:
- Regulation can stimulate the economy by collecting taxes from users and dispensaries
- Hemp by-products can also stimulate the economy
- Governments will save money because the police will spend less time arresting users who possess small amounts

B. Arguments against:
- Creating and implementing new laws would cost a lot
- Policing will still cost the same, even if attention is redirected
- There may not be enough purchasers to bring in tax revenue—costs would outweigh benefits

C. Your position:
- Considering the financial implications, I believe that . . .

CONCLUSION

1. **Summarize the perspectives:** social aspects, health issues, financial implications
2. **Synthesize:** bring ideas together into one closing idea—a question of weighing the rights of individuals to harm themselves against the broader needs of society as a whole
3. **Answer the question:** I oppose legalization because . . .
4. **End statement:** e.g., speculate about the future: Societies today and in the future need people healthy in body and mind; governments should actively discourage marijuana as a result

TASK 4

The content of the *thematic outline* is the same as the content in the *for-then-against outline*; however, the content of the thematic outline is organized around key themes. Answer the following questions about the thematic outline above.

1. Does the writer clearly list arguments in favour (A), arguments against (B), and his own position (C) in the outline?

____

____

____

____

2. What do you think are the advantages and disadvantages of presenting arguments for, against, and the writer's own position together in the same sections of the essay under relevant themes?

3. Which outline do you think allows for more effective critical analysis, and why?

4. In each outline, the writer has ordered the themes as follows: social aspects, health issues, financial implications. Why do you think the writer has done this? For ideas, you can look back to the Chapter 3 section on ordering principles for paragraphs (page 50).

ADDING SUPPORTING REASONS, EXAMPLES, AND EVIDENCE

The following is an editorial feature for the *Canadian Medical Association Journal* in which the author, Charlotte Gray, argues the case for legalizing marijuana for medical purposes. Read the article and annotate the text. As you take notes, pay particular attention to the arguments that are presented in favour of and against the legalization of medical marijuana and recreational marijuana. Remember to include your feelings or any questions that emerge while you are reading.

Margin Notes

Legalize use of marijuana for medical purposes, MDs and patients plead

Charlotte Gray

In brief

PARA. 1 As debate about the legalization of marijuana continues in Canada, physicians are joining the fray. Ottawa family physician Don Kilby is working hard to make it easier for ill patients to use the marijuana that alleviates their symptoms. A recent case in Toronto indicates that the courts are starting to share these views.

Jean Charles Pariseau is a 30-year-old Ottawa AIDS patient who, if he had stuck to his legally prescribed medications, would probably be dead by now. At his sickest, Pariseau weighed only 82 lbs. He had to take about 30 pills a day to boost his immune system, fight nausea and stimulate his appetite, but could not keep them down. He was bedridden and miserable. His physician, Don Kilby, gave him less than 3 months to live. PARA. 2

"Jean has a decent prognosis today," reports Kilby, a family physician with an extensive palliative care practice who also serves as director of health services at his alma mater, the University of Ottawa. "He is doing remarkably well because he can now digest his medications. His cerebral toxoplasmosis is in remission, the HIV has been suppressed because he has improved immune function, he has put on weight and he has learned to walk again, with a cane. Most important, he has a decent quality of life. He has regained weight, recovered his appetite and can join his wife and child at the dinner table." PARA. 3

Pariseau owes this startling change of status to the marijuana he smokes each day, half an hour before it is time to take his pills. Since he cannot use marijuana in its pill form, which is legal, because he cannot swallow the pills, Pariseau must buy his on the illegal market. This means he is at risk of purchasing contaminated product and being charged for possession of an illegal substance; the police have already charged him with the latter offence. Police raided his home after receiving a tip that Pariseau was growing marijuana hydroponically. "If he was incarcerated," says Kilby, "God knows what would happen." PARA. 4

Kilby is working hard to eliminate the problems terminally ill patients like Pariseau face if they want to use marijuana. In December, along with Dr. Michele Brill-Edwards and lawyers Eugene Oscapella and Glenn Gilmour, Kilby applied to Health Canada for permission to prescribe marijuana to Pariseau under the Facilitated Access Program, formerly known as the Emergency Drug Release Program. PARA. 5

Although the application was "well received," Kilby says it was turned down because the group lacked access to a legal source for a supply of marijuana. The manufacturer must have a licence under the Controlled Drug and Substance Act to conduct research on a controlled substance; an unlicensed grower would not qualify. PARA. 6

This meant Kilby has had to investigate legal suppliers — pharmaceutical companies, university laboratories or licensed facilities overseas. "I am crossing my fingers that we will have our application accepted before the end of February," he says. "We are looking into the possibility of a supplier in the Netherlands." PARA. 7

Initially Health Canada also argued that Kilby himself must have a special licence to prescribe a controlled substance, but he challenged this successfully by pointing out that physicians can already prescribe controlled substances and opiate derivatives like morphine. Kilby feels that if he could satisfy the legal requirement about a supplier, problems would melt away. "The whole point of the Facilitated Access Program is compassion for patients. You don't have to prove effectiveness or safety when a patient is in the last months of life anyway." He points out that another compound is already being released for cancer patients under the program, despite a lack of evidence about its effectiveness. PARA. 8

Kilby has been involved in the marijuana fray since he first became Pariseau's physician a year ago. Like many doctors involved in palliative care he was aware that 10% to 15% of his patients used marijuana, "but I turned a blind eye." However, he wasn't blind to its beneficial effects on users, who to his knowledge included judges and police officers, or to the resulting improvement in their quality of life. When Pariseau's story became front-page news in the *Ottawa Citizen* in December—he contacted the paper after the police raid on his home—Kilby decided that passive approval was no longer an option: as a physician, he had to take responsibility. Since then he has been overwhelmed by the number of phone calls from people supporting his initiative. PARA. 9

PARA. 10 "Until now I never realized how many people were using marijuana for medicinal purposes, without discussing it with their physicians. Nor did I realize how distressing and frightening it has been for my patients' families, who had to find the supplies."

PARA. 11 He has heard from elderly women who have been forced to go onto the streets to purchase marijuana for their dying husbands—a terrifying prospect for people who have no idea about the quality of what they are buying or whether they are paying a fair price. Kilby is convinced that physicians should move beyond tacit approval: if they are going to support their patients, they must help them secure legal access to a useful substance.

PARA. 12 While Kilby pursued the issue through Health Canada, other challengers have taken the issue to the courts. The campaign to decriminalize marijuana for medical use burst into public view in December when an Ontario judge ruled that 42-year-old Terry Parker of Toronto, who has spent 2 decades battling Canada's marijuana laws, has a legal right to grow, possess and smoke the substance that helps control his epilepsy.

PARA. 13 Before he began using the banned substance he had experienced as many as 12 seizures a day, rendering a normal life impossible. Once he was robbed while lying unconscious in a subway station following a seizure, and he had been arrested repeatedly after his seizure symptoms were mistaken for drunkenness; he cannot ride a bicycle, drive a car or hold a job. However, when he smokes marijuana, the number of seizures declines dramatically; he keeps a careful record of its impact on his health.

PARA. 14 In dismissing the possession charges facing Parker, Judge Patrick Sheppard ruled that restricting his access to marijuana "does not accord with fundamental justice." Sheppard, after listening to expert evidence for and against medical use of the drug, concluded that "regular moderate use of marijuana causes no physical or psychological harm to the vast majority of users."

PARA. 15 Sheppard did not dismiss trafficking charges against Parker, who had told police that he supplied home-grown marijuana to friends who also suffer seizures, but he did point out that his cultivation of marijuana was a logical and defensible activity. "It allowed him to control the quality of the drug smoked, to maximize its benefit and minimize any risks from an unadulterated product. Further, it was an economic necessity for him to grow his own marijuana. All witnesses agreed that at illicit street prices, the marijuana used by Mr. Parker would cost approximately $5000 annually."

PARA. 16 Sheppard's decision has created a comfort zone for other judges dealing with the explosive issue—several other cases involving the use of "medicinal marijuana" are already before the courts. In December AIDS activist Jim Wakeford filed suit, calling for a court declaration allowing people with AIDS to possess and consume marijuana if its use is recommended by a doctor. He also called on the court to order the federal government to supply the drug from the crop grown at Agriculture Canada's Experimental Farm in Ottawa. In April, Lynn Harichy is due to appear in a London, Ont., courtroom to defend her use of marijuana to alleviate her multiple sclerosis symptoms.

PARA. 17 Moves to legalize marijuana for medicinal purposes have solid public support—according to a recent poll, 83% of Canadians believe this type of use should be legal. There have been well-publicized stories about its effectiveness in controlling nausea and relieving symptoms of glaucoma, epilepsy and multiple sclerosis. When the issue arrives in court, much of the argument surrounds scientific proof of its effectiveness, for which little agreement yet exists. The federal government continues to argue that not enough is known about potential dangers posed by the drug.

PARA. 18 Sheppard said his ruling did not extend into the hazy world of recreational drug use but referred only to Terry Parker's Charter rights to life, liberty and security. However, his decision provided a springboard for editorialists across the country. They argued that the harsh penalties for marijuana use contained in the Criminal Code should be eliminated. Pointing to the amount of court and police time that marijuana arrests consume—there were 29,562 arrests in 1996—the *Globe and Mail* concluded that the "marijuana ban should go to pot." Meanwhile, the *Ottawa Citizen* said that legalizing marijuana for medicinal use would simply "invite what amounts to a market in medical prescriptions that is, except for the status quo, the least satisfactory way of dealing with the problem." It said Parliament should act to legalize the possession, consumption and production of marijuana. Several commentators pointed out that it is now 25 years since Gerald Le Dain's royal commission recommended the decriminalization of marijuana use. The Addiction Research Foundation, Canadian Bar Association and Canadian Police Association also want to eliminate criminal penalties.

However, those who are pressing for the release of marijuana for medicinal purposes are less quick to support general access. Kilby shies away from any discussion of recreational use. "In my practice I deal with patients who have addiction problems and need detoxification programs. I don't think there is any question that marijuana is addictive—mildly addictive compared to heroin or cocaine, perhaps, but at least equal to nicotine in both its addictive qualities and its health effects." PARA. 19

He is not interested in seeing a full-scale campaign to take marijuana out of the Criminal Code but does want to encourage other physicians to show compassion for patients who will benefit from smoking marijuana. He would also like to investigate the possibility of finding a legal supply of marijuana to meet patients' needs through Ottawa's Facilitated Access Program. PARA. 20

Source: Charlotte Gray. "Legalize use of marijuana for medical purposes, MDs and patients plead." *Canadian Medical Association Journal* 158.3 (1998): 373–375.

The article is an excellent example of argumentative writing.

The *genre* of the text is an "editorial feature" for an academic journal, in which an editor discusses a topical issue. This genre of argumentative writing is different from the articles in the same journal that base their arguments on data findings. The *audience* is a reader with specialist knowledge of the topic, although as an editorial feature, the article is easier for non-specialists to read. The *context* relates to an ongoing debate about the legalization of marijuana for medical use, one that divides opinions not only in medical circles but also in the country as a whole.

The editorial feature presents opinions on the controversial campaign to legalize medical marijuana, not through direct arguing of the writer, but instead through the eyes and words of patients and doctors. Many of the ideas in the article could be used as supporting reasons, examples, or evidence for the ideas and arguments listed in Outlines 1 and 2 on pages 132 to 135. In order to use the ideas from a text such as this in an argument essay, it is necessary to read actively and critically. You need to infer meaning and figure out how the examples can be brought in to support your own ideas and arguments.

TASK 5

Read the list of sentences or phrases below from the editorial feature. Infer meaning by linking each example to a broader argument in the ongoing debate on legalizing medical marijuana. The first three are done as examples:

1. **Examples that can be used to support arguments in favour of the legalization of medical marijuana:**

PARA. 4

- "Pariseau owes this startling change of status to the marijuana he smokes each day, half an hour before it is time to take his pills."

  This sentence suggests that marijuana has positive health benefits.

- "Since he cannot use marijuana in its pill form, which is legal, because he cannot swallow the pills, Pariseau must buy his on the illegal market."

  This sentence suggests that those suffering have no other choice than to use illegal marijuana.

- "This means he is at risk of purchasing contaminated product."

  This sentence suggests that legalization would reduce the risk of buying contaminated marijuana on the black market.

- "The police have already charged him with the latter offence."

  ____

  ____

  ____

- "'If he was incarcerated,' says Kilby, 'God knows what would happen.'"

  ____

  ____

  ____

PARA. 5

- "In December, along with Dr. Michele Brill-Edwards and lawyers Eugene Oscapella and Glenn Gilmour, Kilby applied to Health Canada for permission to prescribe marijuana to Pariseau under the Facilitated Access Program, formerly known as the Emergency Drug Release Program."

  ____

  ____

  ____

PARA. 8

- "He points out that another compound is already being released for cancer patients under the program, despite a lack of evidence about its effectiveness."

  ____

  ____

  ____

- "However, he wasn't blind to its beneficial effects on users, who to his knowledge included judges and police officers, or to the resulting improvement in their quality of life." PARA. 9

- "'Nor did I realize how distressing and frightening it has been for my patients' families, who had to find the supplies.'" PARA. 10

- "Before he began using the banned substance he had experienced as many as 12 seizures a day, rendering a normal life impossible. . . . However, when he smokes marijuana, the number of seizures declines dramatically; he keeps a careful record of its impact on his health." PARA. 13

- "Sheppard, after listening to expert evidence for and against medical use of the drug, concluded that 'regular moderate use of marijuana causes no physical or psychological harm to the vast majority of users.'" PARA. 14

- "In April, Lynn Harichy is due to appear in a London, Ont., courtroom to defend her use of marijuana to alleviate her multiple sclerosis symptoms." PARA. 16

- "Moves to legalize marijuana for medicinal purposes have solid public support—according to a recent poll, 83% of Canadians believe this type of use should be legal. There have been well-publicized stories about its effectiveness in controlling nausea and relieving symptoms of glaucoma, epilepsy and multiple sclerosis." PARA. 17

2. **Examples that can be used to support arguments against the legalization of medical marijuana:**

PARA. 17

- "Much of the argument surrounds scientific proof of its effectiveness, for which little agreement yet exists."

- "The federal government continues to argue that not enough is known about potential dangers posed by the drug."

3. **Examples that can be used to support arguments in favour of the legalization of recreational marijuana:**

PARA. 18

- "They argued that the harsh penalties for marijuana use contained in the Criminal Code should be eliminated."

- "It said Parliament should act to legalize the possession, consumption and production of marijuana. Several commentators pointed out that it is now 25 years since Gerald Le Dain's royal commission recommended the decriminalization of marijuana use. The Addiction Research Foundation, Canadian Bar Association and Canadian Police Association also want to eliminate criminal penalties."

4. **Examples that can be used to support arguments against the legalization of recreational marijuana:**

PARA. 19

- "However, those who are pressing for the release of marijuana for medicinal purposes are less quick to support general access."

- "Kilby shies away from any discussion of recreational use. 'In my practice I deal with patients who have addiction problems and need detoxification programs. I don't think there is any question that marijuana is addictive—mildly addictive compared to heroin or cocaine, perhaps, but at least equal to nicotine in both its addictive qualities and its health effects.'"

- "He is not interested in seeing a full-scale campaign to take marijuana out of the Criminal Code but does want to encourage other physicians to show compassion for patients who will benefit from smoking marijuana." PARA. 20

TASK 6

The author of the editorial feature does not express her opinion explicitly in the article. Why might this be the case? And, based on the examples above, where do you think her sympathies lie, and why?

ANALYZING AN ARGUMENT ESSAY

In this section, you will read a student's argument essay on lowering the legal age for drinking alcohol in British Columbia. The essay was written by James as an assessed research essay in an undergraduate academic writing course. It follows a thematic structure. As you read the essay, take notes in the margin on its strengths and weaknesses, paying particular attention to the following:

- Essay sections (introduction, main body paragraphs, and conclusion)
- Presentation of arguments (Are arguments supported with reasons, examples, and evidence from reliable sources?)
- Coherence (Are arguments logically ordered?)
- Thematic structure (Does the writer effectively present all sides of the argument, including his own position, under each of the themes?)

Margin Notes

Should the legal drinking age be lowered in British Columbia?

1 Because underage drinking can lead to sexual behavior, drunk driving and alcohol dependency, I am opposed to the lowering of the legal drinking age. **2** There is strong evidence to support my thesis, including statistics about deaths from drunk driving, information from censuses about dependency on alcohol with youth, and facts and data about sexual assault and unsafe sex with adolescents. **3** As well, there are arguments in favor of lowering the legal drinking age and my opinion on each separate issue.

4 There are a number of costly consequences when alcohol is introduced into the equation in regards to health issues. **5** Alcohol use interacts with conditions such as depression and stress to contribute to suicide, the third leading cause of death among people between the ages of 14 and 25 (Anderson, 2001; Garlow, 2002). **6** There are a number of serious sexual problems that can occur for adolescents that can be directly influenced by alcohol intake. **7** Sexual assault or rape is very common and occurs most commonly for women in late adolescence and early adulthood. **8** Research suggests that alcohol use by the offender, the victim, or both, increases the likelihood of sexual assault by a male acquaintance (Abbey, 2002). **9** High-risk sex is another important issue to consider. **10** Adolescent alcohol use often leads to high-risk sex. **11** This includes having sex with multiple partners and failing to use condoms. **12** The consequences of high-risk sex are also common in this age group, including unwanted pregnancy and sexually transmitted diseases including HIV/AIDS. **13** Of course, those situations happen in everyday life without alcohol being consumed, so it could be seen as irrelevant to some. **14** Education in school teaches youth about safe sex and alcohol and its negative effects. **15** Parents also have a sizable influence on their children. **16** Adolescents who grow up in positive homes are less likely to get involved with drinking. **17** There are options if the legal drinking age was to be lowered, such as limiting the intake of alcohol, and offering mandatory education. **18** My personal belief on the issue is that I believe it important to keep the drinking age as it is. **19** There are too many negative side effects from drinking and it is only done with protecting adolescents in mind.

20 There is a lot of concern about the linkage between early-age drinking and alcohol dependency. **21** It can have long-lasting consequences on an adolescent. **22** People who begin drinking before age 15 are four times more likely to develop alcohol dependence at some time in their lives compared with those who have their first drink at age 20 or older (Grant & Dawson, 1997). **23** However, it is not clear whether starting to drink at an early age actually causes alcoholism or whether it simply indicates an existing vulnerability to alcohol use disorders (Dawson, 2000). **24** Both early drinking and alcoholism have been linked to personality characteristics such as strong tendencies to act impulsively and to seek out new experiences and sensations. **25** However, there are arguments against this which are just as compelling. **26** Often there is alcohol in the homes of family, and it can be monitored by parents. **27** Adolescents are invited to weddings, where often they can access alcohol, but again it can be limited by parents. **28** Adolescents find themselves in situations all the time where alcohol is present, and they can still drink responsibly without becoming alcoholics. **29** Right or wrong, it happens regardless and they are exposed to it, no matter how hard parents and others will try to prevent it. **30** There needs to be a level of trust too with adolescents that they will make mature decisions. **31** My personal feeling on this matter of alcohol dependency is that I started drinking at a young age, and it definitely made me dependent on alcohol. **32** I didn't know how to handle difficult situations, and ultimately I ran to alcohol to deal with the pressure. **33** Perhaps this wouldn't have happened if I didn't start drinking at a young age.

34 In Canada, the majority of the country has the legal drinking age set at 19. **35** In British Columbia, it is 19. **36** There are many who question why it isn't lowered to 18. **37** However, in the United States, the legal drinking age is 21, making it among the highest legal drinking ages worldwide. **38** Most countries allow people to drink at 16 or 18 years of age. **39** Others, like China, Portugal, and Vietnam, have no minimum drinking age at all. **40** There are arguments that if adolescents can vote, get married, adopt children, purchase firearms, and defend our country, they can be trusted to drink responsibly. **41** Libertarian groups and some conservative economic foundations have long advocated for lowering the drinking age, and in recent years many academics and non-partisan policy groups have joined the cause ("Lowering the legal," n.d.). **42** Those who oppose the lower drinking age argue the law saves lives. **43** Based on the Centers for Disease Control and Prevention's review of nearly 50 peer-reviewed studies, it was found that lowering the minimum drinking age to 18 increases fatalities by 10 percent ("Lowering the legal," n.d.). **44** Motor vehicle crashes are the leading cause of death among youth ages 15 to 20 (National Highway Traffic Safety Administration [NHTSA], 2001). **45** Adolescents already are at increased risk through their relative lack of driving experience (National Institute on Alcohol Abuse and Alcoholism [NIAAA], 2001), and drivers younger than 21 are more susceptible than older drivers to the alcohol-induced impairment of driving skills (National Institute on Alcohol Abuse and Alcoholism, as cited in Zador, Krawchuk & Voas, 2000). **46** The rate of fatal crashes among alcohol-involved drivers between 16 and 20 years old is more than twice the rate for alcohol-involved drivers 21 and older (Yi, Williams, & Dufour, 2001). **47** This is a direct result of drinking and driving and shows a clear lack of judgment and maturity of adolescents. **48** Legislation and laws have been put into place to protect adolescents from being injured or dying as a result of drunk driving. **49** However, by the time adolescents reach 19 or 21, depending on where it is applicable, there are many types of cases where they have been exposed to alcohol illegally through underage drinking. **50** Many people believe for this reason the legal age should be lowered; if the age was lowered, then we could potentially control how much alcohol they could have. **51** However, in this case it would just promote an even lower underage drinking age. **52** However, I agree that drinking causes adolescents to act irrationally, and that drinking can lead to drunk driving, which I am completely against. **53** Safety always comes first in my mind.

54 In this essay I have addressed and explored the issue of lowering the legal age of drinking in British Columbia from 19 to younger, focusing on health concerns, concerns over alcohol dependency, and drinking and driving. **55** I approached these issues from two singular approaches: whether the legal drinking age should be lowered or not. **56** While there are arguments in favor of decreasing the age of consent for drinking alcohol in British Columbia, they are not compelling or strong enough to sway this writer into believing them. **57** There is simply too much corroborating evidence that is too hard to ignore or be unaffected by. **58** For this reason I strongly oppose reducing the legal age of alcohol consumption in British Columbia.

References

Abbey, A. (2002). Alcohol-related sexual assault: A common problem among college students. *Journal of Studies on Alcohol* (Suppl. 14). 118–128.

Anderson, R. N. (2001). Deaths: Leading causes for 1999. *National Vital Statistics Reports, 49*(11) (DHHS Pub. No. PHS 20012–1120). Hyattsville, MD: Centers for Disease Control and Prevention.

Dawson, D. A. (2000). The link between family history and early onset alcoholism: Earlier initiation of drinking or more rapid development of dependence? *Journal of Studies on Alcoholism, 61*(5), 637–646.

Garlow, S. J. (2002). Age, gender, and ethnicity differences in patterns of cocaine and ethanol use preceding suicide. *American Journal of Psychiatry, 159*(4), 615–619.

Grant, B. F., & Dawson, D. A. (1997). Age of onset of alcohol use and its association with DSM–IV alcohol abuse and dependence: Results from the National Longitudinal Alcohol Epidemiologic Survey. *Journal of Substance Abuse, 9,* 103–110.

Lowering the legal drinking age. (n.d.). Retrieved from http://www.drugrehabtreatment.com /legal-drinking-age.html

National Highway Traffic Safety Administration (NHTSA). (2001). *Traffic safety facts 2000: Young drivers* (DOT HS–809–336). Washington, DC: NHTSA.

National Institute on Alcohol Abuse and Alcoholism (NIAAA). (2001). Alcohol and transportation safety. *Alcohol Alert No. 52*. Rockville, MD: NIAAA.

Yi, H. Y., Williams, G. D., & Dufour, M. C. (2001). Trends in alcohol-related fatal crashes, United States, 1979–99. *Surveillance Report No. 56*. Bethesda, MD: NIAAA.

Zador, P. L., Krawchuk, S. A., & Voas, R. B. (2000). Alcohol-related relative risk of driver fatalities and driver involvement in fatal crashes in relation to driver age and gender: An update using 1996 data. *Journal of Studies on Alcohol, 61*(3), 387–395.

TASK 7

Fill in the Argument Essay Evaluation Form below for James' argument essay. In each section, write notes on the strengths or weaknesses of the writing, and include examples and sentence numbers where necessary. It may be useful to review the relevant chapter summaries where necessary.

Argument Essay Evaluation Form	
Introduction	
Does the introduction shift from general to specific?	
Is there a clear thesis statement?	
Does the writer refer to the structure of the essay?	
Does the essay follow that organization?	
Essay structure	
Does the essay successfully follow a thematic structure?	
Main body sections/paragraphs	
Does the writer use topic sentences?	
Does each section keep to one topic?	
Are three levels of critical analysis (argument, counter-argument, and writer's opinion) presented?	
Are arguments supported with reasons, examples, and evidence from reliable sources?	
Does the writer use concluding sentences?	

Are ideas properly attributed (i.e., is it clear who thinks what)?	
Conclusion	
Does the writer clearly signal the beginning of the conclusion?	
Does the conclusion shift from specific to general?	
Does the writer summarize?	
Does the writer synthesize?	
Does the writer answer the question?	
Does the writer round off the essay with an end statement?	
Recommendations for improvement	

TASK 8

Now write an argument essay of four to six pages double-spaced on the legalization of marijuana or on a controversial topic relevant to your subject area. Follow the stages you have studied in this chapter:

- Consider the genre, audience, and context.
- Break down your question according to topic, focus, and task.
- Gather ideas from existing knowledge through exploratory writing, concept mapping, or traditional notes.
- Choose relevant themes around which you can organize your ideas.
- Draw up a thematic outline.
- Do research to find supporting examples and evidence from reliable academic sources.
- Write a first draft.
- Do a self-evaluation and peer review of your first draft using the Argument Essay Evaluation Form.

For the essay, you should follow APA or MLA citation style: refer to Chapter 5 on research essays and to Appendices 1 and 2 for guidelines on citation and referencing.

CHAPTER 7 SUMMARY

In this chapter, you have studied different aspects of argumentative writing: how to gather your ideas; how to organize two types of outlines for argument essays; and how to add supporting reasons, examples, and evidence to your essay. You have also undertaken an analysis of a student's argument essay.

GATHERING YOUR IDEAS

In previous chapters, you have learned about the importance of considering the genre, audience, and context of a text before you read it, as well as the topic, focus, and task of any essay question. In this chapter, you built upon these critical reading skills by practising three ways to gather ideas from existing knowledge: exploratory writing, concept mapping, and traditional notes.

ORGANIZING YOUR IDEAS INTO AN EFFECTIVE OUTLINE

In the section on organizing your ideas, you studied how the notes you have gathered can be transferred to two types of outline for argument essays: a *for-then-against outline* or *thematic outline*. You learned that each outline has its pros and cons, but that, overall, the thematic outline is more effective in ensuring that critical analysis is carried out in each section of the essay.

ADDING SUPPORTING REASONS, EXAMPLES, AND EVIDENCE

The writing process followed in this chapter involves first gathering ideas from your existing knowledge, then forming the outline. The next stage is building upon the outline by searching for supporting reasons, examples, and evidence from reliable academic sources.

In the editorial feature that you read, you practised linking examples and ideas to the arguments in the outlines and to broader arguments in the ongoing debate. You were required to infer meaning and figure out how the examples could be brought in to support these ideas and arguments.

ANALYZING AN ARGUMENT ESSAY

The student argument essay was a very effective example of how to write an argument essay following a thematic structure. The areas for improvement that stood out were the need for clear language of attribution, and consistent ordering of and support for ideas in different essay sections.

CHAPTER 8

Writing about Comparisons

In this chapter, you will study the following aspects of writing about comparisons:

- ✓ Organizing a comparative outline
- ✓ Writing the introduction
- ✓ Writing main body sections and paragraphs
- ✓ Analyzing comparative essays
- ✓ Using the language of comparison

Comparing is something that we do every day of our lives. It is also common in many forms of academic writing: in comparative essays and other essays that include comparisons of one thing with another.

Depending on your subject area, you could be asked to compare and contrast many things, for example, novels, works of art, historical or political leaders, or important theories in your area of study. Comparing involves looking for similarities, while contrasting involves looking for differences. However, it is usually not enough just to describe a list of similarities and differences. You are also normally expected to evaluate and give an opinion as part of the comparison.

ORGANIZING A COMPARATIVE OUTLINE

There are two common approaches to organizing comparative essays. The first is the *case-by-case approach* and involves looking at your topic according to each distinct case—A then B—separately in different sections of the essay. For example, if you were comparing the legal systems of France and the United States, you would first write about the French system in one section, and then the US system in another.

The second is the *thematic approach* and is a variation of the thematic structure you studied in Chapter 7. For a comparative essay on the legal systems of France and the United States, you would compare and contrast the two systems together (in the same essay sections) according to key themes or analytic perspectives such as history, common law, and case law. In this chapter, you will study both approaches to writing about comparisons in essays.

Here is the essay question that you will be working on in this chapter, and the guidelines for writing about it:

> **Question:** Compare and contrast the influences and effects of two major languages in the world today.
>
> **Guidelines:** While comparing and contrasting, you should focus on which language is having greater impact in the world and explain why.

Balanced Comparison

Unless the question asks you to do otherwise, your comparison should be balanced. This means that you should give equal attention and importance to the two things that you are looking at. For example, if you were writing a comparison of the films *Rope* and *Rear Window,* and two-thirds of the essay was about *Rear Window,* the essay would be unbalanced.

A Case-By-Case Outline

Carefully read through Outline 1 below, which is a case-by-case outline for a comparative essay on the influences and effects of English and Mandarin.

Outline 1: Case-by-case outline

INTRODUCTION

1. **Background:** general information on the English and Mandarin languages
2. **Specifics:** set out some similarities and differences, number of speakers, roles in the world (Ethnologue, 2009)
3. **Structure:** the effects of English, then the effects of Mandarin, similarities and differences
4. **Thesis statement:** e.g., English is still the major world language in terms of its effects on other languages and cultures

INFLUENCES AND EFFECTS OF ENGLISH IN THE WORLD TODAY

1. **Other cultures:**
   - English seen as a vehicle for a lot of western culture, and for Americanization in the world, has a lot of influence on other cultures
   - The language of Hollywood films and famous fast-food restaurants found in most countries, McDonaldization (Ritzer, 1996)
2. **Other languages:**
   - Most widely spoken world language in terms of geography and number of speakers (if you include those who speak it as a second or additional language)

- Also the world's largest "lingua franca" (Jenkins, 2006; Seidlhofer, 2005)
- Many languages around the world have borrowed "loan words" from English, e.g., Japanese words *teeburu* (table) and *charenji* (challenge)
- Many young people feel that it is cool and trendy to mix English with the local language
- Also affects the vocabulary and grammar of other languages (e.g., *calques* from English to Spanish: *troca* [truck] *vino p'atrás* [he came back]) (Sayer, 2008)

3. **Media and communications:**
   - Number one world language of technology, digital communication, international organizations, and academic publication
   - English language teaching is a multi-billion–dollar industry; many people around the world need English language skills for their work, especially if they work for international companies or in tourism and hospitality
   - The Roman alphabet and basic grammatical rules make English relatively easy to learn at a basic level at least

INFLUENCES AND EFFECTS OF MANDARIN IN THE WORLD TODAY

1. **Other cultures:**
   - Mandarin has less of an effect on cultures around the world, although its impact is increasing
   - Growing presence with international Chinese-language films, also present in international Chinese cuisine
2. **Other languages:**
   - The most first-language speakers in the world today, and still widely spoken in the Chinese diaspora around the world
   - Less common as a lingua franca
   - Languages around the world have fewer loan words from Mandarin, and Mandarin has relatively few loan words from English (see Yang, 2009)
   - Fewer lexical and syntactic calques
3. **Media and communications:**
   - Less effect in the areas of technology, digital communication, international organizations, and academic publication
   - Slowly becoming more popular as a language to learn in the world today, but still is a long way behind English
   - Chinese characters in the writing system and the ways that meaning changes with tones make Mandarin a very difficult language to learn for many around the world

CONCLUSION

1. **Summarize:** briefly state the major areas of similarity and difference
2. **Synthesize:** bring ideas together into one closing idea—languages reflect economic, political, and cultural power
3. **Answer the question:** e.g., today, English has greater overall influence due to the economic, political, and cultural power historically of the British Empire, and today of the US; as China's power and influence in these areas grows, so too will the world presence of Mandarin and its effects on other languages and cultures
4. **End statement:** e.g., in the future, China's growth will mean the status of English as the world's lingua franca and international language of communication will be challenged by Mandarin

A Thematic Outline

Now carefully read through Outline 2 below, which is a thematic outline for a comparative essay on the influences and effects of English and Mandarin. As you read, think about how the ideas are organized differently in this outline.

Outline 2: Thematic outline

INTRODUCTION

1. **Background:** general information on the English and Mandarin languages
2. **Specifics:** set out some similarities and differences, number of speakers, roles in the world (Ethnologue, 2009)
3. **Structure:** 3 themes: influences and effects on *other cultures*, *other languages*, and *media and communications*, looking at similarities and differences of each case under each theme
4. **Thesis statement:** e.g., English is still the major world language in terms of its effects on other languages and cultures

INFLUENCES AND EFFECTS ON OTHER CULTURES

1. **English:**
   - English is seen as a vehicle for a lot of western culture, and for Americanization in the world, it has a lot of influence on other cultures
   - English is the language of Hollywood films and famous fast-food restaurants that can be found in most countries, McDonaldization (Ritzer, 1996)
2. **Mandarin:**
   - Mandarin has less of an effect on cultures around the world, although its impact is increasing
   - The language has a growing presence with international Chinese-language films, also present in international Chinese cuisine
3. **Greater effect?**
   - Overall, English has more effect, helped by globalization

INFLUENCES AND EFFECTS ON OTHER LANGUAGES

1. **English:**
   - English is the most widely spoken world language in terms of geography and number of speakers (if you include those who speak it as a second or additional language)
   - Also the world's largest "lingua franca" (Jenkins, 2006; Seidlhofer, 2005)
   - Many languages around the world have borrowed words from English, e.g., Japanese words such as *teeburu* (table) and *charenji* (challenge)
   - Many young people feel that it is cool and trendy to mix English with the local language
   - Also affects the vocabulary and grammar of other languages (e.g., *calques* from English to Spanish: *troca* [truck] *vino p'atrás* [he came back]) (Sayer, 2008)
2. **Mandarin:**
   - Mandarin is the language with the most first-language speakers in the world today, and is also still widely spoken in the Chinese diaspora around the world

- Less common as a lingua franca
- Languages around the world have fewer loan words from Mandarin, and Mandarin has relatively few loan words from English (see Yang, 2009)
- Few lexical and syntactic calques

3. **Greater effect?**
   - English still has more impacts than Mandarin, despite Mandarin's growing presence

INFLUENCES AND EFFECTS ON MEDIA AND COMMUNICATIONS

1. **English:**
   - English is the number one world language of technology, digital communication, international organizations, and academic publication
   - English language teaching is a multi-billion–dollar industry; many people around the world need English language skills for their work, especially if they work for international companies or in tourism and hospitality
   - The Roman alphabet and basic grammatical rules make it relatively easy to learn at a basic level at least
2. **Mandarin:**
   - Mandarin has less effect in the areas of technology, digital communication, international organizations, and academic publication
   - Mandarin is slowly becoming more popular as a language to learn in the world today, but still is a long way behind English
   - The use of Chinese characters in the writing system, and the ways that meaning changes with tones make Mandarin a very difficult language to learn for many around the world
3. **Greater effect?**
   - Perhaps the writing system and tonal grammar limit Mandarin's impact in this area more than anything else

CONCLUSION

1. **Summarize the analytic perspectives:** state briefly the influences and effects according to three themes: other cultures, other languages, media and communications
2. **Synthesize:** bring ideas together into one closing idea, e.g., languages reflect economic, political, and cultural power
3. **Answer the question:** e.g., today, English has greater overall influence due to the economic, political, and cultural power historically of the British Empire, and today of the US; as China's power and influence in these areas grows, so too will the world presence of Mandarin and its effects on other languages and cultures
4. **End statement:** e.g., in the future, China's growth will mean the status of English as the world's lingua franca and international language of communication will be challenged by Mandarin

TASK 1

Write what you consider to be the advantages and disadvantages of the two outlines above.

OUTLINE 1: CASE BY CASE

Advantages:

Disadvantages:

OUTLINE 2: THEMATIC

Advantages:

Disadvantages:

WRITING THE INTRODUCTION

In many ways, writing an introduction to a comparative essay is no different from writing an introduction to any other type of essay. Your introduction would typically shift from general to specific, have some kind of thesis statement, and give your reader an idea of the structure of the forthcoming sections.

In comparative essay introductions, writers commonly begin by making some general background statements about the similarities and differences between the two things being compared. Then, they often follow with a shift to the specific focus of the essay.

Read the introductory paragraph below from a comparative essay on English and Mandarin and answer the questions that follow.

1 Both English and Mandarin are major world languages: while there are 328,008,138 native speakers of English in the world today ("English," 2009), over 1.2 billion people speak Mandarin ("Chinese," 2009). **2** Each language has billions of speakers (including first- and second-language speakers), is attached to strong nation-states, has a strong international presence, and is learned by students and professionals around the world for business and pleasure. **3** While Mandarin, as the official and main language of China, has a long history of thousands of years as a spoken and written language, English is a relative newcomer in the world, having slowly emerged from a coming together of Norman French and Anglo-Saxon around a thousand years ago. **4** Yet, as first the language of the British Empire, and later as the language of US cultural and economic influence in the twentieth century, English has become *the* world language in recent years. **5** Mandarin, however, is starting to catch up, rapidly increasing its international presence as China's influence in the world grows. **6** Each language is affecting the world in similar and different ways. **7** Where these similarities and differences are most evident is in their effects upon other cultures, other languages, and on media and communications.

TASK 2

Look at each sentence in the introductory paragraph and complete the corresponding information below.

Which sentence(s) carries out the following functions of an introduction? Write the sentence number(s) in the blank.

a) Sentence _______ describes a broad similarity and provides background statistics.

b) Sentence _______ describes four similarities between the two languages.

c) Sentence _______ changes the focus to the differences between the two languages.

d) Sentences _______ form a kind of thesis statement (i.e., that English has more influence but Mandarin is catching up).

e) Sentence _______ refers to the three main themes of the essay's thematic structure.

Does the introduction shift from general to specific, specific to general, or in another way?

____

WRITING MAIN BODY SECTIONS AND PARAGRAPHS

There are many ways of writing main body sections and paragraphs for comparative essays; the way you write will depend on whether you are following a case-by-case or thematic structure. In this section, the focus is on learning how to write paragraphs that follow a thematic structure.

TASK 3

Read Example 1 below, in which the influences and effects of English and Mandarin on other languages are discussed. Pay special attention to how the information is organized.

Where new information is introduced for comparison, the sentence is highlighted in **boldface**, then followed by supporting information. In the margin (next to each of the sentences in bold), note the information about English by writing **E1, E2, E3** in order of appearance in the paragraph. Do the same for Mandarin, by writing **M1, M2,** and **M3.**

Margin Notes

EXAMPLE 1: Effects on other languages

1 Another area where both English and Mandarin are having a significant impact in the world today is on other languages. 2 With its status as the most widely spoken language in the world today in terms of geography and number of speakers (including speakers of English as a second/additional language), **English is, in effect, a "lingua franca"** (Jenkins, 2006; Seidlhofer, 2005). 3 It is, therefore, inevitably having a significant effect on the many languages that it is coming into contact with. **4 Many languages around the world have borrowed words from English,** and in some cases, these English-origin words are replacing words with the same meaning in other languages. 5 The presence of English in the Japanese language is a case in point. 6 Words such as *teeburu* (table), and *charenji* (challenge) are commonly used in Japanese today, and in many cases, especially with young people, they have replaced an original Japanese word. 7 In fact, many young people feel that it is cool and trendy to mix English words with their local language, which serves only to increase the presence of English. **8 English is also affecting the vocabulary and grammar of other languages in the form of *calques*** (English grammar or vocabulary structures that are translated into other languages). 9 For example, as highlighted by Sayer (2008) in his study of young people mixing Spanish and English in schools, in the southwestern states of the US, Spanish speakers use terms like *troca* (from the English "truck") and *vino p'atrás* (from the English "he came back").

10 Mandarin, like English, also has a very large number of speakers. 11 It is unquestionably the language with the most speakers in the world if second/additional language speakers are excluded. 12 It is also spoken all over the world, with a strong presence in the Chinese diaspora, along with other Chinese languages such as Cantonese. **13 It does not, however, have the status of being a world lingua franca as does English.** 14 Consequently, it is having less of an effect on other world languages. **15 There are also comparatively few Mandarin-origin loan words in other languages of the world,** when comparing with English (see Yang, 2009, for a detailed discussion on Mandarin loan words in English). 16 Perhaps the area of Chinese food is the only area where Mandarin (and other Chinese) words are widely used in other languages. **17 Equally, lexical and syntactic calques that originate in Mandarin are virtually non-existent in most other languages.**

18 To sum up this section, when comparing the effects of English and Mandarin on other languages of the world, English is clearly having greater influence on other languages, particularly when it comes to speakers of other languages borrowing foreign words and incorporating them into their everyday conversations. 19 The degree of influence that either English or Mandarin may have on everyday conversations in other languages is also closely related to their presence in the media and modes of communication in other societies.

Which of the following illustrates the notes that you took?

a) **E1** + **E2** + **E3** then **M1** + **M2** + **M3**
b) **E1** + **M1** then **E2** + **M2** then **E3** + **M3**

TASK 4

Read Example 2 below, and repeat the exercise outlined in Task 3.

EXAMPLE 2: Effects on other languages

Margin Notes

1 Another area where both English and Mandarin are having a significant impact in the world today is on other languages. **2** With its status as the most widely spoken language in the world today in terms of geography and number of speakers (including speakers of English as a second/additional language), **English is, in effect, a "lingua franca"** (Jenkins, 2006; Seidlhofer, 2005). **3 Mandarin, like English, also has a very large number of speakers, and is unquestionably the language with the most speakers in the world, if second/additional language speakers are excluded. 4 Mandarin is also spoken all over the world, with a strong presence in many Chinese diasporas, along with other Chinese languages such as Cantonese. 5 Mandarin does not, however, have the status of being a world lingua franca as does English**. **6** The number of speakers of a language and its geographical scope relate closely to how the languages are affecting other languages that they are coming into contact with. **7** Looking at the example of loan words is one way to illustrate this.

8 Many languages around the world have borrowed words from English, and in some cases, these English-origin words are replacing words with the same meaning in other languages. **9** The presence of English in the Japanese language is a case in point. **10** Words such as *teeburu* (table) and *charenji* (challenge) are commonly used in Japanese today, and in many cases, especially with young people, they have replaced an original Japanese word. **11** In fact, many young people feel that it is cool and trendy to mix English words with their local language, which serves only to increase the presence of English. **12** In contrast, **there are comparatively few Mandarin-origin loan words in other languages of the world,** when comparing with English (see Yang, 2009, for a detailed discussion on Mandarin loan words in English). **13** Perhaps the area of Chinese food is the only area where Mandarin (and other Chinese) words are widely used in other languages. **14 English is also affecting the vocabulary and grammar of other languages in the form of *calques* (English grammar or vocabulary structures that are translated into other languages). 15** For example, as highlighted by Sayer (2008) in his study of young people mixing Spanish and English in schools in the southwestern states of the US, Spanish speakers use terms like *troca* (from the English "truck") and *vino p'atrás* (from the English "he came back"). **16** In comparison, **lexical and syntactic calques that originate in Mandarin are virtually non-existent in most other languages.**

17 To sum up this section, when comparing the effects of English and Mandarin on other languages of the world, English is clearly having far greater influence on other languages, particularly when it comes to speakers of other languages borrowing foreign words and incorporating them into their everyday conversations. **18** The degree of influence that either English or Mandarin may have on everyday conversations in other languages is also closely related to their presence in the media and modes of communication in other societies.

Which of the following illustrates the notes that you took?

a) **E1 + E2 + E3** then **M1 + M2 + M3**
b) **E1 + M1** then **E2 + M2** then **E3 + M3**

Examples 1 and 2 show two ways to compare information in a comparative essay that follows a thematic approach. Both can be effective methods. Of the two, many would argue that Example 2 is more effective as it allows the reader to make more immediate comparisons while reading.

TASK 5

The following statements refer to Examples 1 and 2 on pages 156 and 157. Read the statements and match them to either example by writing *Example 1* or *Example 2* in the margin. If a statement applies to both examples, you should write *Examples 1 and 2*.

Margin Notes

1. In this example, the comparative analysis is reasonably balanced as the writer considers both languages more or less equally.
2. In this example, the comparative analysis is more immediate because the reader does not have to wait until the next paragraph or section for a comparison.
3. In this example, the writer is making the reader work a little harder because the reader has to think back to the order of the previous paragraph as comparisons are made.
4. This example represents effective comparative analysis.

ANALYZING COMPARATIVE ESSAYS

In this section, you will read two comparative essays.

In the first essay, the writer compares and contrasts the influences and effects of English and Mandarin. The second essay was written by Tony, a second-year undergraduate student, as an unassessed essay in an academic writing course, and compares and contrasts the public transport systems of Vancouver and Toronto.

As you read each essay, take notes in the margin on the strengths and weaknesses of the essay, paying particular attention to the following:

- Structure (Is it case by case or thematic?)
- Essay sections (introduction, main body paragraphs, conclusion)
- Presentation of comparisons (Are arguments supported with reasons, examples, and evidence from reliable sources?)
- Coherence (Are themes and arguments logically ordered?)

COMPARATIVE ESSAY 1

Margin Notes

A comparison of two major world languages: English and Mandarin

Introduction

1 Both English and Mandarin are major world languages: while there are 328,008,138 native speakers of English in the world today (English, 2009), over 1.2 billion people speak Mandarin (Chinese, 2009). **2** Each language has billions of speakers (including first- and second-language speakers), is attached to strong nation-states, has a strong international presence, and is learned by students and professionals around the world for business and pleasure. **3** While Mandarin, as the official and main language of China, has a long history of thousands of years as a spoken and written language, English is a relative newcomer in the world, having slowly emerged from a coming together of Norman French and Anglo-Saxon around a thousand years ago. **4** Yet, as first the language of the British Empire, and later as the language of US cultural and economic influence in the twentieth century, English has become *the* world language in recent years. **5** Mandarin, however, is starting to catch up, rapidly increasing its international presence as China's influence in the world grows. **6** Each language is affecting the world in similar and different ways. **7** Where these similarities and differences are most evident is in their effects upon other cultures, other languages, and on media and communications.

Effects on other cultures

8 Language and culture have such a close interrelationship that it is difficult to discuss one without mentioning its close interconnectedness with the other. **9** This applies to both English and Mandarin. **10** The English language in the world today is closely associated with the pervasive spread of American culture, making its influence and effects on cultures around the world even greater. **11** Mandarin, on the other hand, currently has less effect on other world cultures, due perhaps to the different role that Chinese culture plays around the world. **12** The examples of films and food illustrate this point well. **13** English is the language of Hollywood movies and of American fast-food giants. **14** Whether it is a cinema audience watching *Die Hard* in Lebanon or a family eating at McDonald's in Thailand, the Americanized cultural activity, or even McDonaldization (Ritzer, 1996), is characterized by a strong dose of English. **15** Even if the film *Die Hard* is dubbed into Arabic, the street signs, the names, and the images are related to the English language. **16** Similarly, the McDonald's meal in Bangkok involves English signs and names that carry the American culture into the local family's life. **17** A number of Chinese blockbuster films are also seen worldwide in other cultures, either dubbed or with subtitles. **18** In the 1980s and 1990s, films such as *Ju Dou* and *Raise the Red Lantern* enjoyed great commercial success and acclaim from critics around the world. **19** And of course, people around the world eat Chinese food in restaurants where Chinese languages are heard and seen. **20** In some cases, however, it is Cantonese rather than Mandarin that is spoken.

21 For every Chinese film seen around the world, perhaps one hundred Hollywood movies are also seen. **22** The same could be said for food. **23** English, or the American culture that often carries it, has clearly had more impact on the world's cultures in recent years. **24** This process has been helped along by globalization in its many forms. **25** And the impact on other cultures has been accompanied by impacts on the languages associated with those cultures.

Effects on other languages

26 Another area where both English and Mandarin are having a significant impact in the world today is on other languages. **27** With its status as the most widely spoken language in the world today in terms of geography and number of speakers (including speakers of English as a second/additional language), English is today, in effect, a world language, or "lingua franca" (Jenkins, 2006; Seidlhofer, 2005). **28** Mandarin, like English, also has a very large number of speakers, and is unquestionably the language with the most speakers in the world, if second/additional language speakers are excluded. **29** Mandarin is also spoken all over the world, with a strong presence in the Chinese diaspora, along with other Chinese languages such as Cantonese. **30** Mandarin does not, however, have the status of being a world lingua franca as does English. **31** The number of speakers of a language and its geographical scope relate closely to how the languages are affecting other languages that they are coming into contact with. **32** Looking at the example of loan words is one way to illustrate this.

33 Many languages around the world have borrowed words from English, and in some cases, these English-origin words are replacing words with the same meaning in other languages. **34** The presence of English in the Japanese language is a case in point. **35** Words such as *teeburu* (table), and *charenji* (challenge) are commonly used in Japanese today, and in many cases, especially for young people, they have replaced an original Japanese word. **36** In fact, many young people feel that it is cool and trendy to mix English words with the local language, which serves only to increase the presence of English. **37** In contrast, there are comparatively few Mandarin-origin loan words in other languages of the world, when comparing with English (see Yang, 2009, for a detailed discussion on Mandarin loan words in English). **38** Perhaps the area of Chinese food is the only area where Mandarin (and other Chinese) words have historically been most widely used in other languages. **39** English is also affecting the vocabulary and grammar of other languages in the form of *calques* (English grammar or vocabulary structures that are translated into other languages). **40** For example, as highlighted by Sayer (2008) in his study of young people mixing Spanish and English in schools in the southwestern states of the US, Spanish speakers use terms like *troca* (from the English "truck") and *vino p'atrás* (from the English "he came back"). **41** In comparison, lexical and syntactic calques that originate in Mandarin are less common in most other languages.

42 To sum up this section, when comparing the effects of English and Mandarin on other languages of the world, English is clearly having greater influence on other languages, particularly when it comes to speakers of other languages borrowing foreign words and incorporating them into their everyday conversations. **43** The degree of influence that either English or Mandarin may have on everyday conversations in other languages is also closely related to their presence in the media and modes of communication in other societies.

Media and communications

44 Both English and Mandarin are major world languages in the areas of media and communications. **45** Few would question the view that English is today the number one world language of technology, digital communication, international organizations, and academic publication. **46** In these areas, Mandarin is less present and has much less impact than English. **47** The English language is also the product of the multibillion-dollar English language teaching industry. **48** As many people around the world need English language skills for their work, the demand for language classes is massive, especially for employees who work in tourism and hospitality or for international companies that require English. **49** Nonetheless, Mandarin is slowly becoming more popular as a language to learn in the world today. **50** In schools, universities, and private institutes, the demand for Mandarin classes is growing considerably. **51** In cities such as Vancouver, Canada, local education boards are even considering setting up Mandarin immersion programs that will allow local schoolchildren to take part of their schooling in Mandarin. **52** These children will not all be native speakers of Mandarin; parents will choose a Mandarin immersion environment due to the perceived future benefits that will come with being able to speak Mandarin in today's world. **53** It has to be stated, however, that Mandarin remains a long way behind English. **54** I would suggest that the difficulty of learning Mandarin also plays an additional role in its slower progress. **55** Certainly, the use of Chinese characters in the writing system and the ways that meaning changes with tones make Mandarin a very difficult language to learn for many around the world. **56** In contrast, the Roman alphabet and basic grammatical rules of elementary English make the language comparatively easy to learn at a basic level at least.

Conclusion

57 The role of English and Mandarin in the world today has been discussed in terms of how they are affecting other cultures, other languages, and media and communications. **58** One important factor underpins each of the points discussed, that is, that languages reflect the economic, political, and cultural power of the nation-states with which they are associated. **59** Today, it is the English language which has greater overall influence. **60** This is due to the economic, political, and cultural power of, historically, the British Empire, and currently of the United States. **61** Nonetheless, as China's power and influence in these areas grows, so too will the world presence of Mandarin and its effects on other languages and cultures. **62** In the future, the growth of China will mean the status of English as the world's lingua franca and international language of communication will be challenged by Mandarin.

References

Chinese. (2009). In M. Paul Lewis (Ed.), *Ethnologue: Languages of the world* (16th ed.). Retrieved from http://www.ethnologue.com/show_language.asp?code=zho

English. (2009). In M. Paul Lewis (Ed.), *Ethnologue: Languages of the world* (16th ed.). Retrieved from http://www.ethnologue.com/show_language.asp?code=eng

Jenkins, J. (2006). Current perspectives on teaching world Englishes and English as a lingua franca. *Tesol Quarterly, 40*(1), 157–181.

Ritzer, G. (1996). The McDonaldization thesis: Is expansion inevitable? *International Sociology, 11*(3), 291–308.

Sayer, P. (2008). Demystifying language mixing: Spanglish in school. *Journal of Latinos and Education, 7*(2), 94–112.

Seidlhofer, B. (2005). English as a lingua franca. *ELT Journal, 59*(4), 339–341.

Yang, J. (2009). Chinese borrowings in English. *World Englishes, 28*(1), 90–106.

COMPARATIVE ESSAY 2

Margin Notes

A comparison of two cities' public transit systems

Introduction

1 It is a human trait to compare things and to make judgments about whether one thing or place is better than the other. **2** It is, therefore, no surprise that, as I wait twenty-five minutes for my bus in the Vancouver rain on my hour-long journey home, I think back to my student days in Toronto when I covered a similar distance by subway in a mere twenty-five minutes. **3** Toronto transit, or the TTC, is the backbone of the largest city in Canada. **4** Vancouver transit, or TransLink as it is more affectionately called, is little more than an alternative mode of transportation. **5** To compare the transit of Toronto and that of Vancouver would be like comparing a nimble sports car to a slow awkward tank. **6** To make an accurate comparison between the two, the cost, efficiency, and accessibility are just a few factors to take into consideration.

Section 1

7 Transit fares are quite similar in both cities. **8** The major difference would be the zone system that operates in Vancouver. **9** It seems that very little is known about the zoning though. **10** An informal survey conducted by my friends and I concluded that even we riders know almost nothing about how the zone system works. **11** Luckily, in Toronto, such a feature does not exist. **12** For $2.75, one can take the transit all day as long as the "connection" of routes is not broken. **13** The lack of turnstiles or ticket booths in Vancouver is also quite confusing. **14** It seems that the rider has the option of paying at the SkyTrain or just walking on and hoping that the transit police are not on the same train. **15** A troubling statistic that I have read stated that fare evasion cost TransLink just under $6.4 million in lost revenue (2.1 per cent of revenue) in 2006 (TransLink, n.d.). **16** That is a very hefty amount for a fairly small system. **17** The elimination of zone systems would ease confusion (especially for tourists) or those new to the city.

Section 2

18 The efficiency is somewhat better in Vancouver. **19** Although the trains arrive with less frequency, there is always room to board. **20** The busyness of Toronto buses and trains can be stunning to inexperienced riders. **21** During rush hour, it is very likely that one will miss at least one train or bus due to overcrowding. **22** For a system that moves just around 1.4 million users daily (CTV, 2005), this should not be a surprise. **23** Luckily, subways and buses arrive frequently to pick up those disgruntled riders. **24** In comparison with Toronto, the accessibility is very disappointing. **25** Transit to the suburbs in Vancouver is very slow and at times non-existent. **26** With the "speed" of TransLink, there are times when it is possibly faster to walk to a destination than waiting for the bus. **27** Considering the fact that Vancouver is a smaller city, with a smaller budget and smaller ridership, this comes as no surprise.

Section 3

28 With the arrival of the 2010 Olympics, TransLink has spent a huge amount on expansion and further additions to the system. **29** Construction has already taken place and the system is being improved daily. **30** Toronto has been stuck in a hiatus for the past ten years. **31** There has been very little in terms of tangible developments. **32** From planning committees to environmental committees to community committees, expansion proposals have been moving at a snail's pace. **33** Although planning and committees are important, actions are also quite necessary. **34** There needs to be more motivation for municipal governments to get the job done. **35** At the same time, such rapid expansion may one day come at a cost to Vancouver. **36** The future is still uncertain regarding ridership after the Olympics. **37** There is a chance that such expansions may be a detriment to the city.

Conclusion

38 TransLink is a very impressive system for the city it moves. **39** It has exceeded expectations and is still very speedy. **40** It is aesthetically appealing and much cleaner. **41** Toronto attempts to work with the bare minimum. **42** With the traffic that passes through daily, cleanliness and aesthetics are the least of its concerns. **43** Instead, the focus is on efficiency and budgeting. **44** It is easy to compare and contrast, but it is very difficult to name a winner. **45** Both systems function, and function very well. **46** Both provide exceptional and essential service to the community.

References

CTV News. (2005, April). *Toronto transit workers set strike for Monday.* Retrieved from http://www.ctv.ca/servlet/ArticleNews/story/CTVNews/1112986187732_68/?hub=Canada

TransLink. (n.d.). *Independent audit confirms fare evasion estimate—Evasion rate and revenue loss lower than the public perceives.* Retrieved from http://www.translink.ca/en/About-TransLink/Media/2008/July/Independent-audit-confirms-fare-evasion-estimate-Evasion-rate-and-revenue-loss-lower.aspx

TASK 6

Fill in the sections of the Comparative Essay Evaluation Form below for each of the comparative essays. In each section, write notes on the strengths or weaknesses of the writing, and include examples and sentence numbers where necessary.

Comparative Essay Evaluation Form		
Introduction	Comparative Essay 1	Comparative Essay 2
Does the introduction shift from general to specific?		
Does it describe similarities and differences between the two things being compared?		
Is there a clear thesis statement?		
Does the writer refer to the structure of the essay?		
Does the essay follow that organization?		
Essay structure	Comparative Essay 1	Comparative Essay 2
Does the essay follow a case-by-case or thematic structure?		
Is the comparison balanced?		
Main body sections/ paragraphs	Comparative Essay 1	Comparative Essay 2
Does the writer use topic sentences?		
Does each section keep to one topic?		
Are comparisons presented in a logical order that is easy to read?		
If thematic: within each section, is the ordering principle **A1 + A2 + A3 then B1 + B2 + B3,** or **A1 + B1 then A2 + B2 then A3 + B3,** or other?		

Content: Are the examples for comparison well selected?		
Does the writer provide supporting arguments with reasons, examples, and evidence from reliable sources?		
Does the writer use concluding sentences?		
Conclusion	**Comparative Essay 1**	**Comparative Essay 2**
Does the writer clearly signal the beginning of the conclusion?		
Does the conclusion shift from specific to general?		
Does the writer summarize?		
Does the writer synthesize?		
Does the writer give an overall evaluative opinion of the two things being compared?		
Does the writer round off the essay with an end statement?		

Recommendations for improvement	
Comparative Essay 1	Comparative Essay 2

USING THE LANGUAGE OF COMPARISON

Different ways to describe similarities and differences are listed below.

1. **Comparing/describing similarities**
   - English and Mandarin **are both** world languages.
   - **Both** English and Mandarin **are** world languages.

- **Neither** Mandarin **nor** English can be considered a universal language.
- English is a major world language, **as is** Mandarin.
- Mandarin, **like** English, is a major world language.
- English **is similar to** Mandarin **in its** importance in the Asian business world. (+ noun)
- English **is similar to** Mandarin **in that** it is taught in schools as a second language. (+ clause)
- English is a major world language. **The same can be said for** Mandarin.
- English is a major world language. **This also applies to** Mandarin.
- English is a major world language. **This is also the case with** Mandarin.
- Mandarin is spoken by over a billion people. **Similarly/Equally**, English is spoken by many hundreds of millions of people worldwide if we include non-native speakers.
- **Where the similarity between** the two languages **is most evident is in** their potential to expand.

2. Contrasting/describing differences

- English is a world language, **while/whereas** the role of French is declining.
- English is a world language. **However/Yet/In contrast/In comparison**, the role of French is declining.
- **Unlike** French, the role of English in the world today is growing.
- The role of English in the world today **is greater than** that of French.
- English is a common lingua franca in Asia. **The same cannot be said of** Spanish.
- **A key distinguishing feature between** English and French in the world today is the number of speakers.
- **One of the (main) differences between** English and French in the world today is the number of speakers.
- **Where the difference between** Mandarin and English **is most evident is in** their writing systems.

TASK 7

Now look back at Comparative Essay 1 and highlight the language used to compare and contrast English and Mandarin.

TASK 8

Now read Comparative Essay 2 again and highlight the language used to compare and contrast the public transit systems of Vancouver and Toronto.

TASK 9

Write a comparative essay on two important theories or writers in your subject area. Gather your own information and ideas from researching the subject. Then draw up a case-by-case or thematic outline. Remember to use the language of comparison. Use the categories in the Comparative Essay Evaluation Form for self-evaluation and peer review of your work.

CHAPTER 8 SUMMARY

This chapter has focused on different ways of making comparisons in academic writing. You learned about organizing an outline for a comparative essay, writing the introduction and main body sections and paragraphs, analyzing comparative essays, and using the language of comparison. One idea to remember about comparative writing is that it is usually not enough just to describe similarities and differences; you normally also need to analyze, evaluate, and give an opinion about the things you are comparing.

ORGANIZING A COMPARATIVE OUTLINE

You studied two ways to make an outline for a comparative essay: a case-by-case outline and a thematic outline. The case-by-case approach involves analyzing each case, A then B, separately in different essay sections. This allows for clear and effective comparisons to be made, but can lead to repetition of information in the different sections. The thematic approach involves analyzing each case, A and B, together under relevant themes. This approach allows for the comparative analysis to be present throughout the essay; it also requires the use of more advanced language of comparison.

Whichever approach you may follow, it is important to organize your themes and information logically, and to bring in reasons, examples, statistics, and evidence from reliable academic sources.

WRITING THE INTRODUCTION

The introduction to a comparative essay is much the same as any other introduction. However, in comparative essay introductions, it is common for the writer to start by mentioning some broad similarities and differences between the two things being compared, and then to shift to the specific similarities and differences that will be covered in the essay.

WRITING MAIN BODY SECTIONS AND PARAGRAPHS

In this chapter, you studied how to write main body sections and paragraphs for a comparative essay that follows a thematic outline. Two organizing principles were highlighted in the sample essay on the English and Mandarin languages in the world today. One way to organize the information under each theme was to present three aspects of English, E1 + E2 + E3, and then three related aspects of Mandarin, M1 + M2 + M3. The alternative was to analyze each related aspect of English and Mandarin together, E1 + M1, E2 + M2, and E3 + M3, under each theme. Writers are unlikely to stick strictly to either of these ordering principles, and will often adapt them in different ways in different essay sections. Too much inconsistency, however, can make it difficult for your reader to process all of the information smoothly.

ANALYZING COMPARATIVE ESSAYS

Two comparative essays were analyzed using the Comparative Essay Evaluation Form. Each essay followed a thematic outline. The aspects of writing comparative essays that stood out most in the analysis were the following:

- The need for supporting statistics and evidence from reliable academic sources
- The need for a wide range of language of comparison to make the analysis more convincing to the reader

- The need for a clear thesis statement that matches the essay content
- The need for topic sentences that clearly indicate the focus of the paragraph or section

USING THE LANGUAGE OF COMPARISON

This chapter has included examples of comparative language that can be used to compare and contrast information in essays. The first of the two essays you analyzed had a wider range of comparative language, which made the analysis more convincing and effective. Be sure to include a broad range of comparative language when you make comparisons in your academic writing.

CHAPTER 9

Writing about Problems and Solutions

In this chapter, you will study the following aspects of writing about problems and solutions:

- ✓ Organizing an SPSE outline for problem–solution essays
- ✓ Analyzing a problem–solution essay
- ✓ Providing supporting examples and evidence
- ✓ Citing online sources using MLA and APA styles
- ✓ Describing problems and solutions

It is common to write about problems and solutions in different forms of academic writing. You may analyze the solutions to a problem as part of an argument essay, or you may focus exclusively on problems and solutions in a problem–solution essay.

In this chapter, you will look at different ways to write about problems and solutions, focusing on a problem–solution essay writing structure called *SPSE*. You will also learn some academic language that will help you to describe problems and solutions in all types of academic writing.

ORGANIZING AN SPSE OUTLINE FOR PROBLEM–SOLUTION ESSAYS

SPSE (Situation, Problem, Solution, Evaluation) is an essay structure that is effective for writing problem–solution essays.

SPSE Components: Situation, Problem, Solution, and Evaluation

Each component of the SPSE essay has a specific function.

- **Situation:** When you describe the situation, you tell the reader any of the following: the place, definitions of key terms, statistics, or other background information about the problem.
- **Problem:** When you describe the problem, you focus on what is wrong with the situation, that is, the specific problems that need to be solved. This often involves looking at the causes of the problem(s). In the problem section, you need to order the problems logically and provide supporting examples and statistics to illustrate to your reader the nature of the problem. Sometimes there is overlap between the descriptions of the situation and the problem, in which case both can be presented together in one section.
- **Solution:** When you describe the solutions, you present ideas to solve each of the problems raised in the previous section. To do this effectively, address only those problems raised in the problem section. Also, it is important to do some research and bring in supporting examples that show how the problems identified have been solved in similar contexts. Doing so will add credibility to your ideas.
- **Evaluation:** When you write the evaluation section, your focus should be on the potential validity of your suggested solutions, or, put simply, the chances of your suggestions being implemented successfully. In this section, you need to think about the wider contextual factors that may affect the potential success of your suggested solutions, such as financial constraints and political concerns.

TASK 1

Identify the situation, problem, solution, and evaluation in the paragraph below, which was written by a student during her first week at university. Read the paragraph and fill in the table on the next page.

Week 1 on campus

1 It's my first week at university, the new campus must be at least 50 times bigger than my high school, and there are thousands of students! **2** Getting from one class to another is a real challenge as the university is like a maze of corridors, halls, open spaces, offices, and classrooms. **3** Settling in to this new environment has been really difficult for me: I feel lost. **4** I don't know anyone and I can't find my way around. **5** Somehow, I don't feel like I belong here yet, even though I'm sure that, with time, things will fall into place. **6** I suppose that I should just take things gradually. **7** For a start, I need to get a good campus map. **8** But I also need to get up the courage to start talking to some people to make friends. **9** Getting a map will be easy, but making friends is easier said than done.

SPSE components	Sentence number
Situation	
Problem	
Solution	
Evaluation	

The Outline for an SPSE Essay

The clearest and most common way to organize an SPSE essay is for the sections to follow the order of S, P, S, and E. If you follow this order, you would describe the situation in the introduction, identify the problem(s) and solutions in the next two sections, and provide an evaluation in the conclusion. (The introduction can describe the situation and problem together if they are closely related.)

It is also possible, but less common, to write an SPSE essay using a thematic essay structure. This would involve looking at problems and solutions together under relevant themes, or analytic perspectives. However, because problems and solutions are usually multifaceted, interrelated, and complex, it is often more effective to look at all of the problems together in one section before suggesting solutions. This is not possible with a thematic approach.

TASK 2

Look at Boxes 1 to 4 below. Each box has a list of ideas for an essay (about homelessness in London, UK) that follows an SPSE structure. The order of the boxes has been jumbled. Label each box Situation, Problem, Solution, or Evaluation. The first one is done as an example.

Here is the essay question:

Question: Describe the problem of homelessness in a city you have lived in and suggest ways of solving the problem.

Guidelines: Your answer should refer to reliable sources for statistics and information, and should give an evaluation of your suggested solutions.

BOX 1: Situation

- There are many homeless people in London.
- There are old and young people sleeping in the streets, in homeless shelters, or in temporary bed-and-breakfast accommodation.
- There are also families living in temporary accommodation provided by local councils.
- People become homeless for many reasons, ranging from unemployment to addiction.
- It is necessary to understand the complex nature of the problem in order to find viable solutions.
- Define "homeless."

BOX 2: ....

- Two issues to consider when evaluating possible success: cost and "victim of own success."
- Cost: an integrated solution that addresses the social, economic, and health causes of homelessness will cost a lot of money. Are taxpayers willing to pay for it?
- Victim of own success: many young homeless people come to London from other parts of the country to escape unemployment, abuse in the home, or boredom; some come to London and end up homeless; if they are offered expensive integrated support, this may attract more people to London.
- "Cost" and "victim of own success": both could limit chances for successful application of solutions.
- To succeed, solutions need to be long term and address the underlying causes of homelessness.

BOX 3: ....

- Poverty is a major problem: people lose jobs and income and end up on the streets.
- Also, mental illness can be a factor: psychiatric hospitals closed as part of "care in the community"; former patients couldn't manage in sheltered housing, stop taking medicine, become homeless.
- Drug addiction and alcoholism can be factors: people suffering from addiction lose jobs and homes, need money for their next drink or fix—begging, theft, prostitution.
- They lead to a vicious circle: no job = no home; no home = no job.

BOX 4: ....

- Poverty: the poor need social security support from government.
- Mental illness: centres need to be set up to help the mentally ill get off the streets.
- Addiction: not enough to just find homes for addicts; they also need long-term treatment plans and support networks.
- The vicious circle needs to be broken: few employers want to hire homeless people.
- These solutions need to be developed all together: support centres for homeless people, and help finding employment, treatment for illness, and temporary accommodation.

ANALYZING A PROBLEM–SOLUTION ESSAY

Carefully read the essay below on homelessness in London. It has been written as a first draft without supporting examples and evidence from reliable academic sources. You will see capital letters in square brackets between some sentences, which correspond to the instructor's comments. You will look at these comments later in Task 6.

Homelessness in London: A complex problem with no easy solution

Section 1

1 Like most other large cities, London has many problems, and homelessness is one of them. **2** There are many kinds of homeless people in London. **3** It is not uncommon to see young and old alike sleeping in shopfronts, in parks, and in other public places. **4** These are the visible homeless that theatre-goers, tourists, and commuters see every day. **5** There are also many less visible homeless people in the city: people of all ages who have nowhere to call home and who live in temporary homeless shelters or bed-and-breakfast "hotels," and other temporary accommodation funded by government. [**A**] **6** No one knows exactly how many homeless people there are in London today, but most studies suggest many thousands. [**B**] **7** People in London, just like anywhere else, become homeless for many reasons, ranging from becoming unemployed to suffering from addiction. **8** It is necessary, therefore, to understand the complex nature of the problem in order to find viable solutions to homelessness in London.

Section 2

9 There is no single underlying cause, or problem, of homelessness to be solved. [**C**] **10** Instead, there is a long list of additional reasons why people in London, and elsewhere, become homeless. [**D**] **11** One problem that would come to many people's minds when thinking about homelessness is poverty. **12** Few would argue that homelessness and poverty are closely interrelated. **13** When people lose their jobs and incomes, some can no longer afford to pay the rent or mortgage on the home that they live in, or the weekly bills, and they end up homeless. **14** However, not all of London's homeless have gone from being in the workforce to being on the streets. **15** A large number of homeless people have instead moved from government institutions to the streets: from psychiatric hospitals and children's homes to the streets or homeless hostels of London. **16** As part of the well-intentioned but misguided policy of "care in community," it was felt that large psychiatric hospitals were not the place where many mentally ill people should be kept. **17** Consequently, many hospitals were closed and patients moved to smaller care centres or sheltered housing, resulting in many of the former patients becoming homeless, unable to cope with controlling their own medicine and the wider demands of living in society. **18** Mental illness is, therefore, clearly a significant cause of homelessness. [**E**] **19** Others gain their first experience of being homeless when they leave, or run away from, children's homes, heading for the "bright lights of London." **20** And finally, a significant number of homeless people in London are veterans who, having served in the armed forces for several years, are unable to find secure accommodation and employment after leaving the services.

21 Another major problem that comes with attempting to solve homelessness is dealing with individuals suffering from both addictions and mental illness. [**F**] **22** There are also the added health and crime risks that come with feeding an addiction. **23** For example, someone who has no job or home but who needs to feed an addiction has to find money to pay for their next fix or drink: begging, theft, and prostitution are usually the means to meeting this end. **24** Addiction and its effects add to the problem of being marginalized and excluded from the rest of society and create major obstacles to getting many homeless people successfully off the streets and into permanent accommodation and employment.

25 When added together, these problems associated with homelessness feed into a broader vicious circle that usually comes with being homeless. **26** Homeless people often cannot get homes from landlords without being able to prove that they have a job that will provide enough income to pay the rent. **27** Yet, in order to get that elusive job, they need to have a home. **28** Few employers will hire or even interview job candidates who identify their home on the application form as a homeless hostel, or a park bench.

Section 3

29 Complex multifaceted problems require complex multifaceted solutions. **30** The problems highlighted above are multiple: poverty, people becoming homeless after being in institutions (psychiatric hospitals, children's homes, and the armed forces), addiction and crime, and a vicious circle of *no job = no home*. **31** In order to solve the problems of homelessness, national and local government policies need to be coordinated, and should involve the work of non-governmental organizations (NGOs). [**G**] [**H**] **32** However, the problems cannot be addressed in isolation from each other. **33** Instead, an integrated, long-term approach is needed, in which the problems are understood as being multifaceted and interrelated.

34 The poverty that underlies many cases of homelessness cannot easily be solved. **35** Rather than targeting poverty alone, policy-makers should perhaps focus on breaking the poverty–homelessness link, that is, the causal link that allows poverty to lead to homelessness. **36** This causal link can come in many forms, for example, an unpaid mortgage leading to the loss of a home, or eviction from rented accommodation due to inability to pay the rent. **37** In each case, systems should be put in place to help those in need. **38** The problems of people losing their homes could be at least alleviated if mortgage lenders were encouraged to give people more time to meet payments or to reschedule loans. [I] **39** Perhaps the UK could even follow the example of Canada, where payment protection insurance is often compulsory for high-risk mortgage borrowers. **40** In terms of private tenants who become evicted from rented accommodation, more help through temporary government accommodation should also be provided. [J] **41** Although the cost may be high, if such measures allow people to get back to work and/or get stable accommodation in the longer term, and to contribute to society as taxpayers, then the long-term savings will outweigh the shorter-term costs.

42 Homeless people with mental health problems also need special, targeted care. **43** Providing a home is not enough. **44** Although homeless people with mental health problems may indeed take up offers of a roof over their head, without focused and concerted treatment and monitoring of the illness, it is unlikely that the provision of accommodation alone will suffice. **45** The same applies for homeless people with addiction problems. **46** In this case, as in the case of the other solutions suggested above, cost is a major factor. **47** Who will pay for all of these measures and will they be cost-effective as well as beneficial to the homeless?

Section 4

48 When the stage character Dick Whittington sets off to London to make his fortune, he believes that the streets of London are paved with gold. **49** In his story of hardship, he eventually wins though, becoming London's mayor three times over. **50** Today, some people come to the city with the same hope, as the bright lights of London still have that same allure for many who are looking for an escape from their lives in other towns across the UK, and from other countries around the world. **51** For those who end up living on the city's streets, or in temporary accommodation, there is rarely such a happy ending. **52** Becoming homeless is the result of a wide array of problems, some of which have been highlighted in the paragraphs above. **53** The key to success—and success may indeed be hard to come by in many cases—is to look at solving the problems of homelessness in an integrated way, understanding that the problems are interrelated. **54** Moreover, any integrated strategy that finds homes for the homeless is unlikely to succeed in the long term if the underlying causes of homelessness are not addressed fully. [K] **55** As usual, money is central to success. **56** An integrated strategy to combatting homelessness in London, and in other cities, requires long-term investment. **57** Yet, homelessness cannot be solved solely by throwing money at the problem. **58** Money needs to be spent wisely and in targeted ways that attack the links between poverty and homelessness.

TASK 3

Look at the four sections of the essay above. Fill in the table below to indicate which sections focus on *situation*, *problem*, *solution*, and *evaluation*.

SPSE components	Essay section
Situation	
Problem	
Solution	
Evaluation	

TASK 4

Take notes below on the strengths and weaknesses of each section of the essay.

SECTION 1

Strengths:

Weaknesses:

SECTION 2

Strengths:

Weaknesses:

SECTION 3

Strengths:

Weaknesses:

______

______

______

______

______

SECTION 4

Strengths:

______

______

______

______

______

Weaknesses:

______

______

______

______

______

TASK 5

Sometimes writers have problems with the evaluation section of an SPSE essay, as it can be difficult to speculate about whether the solutions put forward are likely to succeed. Look again at Section 4 of the essay, which is the evaluation section, and answer the following three questions:

1. The writer starts the evaluation by referring to the famous stage character Dick Whittington. Which of the following statements better describes the purpose of this reference? ________

   a) The writer mentions Dick Whittington to answer the question raised at the end of the previous section on solutions.
   b) The writer mentions Dick Whittington to signpost a shift from solutions to evaluation.

2. One way of evaluating in an SPSE essay is to look at the suggestions you have put forward and comment on whether they have a chance of being successful. Which of the following statements better describes the writer's approach? ________

   a) The writer analyzes the chances for success of each of the solutions proposed in the essay.
   b) The writer synthesizes by making an evaluation that applies to all of the suggested solutions.

3. Money is a key idea mentioned in the evaluation. Which of the following statements better reflects what the writer says about money in the evaluation section? _______

a) Money should be spent to break the causal link between poverty and becoming homeless.
b) More money should be given directly to homeless people.

PROVIDING SUPPORTING EXAMPLES AND EVIDENCE

The instructor who marked the first draft of the essay on homelessness commented on the essay's lack of supporting evidence and examples from reliable sources. Here is the instructor's overall advice:

> *"Part of your task was to refer to reliable sources for statistics and information. You haven't done this. Make sure that you do some research for this, and that you address each of the specific points made below, before you hand in the final version of the essay."*

The instructor made 11 specific comments to show the writer how the essay could be improved. Each comment corresponds to the letters in brackets in the essay.

Instructor's Comments

[A] You have described some aspects of homelessness, but you need to provide a more informed definition of homelessness. Look for definitions in some reliable sources, summarize them, and then try to form your own definition for the purposes of your essay.

[B] You need to find some statistics from a reliable source on the number of homeless people, to add credibility to what you are saying.

[C] Actually, several commentators argue that there *is* an underlying cause! Read more and try to bring an underlying cause into your paper.

[D] Before you provide a list of some of the causes of homelessness in this section, you could structure the coming list by categorizing the problems into larger groups.

[E] Yes, mental illness is a significant cause, but try to move beyond thinking of it just as a problem or cause. Remember, mental health problems can also be an effect or result of homelessness. Look for some references to this in the literature.

[F] Experts use the term "dual diagnosis" to refer to homeless people suffering from mental illness and addiction. Try to add something here from a reliable source. This will add credibility to what you are saying.

[G] Give an example of an NGO here, and a few words about what it does.

[H] This is a bit vague. You are talking about national and local governments working together here, but you have failed to mention any examples of national laws that local governments have to follow when looking for solutions to homelessness. Look for something and mention it here.

[I] The idea of helping people who fall into difficulties paying their mortgages is a good one. However, it would be better if you gave details of a specific policy that helps homeowners who are in financial difficulty. Do some research here.

[J] What are the homeless organizations advocating in terms of supporting private tenants?

[K] Are any of the homeless organizations saying anything similar about finding long-lasting solutions to the underlying causes of homelessness? If you can find something, it will add weight to your argument.

TASK 6

The writer of the essay on homelessness followed the instructor's advice and looked for supporting evidence and examples from two reliable online sources: www.shelter.org.uk and www.crisis.org.uk. Both are UK groups that look for solutions to homelessness, and which have statistics and related information on their websites. After taking notes from the online sources, the writer wrote 13 paraphrases in order to add supporting evidence and examples to the essay. Read through the 13 paraphrases and match them with the related letter from the instructor's comments above. Some letters will appear more than once. The first is done as an example.

Comment letter	**Example**
I	**1.** One solution for homeowners who temporarily lose their income is the Homeowner Mortgage Support (HMS) program, which will allow for reduced interest payments on mortgages for up to two years. According to Adam Sampson, the chief executive of Shelter, the program will benefit the estimated half a million households that are expected to be more than three months in arrears with their payments in 2009, and may prevent 75 000 repossessions of properties ("New scheme for homeowners," 2009).
....	**2.** A home is more than just "a roof over your head" ("Homelessness," 2009).
....	**3.** According to Shelter, one of the main underlying causes of homelessness in England is a lack of affordable housing (http://www.shelter.org.uk).
....	**4.** Homelessness is defined by Shelter as the most extreme form of housing need, not only for those sleeping in the streets but also for those who lack a home and have to live in uncertain circumstances in temporary accommodation, often with overcrowding and unsanitary conditions ("Homelessness," 2009).
....	**5.** Shelter categorizes the causes of homelessness according to three possible factors: (1) individual factors, including drug and alcohol misuse, lack of qualifications, lack of social support, debts, poor physical and mental health, relationship breakdown, and crime involvement at an early age; (2) family background, including family breakdown and disputes, sexual and physical abuse in childhood or adolescence, having parents with drug or alcohol problems, and previous experience of family homelessness; and (3) institutional background, including having been in care, the armed forces, or in prison ("What causes homelessness?" 2009).
....	**6.** Defining who is and who is not homeless is not always a straightforward matter. Being homeless does not just mean that someone is living on the streets. The definition extends to people living in homeless hostels and in temporary accommodation provided by their local councils. Some definitions

would also include the "hidden homeless," defined as people "who are in unstable accommodation, with friends or family or otherwise without their own home" (Rees, 2009, p. 9).

.... **7.** According to a discussion paper written by Sian Rees (2009), mental health problems can be understood as a cause and an effect of homelessness: that is, mental health problems are not only a factor in the circumstances that lead to people losing their accommodation, "mental health problems may also be exacerbated by the stresses associated with being homeless, which in turn will make it even harder for that person to achieve stability in their housing" (p. 5).

.... **8.** According to Shelter, a major support organization for the homeless in the UK, the solutions to homelessness are not only about getting people off the streets, they are also about finding lasting solutions to preventing people from becoming homeless ("Homelessness," 2009).

.... **9.** Rees (2009) also suggests that homeless people living on the street may be 50 to 100 times more likely to have a psychotic disorder than the general population, and highlights the link between what she describes as homeless people with a "dual diagnosis," that is, mental illness and alcohol/substance abuse (2009, p. 5). Rees suggests that, according to most studies, around 10 to 20 percent of the homeless population would fulfill the criteria for dual diagnosis (2009, p. 5).

.... **10.** Under the national UK Homelessness Act of 2002, all local authorities are required to develop a homelessness strategy for their area.

.... **11.** Shelter argues that every local authority should have a "tenancy sustainment service" to help vulnerable people in private rentals stay in their homes, and that the housing benefit system should work better. The main solution suggested by Shelter, however, is for more affordable homes to be built ("Homelessness," 2009).

.... **12.** Accurate figures for the number of homeless people in London are difficult to come by. Shelter, a UK organization that advocates in favour of the homeless, estimates there are between 310 000 and 380 000 single homeless people in the UK with approximately one-quarter living in hostels or B&B accommodation, or facing imminent eviction due to debt. The figure is based on a definition of "homeless" that includes the following groups: rough sleepers; people staying in hostels and shelters; people staying in bed and breakfasts and other boarded accommodation; squatters; and concealed households—those residing with friends or family, but without any explicit right to do so and in accommodation that is in some way unsatisfactory (http://www.shelter.org.uk, 2009).

.... **13.** Shelter is one such NGO that helps people find and keep a home, and campaigns for decent housing for all (http://www.shelter.org.uk).

CITING ONLINE SOURCES USING MLA AND APA STYLES

In Chapter 5, you learned how to cite online sources in your text (in-text citations) and how to include online sources, with and without an author, in a reference at the end of your work using MLA and APA styles. You will now review both styles. You can refer to Appendices 1 (MLA) and 2 (APA) for more guidelines.

TASK 7

The two excerpts below are from online sources that will be cited in the final version of the essay on homelessness. Using either MLA or APA style, write the reference entries for the two excerpts.

Excerpt 1 Adding an online source with a stated author to your references using MLA or APA style: start the reference entry with the author's name.

Text added to the essay (MLA)
According to a discussion paper written by Sian Rees, mental health problems can be understood as a cause and an effect of homelessness: that is, mental health problems are not only a factor in the circumstances that lead to people losing their accommodation, "mental health problems may also be exacerbated by the stresses associated with being homeless, which in turn will make it even harder for that person to achieve stability in their housing" (5).

Text added to the essay (APA)
According to a discussion paper written by Sian Rees (2009), mental health problems can be understood as a cause and an effect of homelessness: that is, mental health problems are not only a factor in the circumstances that lead to people losing their accommodation, "mental health problems may also be exacerbated by the stresses associated with being homeless, which in turn will make it even harder for that person to achieve stability in their housing" (p. 5).

Citation information
Organization: Crisis UK
URL: http://www.crisis.org.uk/publications_djhsearch .php?submitted=search &fullitem=235
Document title: Mental ill health in the adult single homeless population: A review of the literature
Stated author: Sian Rees
Publication date: 2009
Date accessed: May 7, 2009
Page cited: 5

Use this order for MLA
Surname, Name. "Title of the Document." *Title of the Site*. Sponsor or publisher, date of publication. Medium of publication. Access date.

EXAMPLE MLA:
Jones, Sally. "Writing Reference Lists for Essays." *Sally Jones Website.* Jonesessay, 14 October 2007. Web. 7 May 2009.

Use this order for APA
Surname, Initials. (year, month day). *Title of the document.* Retrieved from URL

EXAMPLE APA:
Jones, S. (2007, October 14). *Writing reference lists for essays*. Retrieved from http://www.jonesessay.com/references

Now write the reference entry for Excerpt 1 using MLA or APA style.

____

____

Excerpt 2 Adding an online source without a stated author to your references using MLA or APA style: start the reference entry with the document title.

Text added to the essay (MLA)
Shelter categorizes the causes of homelessness according to three possible factors: (1) individual factors, including drug and alcohol misuse, lack of qualifications, lack of social support, debts, poor physical and mental health, relationship breakdown, and crime involvement at an early age; (2) family background, including family breakdown and disputes, sexual and physical abuse in childhood or adolescence, having parents with drug or alcohol problems, and previous experience of family homelessness; and (3) institutional background, including having been in care, the armed forces, or in prison ("What Causes Homelessness?").

Text added to the essay (APA)
Shelter categorizes the causes of homelessness according to three possible factors: (1) individual factors, including drug and alcohol misuse, lack of qualifications, lack of social support, debts, poor physical and mental health, relationship breakdown, and crime involvement at an early age; (2) family background, including family breakdown and disputes, sexual and physical abuse in childhood or adolescence, having parents with drug or alcohol problems, and previous experience of family homelessness; and (3) institutional background, including having been in care, the armed forces, or in prison ("What causes homelessness?" 2009).

Citation information
Organization: Shelter
URL: http://england.shelter.org.uk/housing_issues/homelessness/What_causes_homelessness
Document title: What causes homelessness?
Stated author: none
Publication date: 2009
Date accessed: May 7, 2009
Page number: none

Use this order for MLA
"Title of the Document." *Title of the Site*. Sponsor or publisher, date of publication. Medium of publication. Access date.

EXAMPLE (MLA):
"Writing Reference Lists for Essays." *Sally Jones Website.* Jonesessay, 14 October 2007. Web. 7 May 2009.

Use this order for APA
Title of the document. (year). Retrieved from URL

EXAMPLE (APA):
Writing reference lists for essays. (2009). Retrieved from http://www.jonesessay.com/references

Now write the reference entry for Excerpt 2 using MLA or APA style:

____

____

DESCRIBING PROBLEMS AND SOLUTIONS

Different ways to write about problems, solutions, and evaluation are listed below.

Describing Problems

- There are Y (main/major/key) problems to consider when looking at X.
- One of the main problems to consider with regard to X is . . .
- Health/financial problems can be understood as a major cause of . . .
- The problems of X can be categorized according to . . .
- One problem that would come to many people's minds when thinking about X is . . .

Describing Solutions

- The problems highlighted above require simple/complex/multiple solutions.
- An effective solution would be to . . .
- One solution for homeowners is/would be . . .
- One solution to the problem of X is/would be to . . .
- The main solution suggested by X is to . . .
- An example of how this problem can be solved is . . .
- Local governments/politicians should . . . in order to solve the problem of X.
- An integrated/long-term approach is needed to address/solve the problem of X.
- Rather than . . . ing X, policy-makers should . . .
- In each case, systems/measures/policies should be put in place/enacted/implemented in order to . . .
- The problem of X could be improved/alleviated/solved if . . .
- Perhaps the government could/should/might even consider . . .
- More help should also be provided to . . .

Evaluating

- X is likely/unlikely to succeed/be successful if/unless . . .
- It is likely/unlikely that X will solve the problem/succeed due to/unless . . .
- The chances of the solutions suggested above succeeding are/depend on . . .
- X will have significant/little impact/effect on . . .
- The solution/s can be generally regarded as . . .
- X cannot be solved by . . .

Now read the final version of the essay on homelessness in London below. The supporting evidence and examples have been added in response to the instructor's comments. They are added below in **boldface** with some minor changes and additions made to incorporate the excerpts smoothly into the text. Pay special attention to the language used to describe problems and solutions and to evaluate.

Homelessness in London: A complex problem with no easy solution

Section 1

1 Like most other large cities, London has many problems, and homelessness is one of them. **2** There are many kinds of homeless people in London. **3** It is not uncommon to see young and old alike sleeping in shopfronts, in parks, and in other public places. **4** These are the visible homeless that theatre-goers, tourists, and commuters see every day. **5** There are also many less visible homeless people in the city: people of all ages who have nowhere to call home and who live in temporary homeless shelters or bed-and-breakfast "hotels," and other temporary accommodation funded by government. **Homelessness is defined by Shelter, a UK organization that advocates in favour of the homeless, as the most extreme form of housing need, not only for those sleeping in the street but also for those who lack a home and have to live in uncertain circumstances in temporary accommodation, often with overcrowding and unsanitary conditions ("Homelessness," 2009). As stated by Rees (2009), defining who is and who is not homeless is not always a straightforward matter. Being homeless does not just mean that someone is living on the streets. The definition extends to people living in homeless hostels and in temporary accommodation provided by their local councils. Some definitions would also include the "hidden homeless," defined as people "who are in unstable accommodation, with friends or family or otherwise without their own home" (Rees, 2009, p. 9). In sum, "Having a home is more than just having a roof over your head" ("Homelessness," 2009, para. 3).**

6 No one knows exactly how many homeless people there are in London today, but most studies suggest many thousands. **Accurate figures for the number of homeless people in London are also difficult to come by. Shelter estimates there are between 310 000 and 380 000 single homeless people in the UK, with approximately one-quarter living in hostels or B&B accommodation, or facing imminent eviction due to debt. The figure is based on a definition of "homeless" that includes the following groups: rough sleepers; people staying in hostels and shelters; people staying in bed-and-breakfasts and other boarded accommodation; squatters; and concealed households—those residing with friends or family, but without any explicit right to do so and in accommodation which is in some**

way unsatisfactory (http://www.shelter.org.uk). 7 People in London, just like anywhere else, become homeless for many reasons, ranging from becoming unemployed to suffering from addiction. **8** It is necessary, therefore, to understand the complex nature of the problem in order to find viable solutions to homelessness in London.

Section 2

9 According to Shelter, one of the main underlying causes of homelessness in England is a lack of affordable housing (http://www.shelter.org.uk). 10 There is a long list of additional reasons why people in London, and elsewhere, become homeless. **Shelter categorizes the causes of homelessness according to three possible factors: (1) individual factors, including drug and alcohol misuse, lack of qualifications, lack of social support, debts, poor physical and mental health, relationship breakdown, and crime involvement at an early age; (2) family background, including family breakdown and disputes, sexual and physical abuse in childhood or adolescence, having parents with drug or alcohol problems, and previous experience of family homelessness; and (3) institutional background, including having been in care, the armed forces, or in prison ("What causes homelessness?" 2009).**

11 One problem that would come to many people's minds when thinking about homelessness is poverty. **12** Few would argue that homelessness and poverty are closely interrelated. **13** When people lose their jobs and income, some can no longer afford to pay the rent or mortgage on the home that they live in, or the weekly bills, and they end up homeless. **14** However, not all of London's homeless have gone from being in the workforce to being on the streets. **15** A large number of homeless people have instead moved from government institutions to the streets: from psychiatric hospitals and children's homes to the streets or homeless hostels of London. **16** As part of the well-intentioned but misguided policy of "care in community," it was felt that large psychiatric hospitals were not the place where many mentally ill people should be kept. **17** Consequently, many hospitals were closed and patients moved to smaller care centres or sheltered housing, resulting in many of the former patients becoming homeless, unable to cope with controlling their own medicine and the wider demands of living in society. **18** Mental illness is, therefore, clearly a significant cause of homelessness. **According to a discussion paper written by Sian Rees (2009), mental health problems can be understood as a cause *and* an effect of homelessness: that is, mental health problems are not only a factor in the circumstances that lead to people losing their accommodation, "mental health problems may also be exacerbated by the stresses associated with being homeless, which in turn will make it even harder for that person to achieve stability in their housing" (Rees, 2009, p. 5). 19** Others gain their first experience of being homeless when they leave, or run away from, children's homes, heading for the "bright lights of London." **20** And finally, a significant number of homeless people in London are veterans who, having served in the armed forces for several years, are unable to find secure accommodation and employment after leaving the services.

21 Another major problem that comes with attempting to solve homelessness is dealing with individuals suffering from both addictions and mental illness. **Rees also suggests that street homeless people may be 50 to 100 times more likely to have a psychotic disorder than the general population, and highlights the link between what she describes as homeless people with a "dual diagnosis," that is, mental illness and alcohol/substance abuse (2009). Rees suggests that, according to most studies, around 10 to 20 percent of the homeless population would fulfill the criteria for dual diagnosis (Rees, 2009, p. 5). 22** There are also the added health and crime risks that come with feeding an addiction. **23** For example, someone who has no job or home but who needs to feed an addiction has to find money to pay for his or her next fix or drink: begging, theft, and prostitution are usually the means to meeting this end. **24** Addiction and its effects add to the problem of being marginalized and excluded from the rest of society and create major obstacles to getting many homeless people successfully off the streets and into permanent accommodation and employment.

25 When added together, these problems associated with homelessness feed into a broader vicious circle that usually comes with being homeless. **26** Homeless people often cannot get homes from landlords without being able to prove that they have a job that will provide enough income to pay the rent. **27** Yet, in order to get that elusive job, they need to have a home. **28** Few employers will hire or even interview job candidates who identify their home on the application form as a homeless hostel, or a park bench.

Section 3

29 Complex multifaceted problems require complex multifaceted solutions. **30** The problems highlighted above are multiple: poverty, people becoming homeless after being in institutions (psychiatric hospitals, children's homes, and the armed forces), addiction and crime, and a vicious circle of *no job = no home*. **31** In order to solve the problems of homelessness, national and local government policies need to be coordinated, and should involve the work of non-governmental organizations (NGOs) **such as Shelter, which helps people find and keep a home, and campaigns for decent housing for all. An example of this national–local connection can be found in the national *UK Homelessness Act* of 2002, under which local authorities have to develop a homelessness strategy for their area.** **32** However, the problems cannot be addressed in isolation from each other. **33** Instead, an integrated, long-term approach is needed, in which the problems are understood as being multifaceted and interrelated.

34 The poverty that underlies many cases of homelessness cannot easily be solved. **35** Rather than targeting poverty alone, policy-makers should perhaps focus on breaking the poverty–homelessness link, that is, the causal link that allows poverty to lead to homelessness. **36** This causal link can come in many forms, for example, an unpaid mortgage leading to the loss of a home, or eviction from rented accommodation due to inability to pay the rent. **37** In each case, systems should be put in place to help those in need. **38** The problems of people losing their homes could be at least alleviated if mortgage lenders were encouraged to give people more time to meet payments or to reschedule loans. **One solution for homeowners who temporarily lose their income is the Homeowner Mortgage Support (HMS) program, which will allow for reduced interest payments on mortgages for up to two years. According to Adam Sampson, the chief executive of Shelter, the program will benefit the estimated half a million households that are expected to be more than three months in arrears with their payments in 2009, and may prevent 75 000 repossessions of properties ("New Scheme for Homeowners," 2009).** **39** Perhaps the UK could even follow the example of Canada, where payment protection insurance is often compulsory for high-risk mortgage borrowers. **40** In terms of private tenants who become evicted from rented accommodation, more help through temporary government accommodation should also be provided. **Shelter argues that every local authority should have a "tenancy sustainment service" to help vulnerable people in private rentals stay in their homes, and that the housing benefit system should work better. The main solution suggested by Shelter, however, is for more affordable homes to be built ("Homelessness," 2009).** **41** Although the cost may be high, if such measures allow people to get back to work and/or get stable accommodation in the longer term, and to contribute to society as taxpayers, then the long-term savings will outweigh the shorter-term costs.

42 Homeless people with mental health problems also need special, targeted care. **43** Providing a home is not enough. **44** Although homeless people with mental health problems may indeed take up offers of a roof over their head, without focused and concerted treatment and monitoring of the illness, it is unlikely that the provision of accommodation alone will suffice. **45** The same applies for homeless people with addiction problems.

46 In this case, as in the case of the other solutions suggested above, cost is a major factor. **47** Who will pay for all of these measures and will they be cost-effective as well as beneficial to the homeless?

Section 4

48 When the stage character Dick Whittington sets off to London to make his fortune, he believes that the streets of London are paved with gold. **49** In his story of hardship, he eventually wins though, becoming London's mayor three times over. **50** Today, some people come to the city with the same hope, as the bright lights of London still have that same allure for many who are looking for an escape from their lives in other towns across the UK, and from other countries around the world. **51** For those who end up living on the city's streets, or in temporary accommodation, there is rarely such a happy ending. **52** Becoming homeless is the result of a wide array of problems, some of which have been highlighted in the paragraphs above. **53** The key to success—and success may indeed be hard to come by in many cases—is to look at solving the problems of homelessness in an integrated way, understanding that the problems are interrelated. **54** Moreover, any integrated strategy that finds homes for the homeless is unlikely to succeed in the long term if the underlying causes of homelessness are not addressed fully. **In this regard, the solutions to homelessness are seen by Shelter as not only about getting people off the streets but also about finding lasting solutions to preventing people from becoming homeless ("Homelessness," 2009).** **55** As usual, money is central to success. **56** An integrated strategy to combatting homelessness in London, and in other cities, requires long-term investment. **57** Yet, homelessness cannot be solved solely by throwing money at the problem. **58** Money needs to be spent wisely and in targeted ways that attack the links between poverty and homelessness.

References

Homelessness. (2009). Retrieved from http://england.shelter.org.uk/housing_issues/homelessness

New scheme for homeowners. (2009). Retrieved from http://england.shelter.org.uk/news/april_2009/new_scheme_for_homeowners

Rees, S. (2009). *Mental ill health in the adult single homeless population: A review of the literature.* Retrieved from http://www.crisis.org.uk/publications_djhsearch.php?submitted=search&fullitem=235

What causes homelessness? (2009). Retrieved from http://england.shelter.org.uk/housing issues/homelessness/What_causes_homelessness

Note: In APA style, when citing an entire website, an in-text citation with the site's address is sufficient.

In the essay above, the writer has described the situation and its associated problems, suggested solutions, and provided an evaluation of those solutions in separate sections. Supporting examples, statistics, and evidence from reliable sources have been added to the earlier draft, thus making the essay more convincing.

TASK 8

Select a major problem in your subject area. Write a problem–solution essay, following an SPSE structure. Use some of the language for describing problems and solutions that you have studied in this chapter. Remember to support your ideas with relevant examples, statistics, and evidence from reliable online sources.

CHAPTER 9 SUMMARY

The aspects of writing about problems and solutions that you have studied in this chapter will help you to write not only problem–solution essays but also other essays in which you are required to write about problems and solutions.

In this chapter, you studied the following: organizing and writing a problem–solution essay using an SPSE structure, providing supporting examples and evidence from reliable academic sources when describing problems and solutions, citing online sources using MLA and APA citation styles, and using language to describe problems and solutions.

ORGANIZING AN SPSE OUTLINE FOR PROBLEM–SOLUTION ESSAYS

SPSE stands for Situation, Problem, Solution, Evaluation. When you organize an outline for an SPSE essay, it is most common to analyze the four components separately, each in a different essay section. Although it would be possible to write an SPSE essay using a thematic structure, as described in Chapters 7 and 8, doing so could be problematic. Often, many different problems are closely interrelated and need to be considered together before thinking about solutions. In a thematic structure, the problems would be separated under different themes, breaking up this interconnectedness.

PROVIDING SUPPORTING EXAMPLES AND EVIDENCE

The first draft of the essay on homelessness lacked supporting examples, statistics, and evidence from reliable academic sources. These shortcomings were indicated in the instructor's comments. In the final draft of the essay, the writer responded to each of the instructor's comments by adding examples, statistics, and evidence from academic and professional/non-governmental organization sources. The revisions made the essay much more comprehensive, thorough, and convincing.

DESCRIBING PROBLEMS AND SOLUTIONS

You have also studied different language to describe problems and solutions and to evaluate. Remember to use these and other language structures when you are describing problems and solutions, and evaluating in academic writing. If you use a broad range of effective language, your ideas will be more convincing to your reader.

CHAPTER 10

Writing about Causes and Effects

In this chapter, you will study the following aspects of writing about causes and effects:

- ✓ Understanding causality
- ✓ Thinking critically about causality: Avoiding generalizations
- ✓ Using the language of causality in academic and professional texts
- ✓ Organizing an outline for a cause-and-effect essay
- ✓ Describing causal relations
- ✓ Improving style: Formality and effectiveness of expression

In this chapter, you will learn how to write a cause-and-effect essay and how to write about causal relations in other types of essays.

An analysis of *causes* (the reasons for things) and *effects* (the results of things) is common in academic writing, and is used in many kinds of essays. In this chapter, you will learn how to write about causal relations, how to organize your ideas, and how to avoid making generalizations when describing causes and effects.

UNDERSTANDING CAUSALITY

Terms such as *causality* and *causal relations* are often used when discussing causes and effects.

Reading and writing about causality requires good critical thinking skills. This is because critical reading and writing demand analysis of the reasons why things may have happened (causes), and the possible consequences of things (effects).

It is sometimes possible to make factual statements about causes and effects, for example, the statement *smoking causes cancer.* This statement is considered factual because it is now scientifically accepted that smoking is a cause of cancer (cause) and that cancer is a result of smoking (effect). However, there is often considerable debate and disagreement about contested causes and effects (i.e., causes and effects that are not agreed upon by all people). One such example is the debate on the causes of global warming. The following statement presents what a writer sees as a factual cause of global warming:

Carbon emissions from vehicles cause global warming.

However, some scientists (and politicians) argue that inadequate evidence exists to make such a statement. They might make the statement as follows in order to reflect their view that scientific proof is lacking:

Carbon emissions from vehicles could be a cause of global warming.

When you write about causes and effects, the language you use reflects whether you think a cause or effect is certain or possible. In this chapter, you will study how to write about causes and effects in different ways. In doing so, you will put into practice some of the critical thinking ideas that you studied in Chapter 2.

TASK 1

In our everyday lives, just as in academic writing, we spend a considerable amount of time thinking and talking about causal relations. Here are four sentences that express causal relations:

1. "We didn't play tennis because it was raining."
2. "It was cold out so I took a warm coat."
3. "It's not my fault that you failed the exam!"
4. "If you don't give up smoking, you'll end up getting cancer."

In each of the sentences above, there is a *cause* and an *effect.* In the first example, the cause is the rain and the effect, or result, of the rain is that we decided not to play tennis.

Identify the cause and effect in sentences 2 to 4:

1. **Example:** "We didn't play tennis because it was raining."
   CAUSE: It was raining.
   EFFECT: We didn't play tennis.
2. "It was cold out so I took a warm coat."
   CAUSE: ....
   EFFECT: ....
3. "It's not my fault that you failed the exam!"
   CAUSE: ....
   EFFECT: ....

4. "If you don't give up smoking, you'll end up getting cancer."
CAUSE: ....
EFFECT: ....

TASK 2

This task involves gathering ideas from existing knowledge through exploratory writing. In Boxes 1 and 2 below, write as many ideas as you can about the causes and effects of climate change. You can write in whatever way you like (e.g., in note form or in paragraphs), and you do not need to worry about formal academic style. The purpose of this activity is to get as many ideas down on paper as you can, and to generate more ideas as you write.

Here is the essay question:

Question: Describe the causes and effects of climate change.

Guidelines: Your answer should refer to reliable sources for statistics and information, and should consider both anthropogenic (meaning "derived from human activities") and non-anthropogenic causes of climate change.

BOX 1: Causes

BOX 2: Effects

____
____
____
____
____
____
____
____
____
____
____
____
____
____
____

THINKING CRITICALLY ABOUT CAUSALITY: AVOIDING GENERALIZATIONS

Writing about causes and effects requires critical thinking skills such as those you studied in Chapter 2, to avoid inappropriate generalizations.

Critical thinking skills are required when you are analyzing a situation and trying to understand how or why it may have happened. You also need to think critically when you are trying to analyze the effects of something, in the past, present, or future.

In Task 1, Sentence 4, above, you identified the cause and effect in the following sentence:

> *"If you don't give up smoking, you'll end up getting cancer."*

This type of statement may be common in everyday conversations; however, in academic writing you need to think carefully and consider a wide range of other possible factors. For Sentence 4, you could ask yourself the following questions about the relationship between smoking and cancer:

- Is it scientifically proven that smoking causes cancer in all cases?
- Could the smoker end up suffering from a disease other than cancer as a result of smoking?
- How old is the smoker?

- What is the smoker's lifestyle like?
- Has the smoker tried to give up smoking before?
- If so, why did the smoker revert to smoking?

By asking such questions, you are engaging critically with causal relations by not immediately accepting the statement as factual, and by considering other possible factors. In academic essays, your reader will engage critically in the same way with the information and ideas that you put forward, and if the writing is assessed, your level of critical thinking will affect the grade that you receive.

Avoiding Generalizations

One common problem that comes up when writers discuss causes and effects is inappropriate generalization. This may occur if a writer presents an effect or result of something as *a certain fact* that applies in all cases, when it is only an opinion or one of many *possible effects or results*. To avoid generalizing when you write about causal relations, you should consider the strategies below.

1. *Strategies for Expressing Causality with Certainty: Present and Past Tense*

Present If you feel that a cause or effect is based on scientific fact (something that is, or can be, scientifically proven and is therefore 100 percent certain), then write your statement with the main verb in the sentence in the present simple tense. This tense is typically used for statements that are generally accepted as scientific fact.

> **EXAMPLE**
> Smoking *causes* cancer.

If you write the statement "smoking causes cancer" in an essay, the reader will understand that you believe there is a scientifically proven link between smoking and getting cancer.

Past If you want to express causality with certainty in your writing about a past cause or effect, use the past simple tense.

> **EXAMPLE**
> The accident *happened* as a result of pilot error.

The past simple tense will indicate to your reader that you believe the statement to be factual, that is, something that has been proven through some form of reliable scientific inquiry.

2. *Strategies for Avoiding Generalizations in Statements of Causality*

Sometimes writers generalize by using the present simple tense in too broad a sense or without necessary evidence.

> **EXAMPLE**
> When the economy is in recession, the Australian public *reduces* travel by car.

In the sentence above, the writer uses the verb *reduces* in the present simple tense. Accordingly, the interpretation of most readers will be that the writer believes this to be a scientifically proven fact. However, the writer is generalizing, as there are obviously some people in Australia who do not reduce car usage as a result of an economic recession, most notably, those who do not own cars. So, how can you avoid the generalization in statements like the one above?

Use the following strategies to avoid uncritical thinking and generalizations in statements about causality:

a) Provide some reliable evidence and specific statistics to back up the statement.

> **EXAMPLE**
> According to an *Economy Today* magazine survey of March 1992, when the economy was in recession in the early 1990s, the Australian public reduced travel by car by 22.5 percent (*Economy Today*, 1992).

The statement is no longer a generalization, as it is now backed up with evidence from a reliable source.

b) Alternatively, if the writer has no evidence, provide some qualifying language to avoid generalizing.

> **EXAMPLE 1**
> When the economy is in recession, *many* Australians reduce travel by car.

The writer has avoided generalizing in Example 1 by adding the quantifier *many* to the sentence. This is no longer a generalization, as the writer is no longer stating that *all* Australians reduce car travel during a recession.

> **EXAMPLE 2**
> *I would suggest/speculate that* when the economy is in recession, Australians reduce travel by car.

Example 2 is not a generalization, as the introductory phrase *I would suggest/speculate that* makes it clear to the reader that the statement that follows should not be interpreted as a proven fact.

c) Use a modal auxiliary verb such as *may, might,* or *could.*

> **EXAMPLE**
> One result of economic recession in Australia *may/might/could* be a reduction in car travel.

This is no longer a generalization about cause and effect, as the use of the modal auxiliary verb *may/might/could* means that a reduction in car travel is being presented only as one possible result of economic recession rather than *the* result in all cases.

d) Use time adverbs of frequency such as *often, at times, sometimes.*

> **EXAMPLE**
> When economies are in recession, people *often* use their cars less.

In this example, using the adverb of frequency *often* avoids generalization. The writer is now stating that less car use is *often* (but not *always*) the result of recession.

e) Use the modal auxiliary verb *can.*

> **EXAMPLE**
> It *can* rain a lot in summer in England.

The modal auxiliary verb *can*, when used to discuss likelihood, gives the general meaning that something is possible and a common feature or occurrence.

In this example, *can* gives the sentence the following meaning: "Rain is a possible and a common feature of the English summer."

You can also use *can* with this meaning if you are not absolutely certain about the causal relations that you are describing or analyzing. For example, when some (but not all) people take certain medicines, they feel drowsy. Therefore, the drug companies need to warn people taking the medicine about this risk, especially as people may have an adverse reaction while driving or operating machinery.

Sufferers of allergic rhinitis, or hay fever as it is also known, often take pills known as antihistamines to control their allergic reactions to pollen and other allergens. Often, the boxes that the antihistamines come in give the following warning:

These pills can cause drowsiness. Avoid driving or using heavy machinery.

By stating that the pills *can cause* drowsiness, rather than the pills *cause* drowsiness, the writer indicates that it is possible and a common feature, but not certain, that the pills will cause drowsiness.

TASK 3

Read the following generalizations about cause and effect. Rewrite each one to avoid the generalization by using one of the language strategies for avoiding generalizations outlined above.

1. Not wearing a seat belt leads to death in road accidents.

   ____

2. Extreme poverty results in violent crime.

   ____

3. Unhealthy diets cause cancer.

   ____

4. Children who watch violence on TV copy it in real life.

____

5. Students who do not study hard get worse grades.

____

USING THE LANGUAGE OF CAUSALITY IN ACADEMIC AND PROFESSIONAL TEXTS

Article 1 below is on the causes of climate change, with a specific focus on Canada. The article was published by the Government of Canada and follows a descriptive, expository writing style. As you read, pay particular attention to the causes of climate change mentioned by the writer and to the language used to describe causal relations.

ARTICLE 1

Climate change 101

GOVERNMENT OF CANADA

1 Climate change is a long-term shift in overall weather conditions over time. **2** It is measured by changes in temperature, precipitation, wind, snow cover and other indicators. **3** When we speak of climate change on a global scale, we are referring to changes in the climate of the earth as a whole.

4 While the earth's climate is naturally variable, its average state is regulated by factors such as the earth's orbit around the sun and the natural greenhouse gas effect. **5** In fact, the earth would not be warm enough to sustain life without the natural greenhouse gas effect. **6** The atmosphere is like a blanket, or greenhouse, trapping heat escaping from the earth's surface. **7** The principal natural greenhouse gases are water vapour and carbon dioxide. **8** By burning fossil fuels such as coal, oil and natural gas, we release more carbon dioxide into this blanket. **9** Changing land use, such as deforestation and the conversion of land to agricultural use, has also contributed carbon dioxide to this blanket.

10 Causes of climate change can be divided into two categories—those related to natural causes and those created by humans.

Natural Causes

11 The climate can be affected by natural factors that are external to the climate system, such as changes in volcanic activity, solar output and the earth's orbit around the sun. **12** It can also be affected by natural internal changes, such as variations in ocean currents, which can influence the climate for periods of decades.

Human Causes

13 Climate change can also be caused by human activities, such as the burning of fossil fuels and the conversion of land for forestry and agriculture. **14** Since the Industrial Revolution began about 250 years ago, climate change due to human influences has increased significantly because of the combustion of fossil fuels (such as oil, natural gas and coal) and, to a lesser extent, because of changes in land use practices. **15** As a result, the amount of heat-trapping gas in the atmosphere has increased, enhancing the warming capability of the natural greenhouse effect.

16 It is this human-induced enhancement of the greenhouse effect that causes the most environmental concern because it has the potential to warm the planet at a rate that has never been experienced in human history, causing glaciers to retreat, sea levels to rise, and climatic zones to shift. **17** Depending upon emissions during the 21st century, most experts agree that average global temperatures could rise by one to six-and-a-half degrees Celsius over this century. **18** In Canada, this could mean an increase in annual mean temperatures in some regions of more than double the increase in the global average.

19 But climate change is more than just a warming trend. **20** Increasing temperatures will lead to changes in many aspects of weather, such as wind patterns, the amount and type of precipitation, and the types and frequency of severe weather events that may be expected to occur. **21** Such climate change could have far-reaching and/or unpredictable environmental, social and economic consequences.

Source: "Climate Change 101." http://www.climatechange.gc.ca/default. asp?lang=En&n=65CD73F4-1. Climate Change, 2010. Reproduced with the permission of the Minister of Public Works and Government Services Canada, 2010.

TASK 4

Which of the following statements best describes the view presented in Article 1 on the causes of climate change? ______

1. Natural causes of the greenhouse effect are insignificant.
2. Human activities are making the natural greenhouse effect worse.
3. The greenhouse effect is caused solely by human activities.

TASK 5

Now read Article 1 again and highlight the language used to describe causes and effects.

Article 2 below is on the effects of climate change, with a more specific focus on Canada. As you read it, pay particular attention to the main effects of climate change mentioned by the writer and to the language used to describe causal relations.

ARTICLE 2

From impacts to adaptation: Canada in a changing climate 2007

NATURAL RESOURCES CANADA

The impacts of changing climate are already evident in every region of Canada.

1 Impacts of changing climate on many physical and biological systems, such as ice and snow cover, river, lake and sea levels, and plant and animal distributions, are unequivocal and have been documented in other recent climate change assessments (Intergovernmental

Panel on Climate Change 2001, 2007; Arctic Climate Impact Assessment, 2005). **2** In addition, increases in the occurrence of heat waves, forest fires, storm-surge flooding, coastal erosion and other climate-related hazards are consistent with observed climate trends. **3** Many of these impacts directly influence human systems. **4** For example, decreases in the thickness and duration of lake and river ice have significantly impacted the viability of many winter road networks that provide access to remote communities and mine sites in northern Canada (including the northern parts of many provinces; Chapters 3, 5, 6 and 7), while coastal erosion has impacted buildings and critical infrastructure, and threatened cultural sites on all of Canada's marine coasts (Chapters 3, 4, 5 and 8).

5 There is also strong evidence that climate change has been a contributing factor to a number of other environmental, social and economic issues. **6** These include the unprecedented outbreak of mountain pine beetle in British Columbia, which encompassed over 9.2 million ha of forest in 2007. **7** Although fire suppression and other historical factors have contributed to this outbreak, the recent predominance of hot summers that favour beetle reproduction, and mild winters that allow their offspring to survive, have been critical factors (Chapter 8). **8** Since 1990 in parts of Atlantic Canada, sea lettuce has been spreading, rendering estuaries less suitable for shellfish or finfish and less attractive to residents and tourists. **9** This spread has been related, in part, to climate-driven reductions in freshwater inflow during summer (Chapter 4).

Climate change will exacerbate many current climate risks, and present new risks and opportunities, with significant implications for communities, industry, infrastructure and ecosystems.

10 Climate change is evidenced by changes in average conditions as well as by changes in climate variability and extreme climate events. **11** Many of the most severe and costly impacts will be associated with projected increases in the frequency and magnitude of extreme climate events and associated natural disasters, including flooding due to high-intensity rainfall and storm surges, ice and wind storms, heat waves and drought (Chapters 2–9). **12** An understanding of future climate extremes is particularly important for the design and maintenance of infrastructure, emergency management, and community health and safety (Chapters 5 and 6).

13 Gradual changes in average temperature, precipitation, and sea level also affect community and ecosystem sustainability. **14** Some of the most significant and pervasive impacts in Canada will be related to water resources. **15** Water-stressed areas will expand due to decreased runoff in many areas resulting from changes in precipitation and increased evapotranspiration (Chapter 2), while reduced water quality and quantity will be experienced on a seasonal basis in every region of Canada (Chapters 3–8). **16** Increasing demands on water resources for agriculture, energy production, communities and recreation will have to be managed in consideration of ecosystem needs (Chapters 4–8). **17** In addition to increasing the impacts already observed, changing climate will bring new risks to some areas, such as the introduction of vector-borne diseases into areas where climate conditions presently inhibit survival of the vector host (Chapters 5, 6 and 9). **18** Climate-related impacts on ecosystems will present new challenges to the management of protected areas (Chapters 6, 7, 8).

19 Climate change will also bring opportunities, including longer and warmer growing seasons, which could increase productivity and allow cultivation of new and potentially more profitable crops and tree species (Chapters 4–8). **20** Although global-scale analysis suggests that climate change should benefit Canadian agriculture and forests, studies in Canada that factor in changes in disturbance regimes and more frequent drought are less optimistic and stress the need for timely and effective adaptation (Chapters 7 and 8). **21** Decreased sea-, river- and lake-ice cover permit longer shipping seasons, although lower lake and river levels could have negative impacts on transportation (Chapters 3, 4 and 6). **22** Increased marine transport in the Arctic would provide opportunities for economic growth, along with environmental and security risks (Chapter 3).

23 Impacts will be cumulative and frequently synergistic. **24** For example, increased frequency and magnitude of heat waves will result in increased peak electricity demand for air conditioning, while decreased runoff from mountain glaciers in western Canada and lower water levels on the Great Lakes are likely to reduce potential for hydroelectricity generation in these areas. **25** Combined with anticipated increases in demand for electricity related to population and economic growth, changing climate could result in increased numbers of black-out and brown-out events (Chapters 6 and 8). **26** The cumulative nature of impacts, and associated cascading uncertainties, makes it likely that climate change will produce "surprises"—impacts related to the crossing of critical thresholds that have not been anticipated. **27** As is the case for all human and managed natural systems, the magnitude of impacts can be reduced through adaptation.

28 Climate change impacts elsewhere in the world, and adaptation measures taken to address these, will affect Canadian consumers, the competitiveness of some Canadian industries, and Canadian activities related to international development, aid and peace keeping.

29 Climate change impacts elsewhere in the world will affect supply-demand dynamics and the competitive advantage of some Canadian industries. **30** This will influence the net economic costs of climate change in Canada. **31** For example, although forest productivity may increase in Canada, greater productivity increases in other countries could result in lower forestry-product prices on the global market and a reduced share of the market for Canadian producers (Chapter 9). **32** For tourism, climate change may reduce the attractiveness of some Canadian natural areas (Chapters 3, 4, 5, 7 and 8). **33** When examined in a global context, however, tourism in Canada is expected to be positively impacted by climate change, as warmer temperatures would make Canada a more attractive destination for foreign tourists and encourage more Canadians to forgo vacations to tropical locations due to less severe winters in Canada (Chapter 9).

34 Climate changes elsewhere in the world will also influence Canadian humanitarian and development activities. **35** In addition to commitments to assist developing countries in their efforts to adapt to climate change, changing climate will increase the need for disaster relief. **36** Observed trends toward increases in the frequency of extreme climate events are expected to continue in the future. **37** Extreme events are also expected to become more intense. **38** Environmental stress and scarcity issues (primarily related to food and water) caused by climate changes can exacerbate political, social, economic, ethnic, religious or territorial conflicts, leading to increased political instability and displacement of populations (Chapter 9).

Source: "From Impacts to Adaptation: Canada in a Changing Climate 2007." http://adaptation.nrcan.gc.ca/assess/2007/synth/impact_e.php. National Resources, 2007. Reproduced with the permission of the Minister of Public Works and Government Services Canada, 2010.

TASK 6

Which of the following statements best represents Article 2's description of the effects of climate change in Canada? ______

1. Climate change is affecting, and will affect, many aspects of life in Canada.
2. Climate change will bring more positive than negative effects to Canada.
3. Climate change will have only environmental impacts in Canada.

TASK 7

Now read Article 2 again and highlight the language used to describe causes and effects.

ORGANIZING AN OUTLINE FOR A CAUSE-AND-EFFECT ESSAY

One common type of university writing assignment in many subject areas is the cause-and-effect essay. Cause-and-effect essays can be organized in two ways, either by looking at causes then effects in separate sections of the essay (*causes-then-effects structure*), or by looking at causes and effects together under relevant themes or analytic perspectives (*thematic structure*).

A Causes-Then-Effects Outline

A clear and effective way to organize a cause-and-effect essay is to look first at the causes then second at the effects, in separate sections.

Read Outline 1 below, which is a causes-then-effects outline for an essay on climate change, and complete the task that follows. Outline 1 was written as an initial outline based on existing knowledge, prior to carrying out research on the topic. Here is a reminder of the essay question:

> **Question:** Describe the causes and effects of climate change.
>
> **Guidelines:** Your answer should refer to reliable sources for statistics and information, and should consider both anthropogenic (meaning "derived from human activities") and non-anthropogenic causes of climate change.

Outline 1: Causes-then-effects outline

INTRODUCTION

1. **Background:** climate change around the world and locally
2. **Specifics:** the range of causes and effects to be analyzed
3. **Structure:** I will look first at causes (anthropogenic and non-anthropogenic) then effects (in general and in North America)
4. **Thesis statement:** e.g., measures should be taken to reduce man-made causes

CAUSES OF CLIMATE CHANGE

- Carbon dioxide emissions from vehicles (e.g., cars and planes)
- Carbon dioxide emissions from factories and power stations
- Sun spot activity
- Volcanoes
- Historical natural cycles of climate change (e.g., ice age, global warming)

EFFECTS OF CLIMATE CHANGE

- Warming temperatures across the world
- Melting ice caps
- Rising sea levels, warming sea temperatures
- Pacific island communities under threat
- Pine beetle problem from Colorado to British Columbia

CONCLUSION

1. **Summarize:** anthropogenic and non-anthropogenic causes and effects
2. **Synthesize:** bring ideas together into one closing idea (e.g., man-made causes most likely to be having greater effect; "non-anthropogenic" studies financed by oil companies and their lobby groups?)
3. **End statement:** e.g., speculate about the future: precautionary principle demands that we do not take a risk; action needs to be taken to reduce man-made causes; this will lead to a reduction in harmful effects

TASK 8

List the strengths and weaknesses of Outline 1.

Strengths:

____

____

____

____

____

____

Weaknesses:

____

____

____

____

____

____

A Thematic Outline

Outline 2 on the next page is a thematic outline in which causes and effects are discussed together under relevant analytic perspectives or themes. Read Outline 2 and complete the task that follows.

Outline 2: A thematic outline

INTRODUCTION

1. **Background:** climate change around the world and locally
2. **Specifics:** the range of causes and effects to be analyzed
3. **Structure:** I will look at causes and effects together under two analytic perspectives—anthropogenic and non-anthropogenic factors
4. **Thesis statement:** e.g., measures should be taken to reduce man-made causes

ANTHROPOGENIC CAUSES AND EFFECTS

1. **Causes:**
   - Most causes are probably the result of human activity
   - Carbon dioxide emissions from vehicles (e.g., cars and planes)
   - Carbon dioxide emissions from factories and power stations
   - Intensive farming of sheep and cattle: food and energy to feed them, methane emissions
2. **Effects:**
   - Global warming and the greenhouse effect
   - Melting ice caps and rising sea levels
   - Desertification
   - Unpredictable weather: storms, floods, hurricanes, tornadoes, and their consequences

NON-ANTHROPOGENIC CAUSES AND EFFECTS

1. **Causes:**
   - Critics argue that climate change has natural causes
   - Sun spot activity
   - Volcanoes
   - Historical natural cycles of climate change (e.g., ice age, global warming)
2. **Effects:**
   - Global warming and the greenhouse effect
   - Melting ice caps and rising sea levels
   - Desertification
   - Unpredictable weather: storms, floods, hurricanes, tornadoes, and their consequences

CONCLUSION

1. **Summarize:** anthropogenic and non-anthropogenic causes and effects
2. **Synthesize:** bring ideas together into one closing idea (e.g., man-made causes most likely to be having greater effect; "non-anthropogenic" studies financed by oil companies and their lobby groups?)
3. **End statement:** e.g., speculate about the future: precautionary principle demands that we do not take a risk; action needs to be taken to reduce man-made causes; this will lead to a reduction in harmful effects

TASK 9

List the strengths and weaknesses of Outline 2.

Strengths:

____

____

____

____

____

____

Weaknesses:

____

____

____

____

____

____

DESCRIBING CAUSAL RELATIONS

In academic writing, causal relations can be described in two ways: *cause-then-effect* and *effect-then-cause*. It is necessary to use different language in each case.

Describing Cause-Then-Effect

1. **Noun phrases to describe causality: cause-then-effect**
   - Greenhouse gases are **a (main/major) cause of** climate change.
   - Greenhouse gases are **a contributing factor in** climate change.
   - Greenhouse gases are **a contributor to** climate change.
2. **Verbs to describe causality: cause-then-effect**
   - Excessive speed **caused/resulted in/led to** the accident.
3. **Linking words/phrases to describe causality: cause-then-effect**
   - Interest rates reached 1.5 percent; **therefore/consequently/thus/hence/ as a result**, the value of the dollar fell.
   - **Because of X,** the value of the dollar fell.
   - **Because** interest rates reached 1.5 percent, the value of the dollar fell.

- **As** interest rates reached 1.5 percent, the value of the dollar fell.
- **Since** interest rates reached 1.5 percent, the value of the dollar fell.

Note: *Since* and *as* are also time conjunctions, so their use to express causality may be confusing unless the context is completely clear.

Describing Effect-Then-Cause

1. **Noun phrases to describe causality: effect-then-cause**
   - Climate change is **the/a (main/major) effect of** greenhouse gases.
   - Climate change is **the result of/a consequence of** greenhouse gases.
2. **Verbs to describe causality: effect-then-cause**
   - The accident was **caused by/brought about by** excessive speed.
3. **Linking words/phrases to describe causality: effect-then-cause**
   - The value of the dollar fell **because of/as a result of** the low interest rate.
   - The value of the dollar fell **due to** the interest rate falling to 1.5 percent.
   - The value of the dollar fell **owing to** the fall in interest rates.
   - The value of the dollar fell **because/as/since** interest rates went down to 1.5 percent.

IMPROVING STYLE: FORMALITY AND EFFECTIVENESS OF EXPRESSION

Read the first draft of the essay below written by a student, Sandy, about the causes and effects of climate change. The essay is written in an expository style in which causes and effects are explained in detail. This first draft was written as an in-class essay based on the student's existing knowledge and, therefore, required no supporting examples and evidence from reliable academic sources.

Man-made causes and effects of global warming

1 Climate change affects the whole world dramatically. **2** Global warming is a widely discussed issue within the debate on climate change. **3** Every few years, the average temperature around the globe increases. **4** Although humans cannot detect these small changes, many plants and animals can and are victims of this disaster. **5** The main examples of global warming are largely the result of human activity.

6 Greenhouse gas is one of the main causes of global warming. **7** It forms a layer around the earth and traps all the heat in. **8** This is called the greenhouse effect. **9** These gases come from many sources: cars, factories and even household products like hairspray. **10** Every time a car is moving, the exhaust pipe gives out a large amount of carbon dioxide. **11** The gas sticks around the atmosphere and stays there for a really long time. **12** But cars aren't the only factor in greenhouse gases. **13** Factories are also a great contributor to the greenhouse effect. **14** It would be understandable if it was only developed countries that had a lot of air-polluting factories because of their advance in technology, but less-developed countries also pollute a lot. **15** They might not have the advanced technology needed to create many of today's products, but many developed countries use less-developed countries as their base for mass production factories. **16** Every day, factories emit tons and tons of harmful chemicals into the air. **17** All these chemicals are also included in the category of greenhouse gas.

18 The effects of global warming are considerable. **19** If one thing in the ecosystem is affected, the chances of it affecting other species of plants or animals or even humans are high. **20** For example, when the climate changes, if many plants are not able to adapt to the slight increase or decrease in temperature, they would die. **21** When a tree dies, not only do many animals whose habitat is there lose their homes, the earth has also lost one of its organisms which recycles the air. **22** Lack of clean air could lead to much greater problems. **23** Lung diseases are one such example. **24** Many people who already suffer from respiratory illnesses could get worse with the bad air that global warming has caused.

25 Climate change could also lead to major environmental problems. **26** For example, the mountain pine beetle crisis is something that is happening because of climate change. **27** The beetles used to die out in the winter but since the average winter temperature in North America is no longer as low as it used to be, the beetles are able to survive and thrive all year round. **28** The consequence of this is that a large amount of pine trees face their death each day from Colorado to British Columbia.

29 Places that people inhabit are not the only places affected. **30** The North Pole is also affected by climate change. **31** With all the icebergs melting, the sea level is going to rise. **32** This affects almost the whole world but it's going to affect the less-developed countries the most. **33** If the sea level does rise, many places on earth are going to flood. **34** Developed countries may have solutions to save their country but less-developed countries can't. **35** They don't have the money to research solutions to save their land. **36** What is going to happen when a flood does occur? **37** We would not know for sure until it happens.

38 Human contribution to climate change is great and it is also important that we do something to prevent it. **39** The effects of even a slight change in climate can lead to much bigger consequences.

TASK 10

The following sentences are taken from Sandy's essay on the causes and effects of climate change. Each one effectively describes causality. However, the formality of each sentence could be improved. Rewrite each sentence to make it more formal. Words and phrases that make the style seem informal for academic writing are underlined. If necessary, refer to Appendix 5 for different ways to improve formality in academic writing.

Sent. 11 The gas <u>sticks around</u> the atmosphere and stays there for a <u>really</u> long time.

____

____

____

Sent. 28 The consequence of this is that a large <u>amount</u> of pine trees face their death each day from Colorado to British Columbia.

____

____

____

Sent. 31 With all the icebergs melting, the sea level <u>is going to</u> rise.

Sent. 32 This affects almost the whole world <u>but it's going to</u> affect the less-developed countries the most.

Sent. 36 <u>What is going to happen when a flood does occur</u>?

TASK 11

The following sentences from Sandy's essay describe causality effectively. To practise adding variety to your own descriptions of cause and effect, rewrite each of Sandy's sentences using some of the language of cause and effect that you have studied in this chapter.

Sent. 6 Greenhouse gas is one of the main causes of global warming.

Sent. 12 But cars aren't the only factor in greenhouse gases.

Sent. 13 Factories are also a great contributor to the greenhouse effect.

Sent. 20 For example, when the climate changes, if many plants are not able to adapt to the slight increase or decrease in temperature, they would die.

____

____

____

Sent. 25 Climate change could also lead to major environmental problems.

____

____

____

TASK 12

Select two academic essays you have written and analyze them for effective expression of causality. Follow the stages below.

Stage 1
Read each essay and underline or highlight any language of cause and effect you find.

Stage 2
Try to add variety or make your expression of causality stronger by using the language of causality you have studied in this chapter.

Stage 3
Ask a friend, classmate, or instructor to read the work and comment on the level of improvement.

CHAPTER 10 SUMMARY

The following aspects of writing about causes and effects have been covered in this chapter:

- Understanding causality
- Thinking critically about causality: avoiding generalizations
- Using the language of causality in academic and professional texts
- Organizing an outline for a cause-and-effect essay
- Describing causal relations
- Improving style: formality and effectiveness of expression

These aspects of writing about causes and effects can be applied when you write about causality in many different forms of academic writing, not only cause-and-effect essays.

THINKING CRITICALLY ABOUT CAUSALITY: AVOIDING GENERALIZATIONS

Whenever you analyze the causes and effects of a situation, critical thinking skills are required in order to avoid generalizations. The words you use to describe causality indicate to your reader your opinion and level of knowledge on a subject. It is, therefore, important to write in a way that shows you are not jumping to simple conclusions.

USING THE LANGUAGE OF CAUSALITY IN ACADEMIC AND PROFESSIONAL TEXTS

The two Canadian government articles on climate change showed a variety of ways to write about causal relations. To write effectively about causality, it is necessary to use a broad range of language to describe causes and effects that reflects different time periods and different degrees of certainty.

ORGANIZING AN OUTLINE FOR A CAUSE-AND-EFFECT ESSAY

There are two common ways to organize an outline for a cause-and-effect essay: by looking at causes then effects in separate sections of the essay (*causes-then-effects structure*) or by looking at causes and effects together under relevant themes, or analytic perspectives (*thematic structure*). The answers to the tasks that involved analyzing two outlines suggested that the thematic approach has one particular disadvantage for this type of essay: the thematic structure does not allow the writer to look at all of the causes together and then describe their collective effects in a non-repetitive way. The causes-then-effects approach avoids this problem.

DESCRIBING CAUSAL RELATIONS

Many different ways to describe causes and effects were presented in this chapter and organized as follows: *causes then effects* (where the cause is mentioned before the effect) and *effects then causes* (when the cause is mentioned after the effect). Using a wide variety of language will hold your reader's attention and make your essay more convincing.

IMPROVING STYLE: FORMALITY AND EFFECTIVENESS OF EXPRESSION

The student essay on the causes and effects of climate change effectively expressed a number of causal relations. To practise using more varied language, you rewrote selected sentences. One stylistic aspect of the essay that required improvement was the level of formality of some of the sentences. The exercises that you did raised your awareness of how to keep your writing appropriately formal. More practice activities can be found in Appendix 5.

Appendices

PART

3

APPENDIX 1

MLA Citation Style: In-Text Citations and List of Works Cited

MLA (Modern Language Association) citation style is commonly used in the humanities for subjects such as English and other modern languages, and literary and cultural studies. MLA citation style includes a comprehensive collection of rules and guidelines about how to format academic papers and how to cite the work of others in the text of your essay and in a list of works cited.

The following is a list of some of the most common MLA style conventions that you will need for referencing and citing sources in academic essays.[1] The latest MLA guidelines can be found in the *MLA Handbook for Writers of Research Papers* (7th edition) and the *MLA Style Manual and Guide to Scholarly Publishing* (3rd edition).

MLA IN-TEXT CITATIONS

MLA citation style requires the use of *in-text citations* that correspond with a *list of works cited* organized in alphabetical order at the end of the essay. MLA style requires parenthetical citations that usually include the author's surname and/or page number(s), with no comma between the two. The following list presents some of the most common formats for MLA in-text citations.

- **Including the author's name in the citation phrase**

  If the author's name is included in the citation phrase, do not repeat it in parentheses.

  > **EXAMPLE**
  > Walsh has suggested that annotation while reading may help readers to internalize information (27).

[1] The examples of in-text citations are not based on real sources; they have been created to illustrate the different formats. The examples of works cited are based on real sources.

- **Not including the author's name in the citation phrase**

  If the author's name is not included in the citation phrase, include it in parentheses.

> **EXAMPLE**
> It has been argued that annotating a text while reading can help readers to internalize information (Walsh 27).

- **Citing a work with two or more authors**

  If there are two authors, separate the surnames with *and*.

> **EXAMPLES (two authors)**
> Walsh and Giggs argue that annotation while reading can help readers to internalize information (45).
>
> It has been argued that annotation while reading can help readers to internalize information (Walsh and Giggs 45).

If there are three authors, separate the surnames with commas and add *and* before the final surname.

> **EXAMPLES (three authors)**
> Walsh, Giggs, and Anderson argue that annotation while reading can help readers to internalize information (14).
>
> It has been argued that annotation while reading can help readers to internalize information (Walsh, Giggs, and Anderson 14).

If there are more than three authors, cite the surname of the first author followed by *et al.* or list all of the authors.

> **EXAMPLES (more than three authors)**
> Meech et al. suggest that passive reading is the primary cause of misunderstanding or misapplying ideas in academic writing (36).
>
> It has been suggested that passive reading is the primary cause of misunderstanding or misapplying ideas in academic writing (Meech et al. 36).
>
> It has been suggested that passive reading is the primary cause of misunderstanding or misapplying ideas in academic writing (Meech, Redfern, Nolan, and Izumi 36).

- **Citing a work with no author**

  If you are citing a work with no author, cite the title of the work, or a shortened version of it, in parentheses. Use quotation marks for short works such as journal articles and italics for longer works such as books.

> **EXAMPLE (journal article)**
> The origin of many problems that students face with referencing, citation, and plagiarism can be found in poor annotation skills ("How to Read Actively" 175).

Although there is no author stated, the reader can use this information to find the full reference in the list of works cited. Note that the title of the full reference in the list of works cited must begin with the same words used in the in-text citation, which in the above case is "How to Read Actively."

- **Citing more than one work by the same author**

  If you are writing a sentence or paragraph in which you cite more than one work by the same author, include the name of the work in parentheses to make it clear which work you are citing.

EXAMPLE (author's name included in the citation phrase)
Although Walsh originally suggested that annotation while reading may help readers to internalize information ("Active Reading Strategies" 27, 51), he later highlighted the need for more research on the topic ("Reading for Research" 251).

EXAMPLE (author's name not included in the citation phrase)
Although it has been argued that annotation while reading can help readers to internalize information (Walsh, "Active Reading Strategies" 7, 51), there is still room for further research in the area (Walsh, "Reading for Research" 251).

- **Citing more than one author at the same time**

If you present ideas that originate in more than one work, cite each work in parentheses, separated by a semicolon.

EXAMPLE
It is now recognized that annotation while reading plays a key role in helping readers to internalize information (Walsh 27; Giggs 32).

- **Citing secondary sources**

If you are citing a work you have read in another author's work, rather than in the original, add *qtd. in* to your in-text citation.

EXAMPLE
Smith suggests that visual learners benefit greatly from multi-modal teaching approaches (qtd. in Larson 22).

- **Using direct quotations of fewer than four lines**

Enclose direct quotations of fewer than four lines in quotation marks. Ensure that punctuation, for example, a question mark, in the original text appears before the closing quotation mark. If you add punctuation, such as a question mark, to the sentence, place the punctuation after the closing parenthesis.

EXAMPLE
According to Walsh and Giggs, annotation is "the cognitive link between active and passive reading practices" (35).

EXAMPLE (with original punctuation before the closing quotation marks)
Walsh and Giggs pose the following question: "Is there a cognitive link between active and passive reading practices?" (40).

EXAMPLE (with added punctuation after the closing parenthesis)
Should we accept, therefore, the view of Walsh and Giggs that "there is a cognitive link between active and passive reading practices" (40)?

- **Using direct quotations of more than four lines**

If the quotation is longer than four lines, do not enclose it in quotation marks. Instead, drop one line and indent the quotation by 2.5 cm (1 inch) from the left margin. Note that with long quotations, the in-text citation follows the punctuation at the end of the quotation.

EXAMPLE
Walsh and Giggs stress the important cognitive and organizational roles of annotation in academic reading and writing as follows:

> One of the key active learning skills for successful academic reading and writing is annotation. Firstly, annotation makes passive reading more active through the reader taking parallel notes in the

> margin of the text. These notes can be key words, questions, or opinions that will be used later in the writing stage. Moreover, the process of writing down information that has just been read, and related ideas, was found in our study to increase long-term memory in most students. (Walsh and Giggs 35)

- **Adding words to quotations**

  Sometimes, to make a quotation clearer for readers, it is advisable to add a word or phrase that was not in the original quotation. In such cases, set off the added words in brackets.

  > EXAMPLE
  > With reference to acquiring academic knowledge through active reading, Sykes states the following: "The [long-term] memory benefits most from internalizing academic concepts" (36).

- **Omitting words from quotations**

  It is common for a writer to omit some words from a quotation, especially if he or she wants to keep the focus on one or two key ideas. MLA citation style requires that three spaced periods (. . .) be inserted where text is omitted.

  > EXAMPLE
  > With reference to acquiring academic knowledge through active reading, Sykes states the following: "The [long-term] memory benefits most from internalizing academic concepts . . . and thus from learning strategies that facilitate acquisition" (36).

- **Citing an idea that appears on more than one consecutive page in the original work**

  If you are presenting information that appears on more than one consecutive page in the work you are citing, separate the beginning and end page numbers with a hyphen.

  > EXAMPLE
  > Walsh has suggested that annotation while reading may, in fact, help readers to internalize information (27-32).

- **Citing an idea that appears in more than one place in the original work**

  If you are citing information that appears in more than one place in the source you are using, include the different page numbers and separate them with a comma.

  > EXAMPLE
  > Walsh has suggested that annotation while reading may, in fact, help readers to internalize information (27, 51).

- **Citing online sources**

  When citing an online source with an identifiable author, cite the author's name. The author's name that you cite in the in-text citation should be the same name used in the full reference in the list of works cited.

  If the online source has no identifiable author, cite the title of the article.

  If the online source does not have an author or title, cite the website's domain name, for example, *CBC.ca*.

  Most information on websites has no page numbers. If the online source being cited includes paragraph numbers, as is sometimes the case, then include the relevant paragraph number(s) in the in-text citation preceded by *par.* or *pars.*

EXAMPLE (with author)
Climate change skeptics argue that there are also many non-anthropogenic causes of global warming (Murray).

EXAMPLE (without author, by article title)
Climate change skeptics argue that there are also many non-anthropogenic causes of global warming ("Climate Change: Fact and Fiction").

EXAMPLE (without author, by website domain name)
Climate change skeptics argue that there are also many non-anthropogenic causes of global warming (Climatedebate.org).

EXAMPLES (with numbered paragraphs)
According to Walsh and Giggs, annotation is "the cognitive link between active and passive reading practices" (par. 3).

According to Walsh and Giggs, annotation is "the cognitive link between active and passive reading practices" (pars. 3-6).

MLA LIST OF WORKS CITED

A full reference for every idea you cite parenthetically in your paper must be included in the list of works cited at the end of your essay. MLA style requires that the medium of publication be stated at the end of each entry in the list of works cited (e.g., *Print*, *Web*, or *Film*). The following list presents some of the more common formats for entries in a list of works cited in MLA style.

The List of Works Cited Format

The list of works cited should start on a separate page at the end of an essay, with the term *Works Cited* (each word capitalized) centred at the top of the page in normal font (no italics or boldface). Entries in the list should be double-spaced. Each entry begins at the left margin, and subsequent lines are indented five spaces (1/2 inch) from the left margin. Entries are listed alphabetically by author surname, or by document title if there is no author.

Books

- **A book with one author**

  Surname, Name. *Title*. Place of publication: Publisher, year. Medium of publication.

  EXAMPLE
  Aitchison, Jean. *The Articulate Mammal: An Introduction to Psycholinguistics.* London: Unwin Hyman, 1989. Print.

- **A book with two authors**

  Surname, Name, and Name Surname. *Title*. Place of publication: Publisher, year. Medium of publication.

  EXAMPLE
  Lave, Jean, and Etienne Wenger. *Situated Learning: Legitimate Peripheral Participation.* Cambridge: Cambridge UP, 1991. Print.

- **A book with three or more authors**

  Surname, Name, Name Surname, and Name Surname. *Title*. Place of publication: Publisher, year. Medium of publication.

EXAMPLE (three authors)
Kalra, Virinder, Raminder Kaur, and John Hutnyk. *Diaspora and Hybridity.* London: Sage, 2005. Print.

EXAMPLE (more than three authors)
Roberts, Celia, Michael Byram, Ana Barro, Shirley Jordan, and Brian Street. *Language Learners as Ethnographers.* Clevedon: Multilingual Matters, 2001. Print.

or

Roberts, Celia, et al. *Language Learners as Ethnographers.* Clevedon: Multilingual Matters, 2001. Print.

- **More than one book by the same author**

  If you are citing more than one book by the same author, list the author's books in alphabetical order. The first entry follows the format for books described above. For subsequent entries, replace the author's name with three hyphens (---) followed by a period. When listing works alphabetically by the same author, disregard words like *a, an,* and *the.*

  Surname, Name. *Title.* Place of publication: Publisher, year. Medium of publication.

  ---. *Title.* Place of publication: Publisher, year. Medium of publication.

  EXAMPLE
  Edwards, John. *Language, Society and Identity.* Oxford: Blackwell, 1985. Print.

  ---. *Multilingualism.* London: Routledge, 1994. Print.

- **A book published by an organization or a corporation**

  Some books are published by organizations or corporations under their name. In such cases, the name of the organization or corporation is considered to be the author's name.

  Organization or corporation name. *Title.* Place of publication: Publisher, year. Medium of publication.

  EXAMPLE
  United Nations. *Human Development Report 2009:* Overcoming Barriers—*Human Mobility and Development.* New York: United Nations Development Programme, 2009. Web.

- **A book without an author**

  If you are citing a book that does not have a stated author, place the title of the book in the position of the author.

  Title. Place of publication: Publisher, year. Medium of publication.

  EXAMPLE
  2010 Encyclopedia Britannica World Atlas. London: Encyclopedia Britannica Editorial, 2010. Print.

- **A chapter in a book of collected works**

  If the entry is for a chapter in an edited book of collected works, cite the chapter first and the book second, as follows:

  Surname, Name "Title of Chapter." *Title of Book.* Ed. Editor's Name(s). Place of publication: Publisher, year. Page numbers. Medium of publication.

EXAMPLE

Zentella, Ana C. "Spanish in New York." *The Multilingual Apple: Languages in New York City*. Ed. Ofelia García and Joshua A. Fishman. Berlin: Mouton de Gruyter, 1997. 176-201. Print.

Articles in Journals, Magazines, and Newspapers

- **An article in a scholarly journal**

Surname, Name. "Title of Article." *Title of Journal* volume number and/or issue number [e.g., 16.6] (year): page number(s). Medium of publication.

EXAMPLE

Bourdieu, Pierre. "The Economics of Linguistics Exchanges." *Social Science Information* 16.6 (1977): 645-68. Print.

Note: The *MLA Handbook* (7th edition) stipulates that the article *the* be omitted from the start of the title of an English-language journal, but retained at the start of the title of a non-English-language journal.

- **An article in a magazine**

Surname, Name. "Title of Article." *Title of Magazine* day month year: page number(s). Medium of publication.

EXAMPLE

Kantrowitz, Barbara. "Men, Women, and Computers." *Newsweek* 16 May 1994: 48–55. Web.

- **An article in a newspaper**

Surname, Name. "Title of Article." *Title of Newspaper* day month year: page number(s). Medium of publication.

EXAMPLE

Watt, Nicholas, and Polly Curtis. "David Cameron Prepares for Hung Parliament as Lead Narrows." *Guardian* 26 Feb. 2010: 1. Print.

Web Publications

It is no longer necessary to provide a URL when listing electronic sources in an MLA list of works cited. It is assumed that a reader will be able to locate the original source with the information provided. However, some instructors may require a full URL. If so, add the full URL inside angled brackets after the access date at the end of the entry. Two common abbreviations are used when listing web publications: *n.p.* when no name is available for the publisher, and *n.d.* when no date is available.

The style guidelines for citing electronic sources change frequently. The following is a list of some of the more common forms of electronic citations that are used in academic research essays.

- **A website**

If you are citing a website in your list of works cited, and the website has an author, begin the full reference with the author's name.

Surname, Name. *Title of Site*. Sponsor or publisher, date of publication (if available). Medium of publication. Access date.

EXAMPLE (with an author)
Chomsky, Noam. *Chomsky.info: The Noam Chomsky Website.* n.p., n.d. Web. 12 Jan. 2010.

If there is no author, start with the title of the site.

Title of Site. Sponsor or publisher, date of publication (if available). Medium of publication. Access date.

EXAMPLE (without an author)
Simon Fraser University Student Learning Commons. Simon Fraser University, n.d. Web. 11 Feb. 2010.

- **A page on a website**

Surname, Name. "Title of Document." *Title of Site.* Sponsor or publisher, date of publication (if available). Medium of publication. Access date.

EXAMPLE (with an author)
Takaro, Tim, and Carol Thorbes. "Childhood Leukemia Increases in Iraq." *Simon Fraser University Website.* Simon Fraser University Public Affairs and Media Relations, 18 Feb. 2010. Web. 23 Feb. 2010.

EXAMPLE (with an author and full URL [as requested by instructor])
Wolfspirit, Darcy. "Writing for University." *Simon Fraser University Website.* Simon Fraser University Student Learning Commons, 19 Aug. 2009. Web. 11 Feb. 2010. <http://learningcommons.sfu.ca/strategies/writing>.

If there is no author, start the entry with the title of the page or article.

EXAMPLE (without an author)
"Thinking About SFU?" *Simon Fraser University Website.* SFU, n.d. Web. 23 Feb. 2010.

- **An article from an online academic journal**

Some academic journals are published only online and may not follow the same pagination formats as print journals. If an article has no pagination, use the term *n. pag.* in the position of the page number(s).

Surname, Name. "Title of Article." *Title of Journal* volume number and/or issue number (year): page number(s). Medium of publication. Access date.

EXAMPLE
Scott, Charles. "Hanging Out: One of the High Arts of Dialogue." *SFU Educational Review* 1.2 (2009): n. pag. Web. 20 Feb. 2010.

- **An article from an online database**

If you are citing an article that you read via an online database, include the name of the database in italics.

Surname, Name. "Title of Article." *Title of Journal* volume number and/or issue number (year): page number(s). *Name of database.* Medium of publication. Access date.

EXAMPLE

Lee, Ena, and Andrea Simon-Maeda. "Racialized Research Identities in ESL/EFL Research." *TESOL Quarterly* 40.3 (2006): 573-94. *ERIC-EBSCO*. Web. 20 Feb. 2010.

- **Email correspondence**

Surname, Name. "Subject Line." Description of message [including recipient's name]. Date of message. Medium of delivery.

EXAMPLE

Ngyen, Shirley. "First Year Academic Literacy?" Message to Joe Bloggs. 20 Dec. 2009. E-mail.

This appendix has provided some common formats for MLA in-text citations and works cited entries. For types of sources not included here, consult the *MLA Handbook* (7th edition) or an online source that is reliable and up-to-date, perhaps from a university library.

APPENDIX 2

APA Citation Style: In-Text Citations and Reference List

APA (American Psychological Association) citation style is commonly used in many social science subjects. The following is a list of some of the most common APA style conventions you will need for referencing and citing sources in academic essays.[1] The latest APA guidelines can be found in the *Publication Manual of the American Psychological Association* (6th edition).

APA IN-TEXT CITATIONS

APA citation style requires *in-text citations* that correspond exactly with a *reference list* organized in alphabetical order at the end of the essay. APA in-text citations usually include the author's surname and year of publication with a comma between the two. Page numbers are included for direct quotations and are separated from the year of publication by a comma and the letter *p* and a period (p.). The latest edition of the *APA Manual* also recommends the inclusion of page numbers for paraphrased information.

The following list presents APA versions of the in-text citations presented in MLA citation style in Appendix 1, where possible.

- **Including the author's name in the citation phrase**

  If the author's name is included in the citation phrase, do not repeat it in parentheses.

  > **EXAMPLE**
  > Walsh (2007) has suggested that annotation while reading may help readers to internalize information (p. 27).

- **Not including the author's name in the citation phrase**

  If the author's name is not included in the citation phrase, include it in parentheses.

[1]The examples of in-text citations are not based on real sources; they have been created to illustrate the different formats. The reference list examples are based on real sources.

EXAMPLE
It has been argued that annotating a text while reading can help readers to internalize information (Walsh, 2007, p. 27).

- **Citing a work with two or more authors**

If there are two authors, separate the surnames with *and* in the citation phrase, and with an ampersand (&) in parentheses.

EXAMPLES (two authors)
Walsh and Giggs (2007) argue that annotation while reading can help readers to internalize information (p. 45).

It has been argued that annotation while reading can help readers to internalize information (Walsh & Giggs, 2007, p. 45).

If there are three to five authors, list all authors in the citation phrase or in parentheses when first cited. Thereafter, cite only the first author's surname followed by *et al.* in the citation phrase or in parentheses.

EXAMPLES (three to five authors: first citation)
Walsh, Giggs, and Anderson (2008) argue that annotation while reading can help readers to internalize information (p. 14).

It has been argued that annotation while reading can help readers to internalize information (Walsh, Giggs, & Anderson, 2008, p. 14).

EXAMPLE (three to five authors: following first citation)
Walsh et al. (2008) go on to define what they mean by internalization in literacy contexts.

If there are six or more authors, use *et al.* in the citation phrase or in parentheses in all citations.

EXAMPLE (six or more authors)
Gonzalez et al. (2001) studied three groups of university students.

- **Citing a work with no author**

If you are citing a work with no authors, cite the title of the work in the citation phrase, or a shortened version of it in parentheses. Use quotation marks for short works such as journal articles and italics for longer works such as books.

EXAMPLE (journal article)
The origin of many problems that students face with referencing, citation, and plagiarism can be found in poor annotation skills ("How to read actively," 2006, p. 175).

The full reference in the reference list must begin with the same words used in the in-text citation, which in the above case is "How to read actively."

- **Citing more than one work by the same author from different years**

If you present ideas that originate in more than one work by the same author published in different years, include the author's surname and the year of each work in parentheses, with the years separated by a comma.

EXAMPLE
It is now recognized that annotation while reading plays a key role in helping readers to internalize information (Walsh, 2006, 2008).

- **Citing more than one work by the same author from the same year**

If you present ideas that originate in more than one work by the same author published in the same year, use the letters *a*, *b*, *c*, etc. after the year. The letters are determined in the reference list, in which works by the same author are ordered by title.

> **EXAMPLE**
> It is now recognized that annotation while reading plays a key role in helping readers to internalize information (Walsh, 2006b, p. 27).

- **Citing more than one author at the same time**

If you present ideas that originate in the work of more than one author, cite each work in parentheses, separated by a semicolon. Cite works alphabetically by the first author's surname.

> **EXAMPLE**
> It is now recognized that annotation while reading plays a key role in helping readers to internalize information (Giggs, 2002, p. 32; Walsh, 2006, p. 27).

- **Citing secondary sources**

If you are citing a work you have read in another author's work rather than in the original, include the name of the original author in your citation phrase and add the citation for the secondary source in parentheses with the words *as cited in*.

> **EXAMPLE**
> Smith suggests that visual learners benefit greatly from multi-modal teaching approaches (as cited in Larson, 1982, p. 22).

- **Using direct quotations of fewer than 40 words**

Enclose direct quotations of fewer than 40 words in quotation marks, with the author's surname, year of publication, and page number(s) in parentheses. Ensure that punctuation, for example, a question mark, in the original text appears before the closing quotation marks. If you add punctuation, such as a question mark, to the sentence, place the punctuation after the closing parenthesis.

> **EXAMPLE (with names in citation phrase)**
> According to Walsh and Giggs (2006), annotation is "the cognitive link between active and passive reading practices" (p. 35).
>
> **EXAMPLE (without names in citation phrase)**
> Annotation has been described as "the cognitive link between active and passive reading practices" (Walsh & Giggs, 2006, p. 35).
>
> **EXAMPLE (with original punctuation before the closing quotation marks)**
> Walsh and Giggs (2006) pose the following question: "Is there a cognitive link between active and passive reading practices?" (p. 40).
>
> **EXAMPLE (with added punctuation after the closing parenthesis)**
> Should we accept, therefore, the view of Walsh and Giggs (2006) that "there is a cognitive link between active and passive reading practices" (p. 40)?

- **Using direct quotations of more than 40 words**

If the quotation is more than 40 words, do not enclose it in quotation marks. Instead, drop one line and indent the quotation five spaces (1/2 inch) from the left margin. Note that with long quotations, the in-text citation follows the punctuation at the end of the quotation.

EXAMPLE

The important cognitive and organizational roles of annotation in academic reading and writing have been described as follows:

> One of the key active learning skills for successful academic reading and writing is annotation. Firstly, annotation makes passive reading more active through the reader taking parallel notes in the margin of the text. These notes can be key words, questions, or opinions that will be used later in the writing stage. Moreover, the process of writing down information that has just been read, and related ideas, was found in our study to increase long-term memory in most students. (Walsh & Giggs, 2006, p. 35)

- **Adding words to quotations**

  If, to enhance clarity, you add a word or phrase that was not in the original quotation, set off the added words in brackets.

EXAMPLE

With reference to acquiring academic knowledge through active reading, Sykes (1996) states the following: "The [long-term] memory benefits most from internalizing academic concepts" (p. 36).

- **Omitting words from quotations**

  APA citation style requires that three spaced periods (. . .) be inserted where text is omitted.

EXAMPLE

With reference to acquiring academic knowledge through active reading, Sykes (1996) states the following: "The [long-term] memory benefits most from internalizing academic concepts . . . and thus from learning strategies that facilitate acquisition" (p. 36).

- **Citing an idea that appears on more than one consecutive page in the original work**

  If you are presenting information that appears on more than one consecutive page in the work you are citing, use *pp.* and separate the beginning and end page numbers with an en dash.

EXAMPLE

Walsh (2008) has suggested that annotation while reading may, in fact, help readers to internalize information (pp. 27–32).

- **Citing an idea that appears in more than one place in the original work**

  If you are citing information that appears in more than one place in the source you are using, include the different page numbers and separate them with a comma.

EXAMPLE

Walsh (2008) has suggested that annotation while reading may, in fact, help readers to internalize information (pp. 27, 51).

- **Citing online sources**

When citing an online source with an identifiable author, cite the author's name and the year of publication, as you would a fixed source. The author's name that you cite in the in-text citation should be the same name used in the full reference in the reference list.

If the online source has no identifiable author, cite the title of the article and the year of publication.

If the year of publication does not appear in the source, write *n.d.* (no date) in the citation.

If the online source does not have an author or title, cite the website address in parentheses. No reference list entry is necessary for this type of citation.

Most information on websites has no page numbers. If the online source being cited includes paragraph numbers, as is sometimes the case, then include the relevant paragraph number(s) in the in-text citation, preceded by *para*.

EXAMPLE (with author)
Climate change skeptics argue that there are also many non-anthropogenic causes of global warming (Murray, 2007).

EXAMPLE (without author, by article title)
Climate change skeptics argue that there are also many non-anthropogenic causes of global warming ("Climate change: Fact and fiction," 2008).

EXAMPLE (without a date)
Climate change skeptics argue that there are also many non-anthropogenic causes of global warming ("Climate change: Our future," n.d.).

EXAMPLE (without author, by website name)
Climate change skeptics argue that there are also many anthropogenic causes of global warming (http://climatedebate.org).

EXAMPLE (with numbered paragraphs)
According to Walsh and Giggs (2006), annotation is "the cognitive link between active and passive reading practices" (para. 3).

APA REFERENCE LIST

APA style guidelines stipulate that a reference list should appear at the end of an essay and should include a full reference for each in-text citation. The following list presents some of the more common formats for reference list entries in APA style.

The Reference List Format

The reference list should start on a separate page at the end of an essay, with the term *References* centred at the top of the page. Entries in the list should be double-spaced. Each entry begins at the left margin, and subsequent lines are indented a 1/2 inch from the left margin. Entries are listed alphabetically by author surname or by document title if there is no author.

Books

- **A book with one author**

Surname, Initial. (year). *Title.* Place of publication: Publisher.

> **EXAMPLE**
> Aitchison, J. (1989). *The articulate mammal: An introduction to psycholinguistics.* London, England: Unwin Hyman.

- **A book with two authors**

Surname, Initial., & Surname, Initial. (year). *Title.* Place of publication: Publisher.

> **EXAMPLE**
> Lave, J., & Wenger, E. (1991). *Situated learning: Legitimate peripheral participation.* Cambridge, England: Cambridge University Press.

- **A book with three to seven authors**

Surname, Initial., Surname, Initial., & Surname, Initial. (year). *Title.* Place of publication: Publisher.

> **EXAMPLE (three to seven authors)**
> Kalra, V., Kaur, R., & Hutnyk, J. (2005). *Diaspora and hybridity.* London, England: Sage.

- **A book with eight or more authors**

If you are citing a book with eight or more authors, list the first six authors' names, add three spaced periods, then list the last author's name.

> **EXAMPLE (eight or more authors)**
> Wasserstein, R., Zappulla J., Rosen E., Gerstman B., Guimard, P., Schutte, N. S., . . . Rock, S. (1994). *Social learning theory.* Englewood Cliffs, NJ: Prentice Hall.

- **More than one book by the same author**

If you are citing more than one book by the same author, list the author's books by year, with the earliest year first. Entries with one author are listed before those with multiple authors that begin with the same surname.

> **EXAMPLE**
> Edwards, J. (1985). *Language, society and identity.* Oxford, England: Blackwell.
>
> Edwards, J. (1994). *Multilingualism.* London, England: Routledge.

If two or more works are published by the same author(s) in the same year, order the works alphabetically by title and add letters (*a*, *b*, *c*, etc.) after the year to differentiate among them.

> **EXAMPLES**
> Edwards, J. (1994a). Ethnolinguistic pluralism and its discontents: A Canadian study, and some general observations. *International Journal of the Sociology of Language, 110*, 5–85.
>
> Edwards, J. (1994b). *Multilingualism.* London, England: Routledge.

- **A book published by an organization or a corporation**

Some books are published by organizations or corporations. In such cases, the name of the organization or corporation is considered to be the author's name.

Organization or corporation name. (year). *Title.* Place of publication: Publisher.

EXAMPLE
United Nations. (2009). *Human development report 2009: Overcoming barriers—human mobility and development.* New York, NY: United Nations Development Programme.

- **A book without an author**

If you are citing a book that does not have a stated author, place the title of the book in the position of the author.

Title. (year). Place of publication: Publisher.

EXAMPLE
2010 Encyclopedia Britannica world atlas. (2010). London, England: Encyclopedia Britannica Editorial.

- **A chapter in a book of collected works**

If the entry is for a chapter in an edited book of collected works, cite the chapter first and the book second as follows:

Surname, Initial. (year). Title of chapter. In Initial. Surname(s) (Ed[s].) *Title of book* (pp. [page numbers]). Place of publication: Publisher.

EXAMPLE
Zentella, A. C. (1997). Spanish in New York. In O. García & J. A. Fishman (Eds.), *The multilingual apple: Languages in New York City* (pp. 176–201). Berlin, Germany: Mouton de Gruyter.

Articles in Journals, Magazines, and Newspapers

- **An article in a scholarly journal**

Surname, Initial. (year). Title of article. *Title of Journal, volume number*(issue number), page number(s).

EXAMPLE
Bourdieu, P. (1977). The economics of linguistic exchanges. *Social Science Information, 16*(6), 645–668.

- **An article in a magazine**

Surname, Initial. (year, month day). Title of article. *Title of Magazine, volume number* (issue number), page number(s).

EXAMPLE
Kantrowitz, B. (1994, May 16). Men, women, and computers. *Newsweek, 123*(20), 48–55.

- **An article in a newspaper**

Surname, Initial. (year, month day). Title of article. *Title of Newspaper,* p. (page number) or pp. (page numbers).

EXAMPLE
Watt, N., & Curtis, P. (2010, February 26). David Cameron prepares for hung parliament as lead narrows. *Guardian*, p. 1.

Web Publications

APA citation style requires that a full URL be included in electronic sources in the reference list (for an exception, see "An article from an online academic journal" below). A retrieval date should be added to the citation only if the source is likely to change over time, as with a wiki.

The style guidelines for citing electronic sources change frequently. The following is a list of some of the more common forms of electronic citations that are used in academic research essays.

- **A website**

  If you have cited an entire website (rather than a webpage or online article) in your text, there is no need to add an entry for the website to the reference list.

- **A page on a website**

  Surname, Initial. (year, month day). *Title of document.* Retrieved from URL

  EXAMPLE (with an author)
  Takaro, T., & Thorbes, C. (2010, February 18). *Childhood leukemia increases in Iraq.* Retrieved from http://www.sfu.ca/pamr/media_releases/media_releases_archives/media_02181001.html

  If there is no author, start the entry with the title of the page or article.

  EXAMPLE (without an author)
  Thinking about SFU? (n.d.). Retrieved from http://www.sfu.ca

- **An article from an online academic journal**

  If the article you are citing has a digital object identifier (DOI)—"doi:xxxxxxx"—then cite it instead of the article's URL (no additional retrieval information is needed).

  Surname, Initial. (year). Title of article. *Title of Journal, volume number* (issue number), page numbers. doi:xxxxxxx

  EXAMPLE (with DOI)
  Howard, K. M. (2010). Social relationships and shifting languages in Northern Thailand. *Journal of Sociolinguistics, 14*(3), 313–340. doi:10.1111/j.1467-9841.2010.00445.x

  EXAMPLE (without DOI)
  Scott, C. (2009). Hanging out: One of the high arts of dialogue. *SFU Educational Review, 1.* Retrieved from http://journals.sfu.ca/sfuer/index.php/sfuer/article/viewFile/50/66

- **An article from an online database**

  If you are citing an article that you found via an online database, it is not necessary to include the database name in your reference because access to journals in databases can change over time. Instead, cite the article as you would an online academic journal.

- **Email correspondence**

  Email correspondence, like other personal communications, is not included in the reference list. It is necessary to cite it only in an in-text citation, as below.

  > EXAMPLE
  > (S. Ngyen, personal communication, December 20, 2009)

This appendix has provided some common formats for APA in-text citations and reference list entries. For types of sources not included here, consult the *APA Manual* (6th edition) or an online source that is reliable and up-to-date, perhaps from a university library.

APPENDIX 3

Common Linking Words in Academic Writing

Linking words provide cohesion to academic writing. They help you connect your ideas and sentences so that your reader can more easily follow your line of thinking. Linking words indicate not only the relationship between ideas and sentences but also any emphasis you want to create. In this section, the focus is on the most common types:

1. Coordinating linking words
2. Subordinating linking words
3. Conjunctive adverbs
4. Correlative conjunctions
5. Additional transitional words and phrases

1. COORDINATING LINKING WORDS

Coordinating linking words (coordinators) are most commonly used to link two independent clauses. In this way, they form compound sentences. Compound sentences are most effective when each independent clause contains equal ideas. The easiest way to remember the seven coordinating linking words is by thinking of the acronym FANBOYS.

FANBOYS Coordinators

for
For is the least common of the coordinators in academic writing, as it has a somewhat literary or poetic style. As a coordinating linking word, it has the same meaning as *because*, for cause and effect.
EXAMPLE: The college basketball team members were happy to reach the final, **for** they had trained hard all year.

and
And is probably the most common coordinating linking word, used to add information or examples.
EXAMPLE: The coach adopted an attacking style, **and** the team won 30 games in total.
nor
Nor has the same coordinating role as *and*, but it is used to indicate a negative relationship between ideas.
EXAMPLE: The team did not lose a single game before the final, **nor*** did the fans give up supporting them. *Note: If *nor* is followed by an independent clause, the order of the subject and verb changes to that of question structure.
but
But is used to join ideas that are being contrasted.
EXAMPLE: Preparation for the final was going well, **but** the team's star player got injured the day before the game.
or
Or is used to join two or more options or possibilities.
EXAMPLE: The coach wasn't sure if the injury was serious **or** if the player would be fit for the next game.
yet
Yet has a similar meaning to *but*. It provides a stronger idea of contrast than *but*, sometimes with an idea of unexpectedness.
EXAMPLE: The team doctor advised him not to play, **yet** he decided to take the risk.
so
So is used to join together ideas when there is a cause and effect.
EXAMPLE: The coach knew the importance of the game, **so** he let his star player play.

2. SUBORDINATING LINKING WORDS

When you introduce a clause with a subordinating linking word (subordinator), the clause becomes dependent. When you join a dependent and an independent clause, they form a complex sentence. Complex sentences are most effective when the idea in one clause, usually the independent clause, carries more emphasis than the idea in the other. Subordinators are most commonly used to introduce a sentence.

> **EXAMPLE**
> **Even though** she didn't study very hard, *Tara got an A for the course.*
>
> **subordinator** → Even though; dependent clause → she didn't study very hard; comma → ,; *independent clause* → Tara got an A for the course.

In the example above, the main emphasis of the complex sentence is that Tara got an A for the course. The subordinator guides the reader by indicating that the independent clause that follows will contain the main focus.

It is also possible to place the dependent clause second, as follows:

> **EXAMPLE**
> *Tara got an A for the course* **even though** she didn't study very hard.
>
> *independent clause* → Tara got an A for the course; **subordinator** → even though; dependent clause → she didn't study very hard.

In the preceding example, there is no comma between the clauses as the dependent clause comes after the independent clause.

Subordinators That Express Contrast

although, even though, while, whereas	
Even though can be used to emphasize more contrast than ***although***.	
EXAMPLES:	They invited 80 guests to the wedding **although** no one was sure how they could afford it. They had decided to get married **even though** he was 20 years her senior.
While and ***whereas*** are usually used when comparing opposites. ***Whilst*** is often used in British English.	
EXAMPLES:	He was quiet and introverted **whereas** she was more outgoing and extroverted. **While** he came from a very wealthy family, she came from a more modest background.

Subordinators That Express Time Relations

before, after, until, as soon as, as long as, when, while	
EXAMPLES:	**Before** the ceremony began, the guests waited in a lounge in the hotel. **After** waiting half an hour, they were invited to watch the ceremony. It didn't start **until** everyone was seated. **As soon as** the couple arrived, everyone got to their feet. The guests stayed on their feet **as long as** the music played. **When** the ceremony was finished, the guests moved on to the banquet hall. **While** the guests were taking their seats, the newlyweds came into the room.

Subordinators That Express Reason

because, as, since	
EXAMPLES:	We couldn't go fishing **because** the lake was frozen. **As** the roads were icy, we were worried about having an accident. **Since** we had a second car with snow tires, it wasn't such a problem.

Subordinators That Express Condition

if, whether, whether or not, unless	
EXAMPLES:	**If** the central bank raises borrowing rates tomorrow, mortgages will be become less affordable. Analysts are unsure **whether** rates will go up or remain the same. **Whether or not** their forecasts are accurate, analysts are heeded by the central bank. **Unless** the central bank takes action soon, inflation will continue to rise.

Subordinators in Relative Clauses

(see Appendix 7 for more details on defining and non-defining relative clauses)

which, that, who, whose, when, where, why	
Use ***which*** and ***that*** to add information about things.	
EXAMPLES:	The central bank, <u>**which** controls borrowing rates</u>, may raise interest rates tomorrow. [non-defining] Mortgage holders <u>**that** have variable rate mortgages</u> may be the first to be affected. [defining]

Use ***who, that,*** and ***whose*** to add information about people.
EXAMPLES: The central bank chairman, **who** has been in the job for just one year, heads the borrowing rate committee. [non-defining clause] He is the person **who** is in charge of making the final decision. [defining clause] He is the person **that** is in charge of making the final decision. [defining clause] He is the person **whose** decision it is. [defining clause]
Use ***when*** to add time-related information.
EXAMPLE: Borrowers will be informed of any increase in mortgage rates **when** they receive their next statement. [defining clause]
Use ***where*** to add place-related information.
EXAMPLE: The committee meets at a private venue **where** no journalists are allowed. [defining clause]
Use ***why*** to add the idea *the reason why.*
EXAMPLE: Reporters are asking **why** such secrecy is necessary. [defining clause]

3. CONJUNCTIVE ADVERBS

Conjunctive adverbs are linking words that are used to join ideas in or between sentences. The conjunctive adverb you use will give your reader an indication of how you understand the link between ideas (e.g., contrast, cause and effect, etc.). Conjunctive adverbs can be positioned at the beginning, middle, or end of an independent clause.

Conjunctive adverbs can be understood as alternative ways of expressing the ideas ***and***, ***but***, and ***so***.

Different Ways to Say *And* with Conjunctive Adverbs

moreover, furthermore, in addition, additionally, similarly, likewise
Use a conjunctive adverb between two independent clauses.
EXAMPLES: Green tea is a refreshing drink; **moreover**, it contains many healthy antioxidants. Green tea is a refreshing drink. **Furthermore**, it contains many healthy antioxidants.
Use a conjunctive adverb within one independent clause.
EXAMPLE: It is, **in addition/additionally**, becoming increasingly popular in western countries.
Use a conjunctive adverb at the end of one independent clause.
EXAMPLE: It is becoming increasingly popular in western countries, **moreover**.
Use a conjunctive adverb between two independent clauses when ideas or things are similar.
EXAMPLE: Green tea is healthy because it is fat-free; **similarly/likewise**, it contains flavonoids, which are strong antioxidants.

Different Ways to Say *But* with Conjunctive Adverbs

however, still, nevertheless, nonetheless
Use a conjunctive adverb between two independent clauses.
EXAMPLES: Red wine may have several health benefits; **however**, these benefits are lost if it is drunk in excess. Red wine may have several health benefits. **Still**, these benefits are lost if it is drunk in excess.
Use a conjunctive adverb within one independent clause.
EXAMPLE: Many people, **nevertheless/nonetheless**, drink too much.

Use a conjunctive adverb at the end of one independent clause.
EXAMPLE: Many people drink too much, **however**.

Different Ways to Say *So* with Conjunctive Adverbs

thus, consequently, as a result, therefore
Use a conjunctive adverb between two independent clauses.
EXAMPLES: Energy drinks often contain large amounts of caffeine; **thus**, children should not drink them. Energy drinks often contain large amounts of caffeine. **Consequently**, children should not drink them.
Use a conjunctive adverb within one independent clause.
EXAMPLES: Shopkeepers, **as a result**, need to be vigilant when selling energy drinks to children. Shopkeepers need to be vigilant, **therefore**, when selling energy drinks to children.
Use a conjunctive adverb at the end of one independent clause.
EXAMPLE: Shopkeepers need to be vigilant when selling energy drinks to children, **therefore**.

4. CORRELATIVE CONJUNCTIONS

Writers use correlative conjunctions together to describe two or more related ideas in a sentence. Many linking words are used in pairs in academic writing. Here are some of the most common.

Different Ways to Say *And* with Correlative Conjunctions

both + and, not only + (but) also
EXAMPLES: The mayor's response to the flooding was **both** swift **and** efficient. The mayor's response to the flooding was **not only*** swift **but also** efficient. [with adjectives] **Not only** did the mayor respond to the crisis swiftly, she **also** organized the rescue teams efficiently. [with clauses] *Note: *Not only* is a negative adverbial phrase that adds emphasis. When a sentence starts with *not only* (as in the third example), the subject and verb are inverted (taking question form).

Different Ways to Say *One or the Other* with Correlative Conjunctions

either + or, neither + nor
EXAMPLES: Students wanting to take the course should have **either** a B grade average **or** relevant work experience. **Neither** qualified teachers **nor** teaching assistants will be able to take the course.

Different Ways to Express Time Relations with Correlative Conjunctions

no sooner + than, hardly + when
When the following correlative conjunctions start a sentence, the subject and verb are inverted (taking question form).
EXAMPLES: **No sooner** had I started taking notes **than** my computer crashed. **Hardly** had I walked into the library **when** my cell phone started ringing.

5. ADDITIONAL TRANSITIONAL WORDS AND PHRASES

Transitions That Indicate Contrast with the Idea in the Previous Clause

on the other hand, as opposed to, in contrast	
EXAMPLES:	Summers in Toronto are usually hot and humid; **on the other hand**, Vancouver normally has mild summer weather. Summers in Toronto, **as opposed to** those in Vancouver, are usually hot and humid.
In contrast can be followed either by an independent clause or by a noun phrase.	
EXAMPLES:	Summers in Toronto are usually hot and humid; **in contrast**, Vancouver normally has mild summer weather. [independent clause] Life in Toronto seems busy and rushed **in contrast** with the more laid-back lifestyle in Vancouver. [noun phrase]

Transitions That Indicate Restatement or Expansion of the Idea in the Previous Clause

in other words, specifically	
EXAMPLE:	The weather in Vancouver is milder than in Toronto; **in other words**, it is cooler in summer and warmer in winter.
Specifically can be followed either by an independent clause or by a noun phrase.	
EXAMPLES:	The weather in Vancouver can be depressing; **specifically**, it rains too much. [independent clause] The weather in Vancouver can be depressing, **specifically**, the endless rain. [noun phrase]

Transitions That Indicate Contradiction with the Idea in the Previous Clause

on the contrary, instead, rather	
EXAMPLES:	The zero-tolerance policing did not reduce crime; **on the contrary**, most crime rates actually increased. The police had hoped that a fall in crime would save money; **instead**, they had to hire more officers. The public response was not positive; **rather**, community leaders called for a more balanced approach.

Transitions That Exemplify

for example, for instance, namely, such as	
For example, ***for instance***, and ***namely*** can be followed by an independent clause or by a noun phrase.	
EXAMPLES:	Tourists often complain about the food in London; **for example**, many find it expensive and badly prepared. [independent clause] Britain's traditional dishes are often criticized as bland, **for instance**, fish and chips and roast beef. [noun phrase] Fish and chips is high in two unhealthy ingredients, **namely**, salt and fat. [noun phrase]

Such as can be followed only by a noun phrase. A comma precedes *such* as in a non-defining noun clause. However, in a defining noun clause, the comma is omitted (see Appendix 7 for information on defining and non-defining clauses).
EXAMPLES: Multiculturalism has led to the adoption of new dishes, **such as** chicken tikka masala. Dishes **such as** fish and chips are now becoming less popular.

Transitions That Enumerate

first/ly, second/ly, third/ly, next, finally
Whether to use ***first*** or ***firstly*** is a matter of preferred style. Usually, when you give a list of examples or explanations in academic writing, it is better to stop at ***third***.
EXAMPLE: Many doctors will not prescribe homeopathic medicine for several reasons. **First**, most homeopathic remedies have not passed rigorous double-blind control trials to prove their efficacy. **Second**, many doctors are unaware of the range of homeopathic medicines available. **Third/Next**, the traditional scientific training of many doctors may make them feel suspicious of homeopathy. And **finally**, some doctors may have a relationship with certain drug companies, and, consequently, a financial interest in prescribing certain medicines.

APPENDIX 4

Punctuation

Proper punctuation is essential in academic writing. The way you punctuate your writing tells your reader a lot about your abilities as a writer. In addition, punctuation errors in your academic writing can reduce the effectiveness of your description or argument.

In order to become a successful academic writer, you need to learn the rules of punctuation. Some are simple, while others are more complicated. Punctuation rules do allow for some subjectivity, which explains why not all writers follow the same rules. Moreover, English punctuation rules can vary from one style guide to another and from one English-speaking country to another. The rules can vary as well depending on the type of text you are writing (genre), who you are writing for (audience), and your aims and purpose (context). (See Chapter 1 for an explanation of genre, audience, and context.) For example, the punctuation you use in an academic essay will be formal as compared with the punctuation you use in an email to a friend. It is important to keep in mind that whatever punctuation rules you follow must be applied consistently in your document.

TASK 1

Read the two email examples below and think about how they are punctuated. Then answer the questions that follow.

EMAIL 1
Dear Dr. Aziz:
Please could you send me notes for yesterday's class, which I missed.
I was absent due to illness.
Thank you.
Stella

EMAIL 2
Hi there Youssef
Could u send me notes for yesterday's class . . . . I know I missed class again ☹
I felt rotten so I stayed home :(
Thanks a lot and c u next time ;)!!
Stella

1. How does the punctuation in Email 1 differ from that in Email 2?
2. How do you think the reader might react to Email 2?

PUNCTUATION AFFECTS MEANING

In 2003, Lynne Truss published her bestselling book *Eats, Shoots and Leaves.* On the cover, a panda stands on a ladder, painting over the comma in the title. It comes as no surprise that the book is about punctuation and how it can affect meaning.

The title of the book is punctuated in three ways below. Consider the meaning of each sentence.

WITHOUT COMMAS
a) Eats shoots and leaves.

WITH COMMAS
b) Eats, shoots and leaves.
c) Eats, shoots, and leaves.

TASK 2

Answer the following questions.

1. Which sentence(s) could be understood as a general statement about the eating habits of a panda?
2. Which sentence(s) could be understood as a statement about someone who has a meal in a restaurant, then goes hunting before leaving?
3. Why do you think there is an additional comma in sentence c)?

The sentences above show two important things about punctuation. First, the inclusion or omission of a comma can change how a reader will understand a sentence. And second, the sentences show that the rules of punctuation in English can vary.

Commas and Relative Clauses

In Appendix 7, you will learn a rule about using commas in defining and non-defining relative clauses.

In defining relative clauses, the relative clause (underlined in the example below) defines a thing in the independent clause; there is no comma before the relative pronoun (*that* in the example).

EXAMPLE: Defining relative clause
The lab class <u>that I missed last week</u> was on how to write lab reports.

In non-defining relative clauses, the relative clause (underlined in the example below) gives extra information about a thing in the independent clause; a comma always comes before the relative pronoun (*which* in the example).

EXAMPLE: Non-defining relative clause
The lab class, <u>which was really interesting</u>, lasted for three hours.

Remember that the comma has a grammatical function. Its use or absence gives a specific meaning to a sentence by making a relative clause defining or non-defining. Keep in mind that if you forget to add a comma to a non-defining relative clause, your reader will understand it as a defining one.

TASK 3

Look at the two sentences below. Each has a relative clause that is underlined.

> **EXAMPLE 1**
> Last night I met your brother, <u>who is really friendly</u>.
>
> **EXAMPLE 2**
> Last night I met your brother <u>who is really friendly</u>.

1. Which example contains a defining relative clause and which contains a non-defining relative clause?
2. What is the difference in meaning between the two sentences? Remember that if the relative clause is defining, it is defining *which brother*.

SELECTED PUNCTUATION RULES

What follows are punctuation rules that tend to be problematic for academic writers.

Commas

Commas are used to set off information at the beginning, middle, or end of an independent clause. These commas can be called *beginning commas*, *middle commas*, and *end commas*.

Commas are also used before coordinating linking words (e.g., and, but, so). These commas can be called *coordinator commas*.

Beginning Commas

Use a comma to set off an introductory phrase, a linking word, or a dependent clause that introduces an independent clause.

1. **Time conjunctions**
   Earlier, the police had asked for the public to be vigilant.
   Next, they asked for witnesses to come forward.

2. **Time phrases**
   When the second half of the twentieth century arrived, late modernity changed western societies.
   When the Berlin Wall came down, Germany was once again united as one country.

3. **Prepositional phrases**
   With 55 percent of the electorate supporting her, the new prime minister took on trade union reform.
   Inside the leader's inner circle, there were few women.

4. **Adverbial conjunctions**
   Therefore, I believe that taxes on high income earners should be increased.
   However, a top income tax rate of 50 percent is likely to lead to greater tax avoidance.

5. **Dependent clauses**
   Because I spent three years in Mexico, I have witnessed first-hand the country's rich cultural diversity.
   Although Mexicans have a strong sense of national identity, many migrate north for economic reasons.

Middle Commas

Use commas to set off extra information (e.g., an extra linking word or non-defining relative clause) in the middle of an independent clause.

1. **Adverbial conjunctions**
   The reason for the 1 percent increase in interest rates**, however,** was to stop inflation.
   Borrowing rates for most mortgages**, therefore,** were raised by 1 percent the same day.
2. **Non-defining relative clauses**
   The Rubik's Cube**, which was invented by the Hungarian professor Erno Rubik,** is one of the most popular toys in the world.
   Erno Rubik**, who invented his toy cube in 1974,** became a very rich man.
3. **Non-defining noun phrases**
   The Rubik's Cube**, one of the world's most popular toys,** was invented by the Hungarian professor Erno Rubik in 1974.
   Erno Rubik, **the inventor of the Rubik's Cube,** was a Hungarian professor.
4. **Non-defining participle phrases**
   The Rubik's Cube**, invented by the Hungarian professor Erno Rubik,** is one of the most popular toys in the world.
   The success of the cube, **lasting through to today,** is its appeal to old and young alike.

End Commas

Use a comma to set off extra information (e.g., an extra linking word or non-defining relative clause) at the end of an independent clause.

1. **Adverbial conjunctions**
   I believe that taxes on high income earners should be increased**, therefore.**
   A top income tax rate of 50 percent is likely to lead to greater tax avoidance**, however.**
   It may even result in less revenue**, too.**
   Higher earners might move their money to off-shore tax havens**, for example.**
2. **Non-defining relative clauses**
   I took the exam yesterday**, which was the last day of the term.**
3. **Non-defining noun phrases**
   I took the exam yesterday**, the last day of the term.**
4. **Non-defining participle phrases**
   I took the exam yesterday**, not wanting to delay any longer.**

Coordinator Commas

Use coordinator commas before coordinating linking words such as *and*, *but*, and *so* in compound sentences. Also use them before the final *and* or *or* in a list of three or more items.

1. **Compound sentences**
   I spent my early childhood in Russia**, and** my family moved to Canada in 2003.
   I love living in Canada**, but** I still miss many things from my old life in Russia.
2. **List of three or more items**
   What I miss most about Russia is my family, our summer house**, and** speaking Russian everywhere.
   In the future, I have three options: stay in Canada, return to Russia**, or** live part of the year in each country.

   Note: In standard British academic writing, coordinator commas are often omitted.

TASK 4

Margin Notes

In the following sentences, the commas are missing. First, identify whether the sentences require beginning commas, middle commas, end commas, or coordinator commas by writing **BC**, **MC**, **EC**, or **CC** in the margin. Then identify the type of comma(s) required by noting the corresponding number from the four sections on commas (pages 236 to 238). Finally, add the missing comma(s) to the sentence. The first sentence has been done as an example.

EXAMPLE

BC 2 — 1. When I came to Pacific University, I studied at Lower Mainland Secondary School.

2. Having been at the school for five years I was definitely ready for a change of scene.
3. My days at Lower Mainland were nonetheless very happy.
4. I remember vividly my last day which was a sunny Friday.
5. At the start of the day everyone in Grade 12 turned up at 11:00 a.m. and we went to our classrooms.
6. Next we gathered for the final school assembly of the year.
7. It was the final assembly of secondary school too.
8. We had reached the end of a journey the last day of school.
9. That sunny Friday a day that I'll never forget was full of so many mixed emotions.
10. I felt sad to be leaving some friends behind excited about the future and glad that the long summer holiday was about to begin.

Semicolons

Semicolons function similarly to periods. Most often, they are used to separate two closely related independent clauses. Less commonly, they are used to separate items in lists.

To Separate Two Closely Related Independent Clauses

Use a semicolon to separate two closely related independent clauses. A period can also be used between two independent clauses, as is shown in Example 1 below.

> **EXAMPLE 1**
> Bilingual education is a controversial topic in the US. In Canada, it is more widely accepted.
>
> **EXAMPLE 2**
> Bilingual education is a controversial topic in the US; in Canada, it is more widely accepted.

Why Use a Semicolon? A semicolon that appears at the end of an independent clause tells the reader that the next independent clause has an idea or information that is closely related to the first clause. A period, on the other hand, suggests that the next clause is newer, less related information. As both clauses in the examples above are closely related, Example 2 is more effective than Example 1.

To Separate Two Independent Clauses with an Adverbial Conjunction

Use a semicolon instead of a period to separate two independent clauses with an adverbial conjunction such as *however* or *therefore* (followed by a comma).

> **EXAMPLE 1**
> Bilingual education is a controversial topic in the US. However, in Canada, it is more widely accepted.
>
> **EXAMPLE 2**
> Bilingual education is a controversial topic in the US; however, in Canada, it is more widely accepted.

Again, the semicolon indicates to the reader that information in the second clause is closely related to that in the first.

To Separate Items in a List—When One or More Items Include a Comma

Sometimes it is necessary to use semicolons instead of commas to separate items in a list. This is the case when one or more of the items in the list already includes a comma. Use a semicolon in such instances so that the reader does not get confused when reading the list.

> **EXAMPLE 1**
> The 2004 tsunami caused major destruction in Indonesia, Sri Lanka, India, and Thailand.
>
> **EXAMPLE 2**
> The 2004 tsunami had a devastating effect on countries around the Indian Ocean: it caused an estimated 200 000 deaths, most of which were in Indonesia; it wiped out whole communities, many of which have yet to fully recover; and it damaged infrastructure, for example, roads, bridges, and sewers.[1]

[1]There is a colon (:) after "the Indian Ocean." The rules for using colons are explained later in this appendix.

In Example 1 above, it is possible to separate the list items with commas without confusing the reader. However, each of the items in Example 2 includes a comma. It is, therefore, necessary to separate each item with a semicolon so that the meaning is clear.

TASK 5

In the following sentences, add semicolons where appropriate. In some sentences, it is not necessary to make any changes. In others, you should replace commas or periods with semicolons. If a period is used to separate two independent clauses that are closely related, change it to a semicolon.

1. Diego Maradona was born in 1960 in Argentina. By the age of 20, he would become the world's greatest soccer player.
2. Maradona's life has been surrounded with the following controversial events: doping scandals, including a failed drug test, cheating allegations, particularly in one famous game in 1986, and even a paternity claim from an Italian woman who claimed that he was the father of her son.
3. Most controversial was a hand-ball goal that he scored against the English team in the 1986 World Cup. The quarter-final goal helped knock England out of the tournament.
4. Maradona later admitted using his hand. He claimed that the goal was scored by "the hand of God."
5. In the same game, however, Maradona scored one of the greatest goals of all time, getting past five English defenders.
6. Maradona remains the greatest. Nonetheless, controversy has followed him everywhere.

Colons

Colons are used to introduce lists, explanations, and direct quotations. Colons are also used to separate main titles and subtitles.

To Introduce a List or an Explanation

The most common use of a colon is to introduce a list or an explanation. However, a colon should be used only when the text that precedes the colon is a complete independent clause (a clause that can stand alone as a sentence).

When Not to Use a Colon to Introduce a List or an Explanation

EXAMPLE 1
The 2004 tsunami caused major destruction in Indonesia, Sri Lanka, India, and Thailand.

EXAMPLE 2
The most worrying effects of climate change are melting ice caps, rising sea levels, and extreme weather.

A colon should not be used in Examples 1 and 2 because the list items are introduced by text that is not an independent clause.

Examples 1 and 2 could be written using colons, but only if the first part of each sentence is revised to an independent clause. A common way to do this is to add an expression such as *the following* or *as follows* before the colon. Another way to do this is to revise the text that comes before the colon to an independent clause.

Using a Colon with *the Following* or *as Follows*

EXAMPLE 1
The 2004 tsunami caused major destruction in the following countries: Indonesia, Sri Lanka, India, and Thailand.

EXAMPLE 2
The most worrying effects of climate change are the following: melting ice caps, rising sea levels, and extreme weather.

EXAMPLE 3
The most worrying effects of climate change are as follows: melting ice caps, rising sea levels, and extreme weather.

Using a Colon after an Independent Clause

EXAMPLE 1
Climate change is having serious negative effects: melting ice caps, rising sea levels, and extreme weather.

EXAMPLE 2
Climate change is having *three* serious negative effects: melting ice caps, rising sea levels, and extreme weather. [rewritten independent clause that states the exact number of list items]

EXAMPLE 3
Climate change is having *numerous* serious negative effects: melting ice caps, rising sea levels, and extreme weather. [rewritten independent clause that states the general number of list items]

Using a Colon to Achieve a More Economical Style When a colon is used to introduce a list or an explanation, the writer can condense the text that follows and achieve a more economical style. By using a colon before a list or an explanation, the writer does not have to repeat introductory linking words in the text that follows the colon.

EXAMPLE 1
In 1998, Gomez cited three weaknesses in existing definitions of bilingualism. First, she mentioned that previous definitions focused only on interactions that involve two languages. The second weakness that she found was considerable confusion between the terms *bilingual* and *multilingual*. And third, she argued that previous definitions ignored monolingual interactions between bilingual speakers.

EXAMPLE 2
In 1998, Gomez cited three weaknesses in existing definitions of bilingualism: a focus only on interactions that involve two languages, considerable confusion between the terms *bilingual* and *multilingual*, and previous definitions that ignored monolingual interactions between bilingual speakers.

The style in Example 2 is more economical than the style in Example 1. The use of the colon in Example 2 tells the reader that a list will follow. It is, therefore, not necessary to use any linking words or expressions after the colon.

To Introduce a Direct Quotation

Use a colon before a direct quotation (that is, a quotation that presents the exact words of a writer). Be sure that the text that precedes the colon is an independent clause.

Short Quotations In academic writing, short quotations of fewer than four lines (MLA) or 40 words (APA) are often run into a paragraph and incorporated grammatically into a sentence, without a colon. However, when an independent clause precedes a short quotation, use a colon before the quotation. A short quotation can also be introduced by a comma, whether or not the text that precedes the quotation is an independent clause.

> **EXAMPLE 1**
> In 1998, Gomez redefined and broadened the term *bilingualism* as "any conversation involving individuals who are able to speak more than one language." [correct]
>
> **EXAMPLE 2**
> In 1998, Gomez redefined and broadened the term *bilingualism* as, "any conversation involving individuals who are able to speak more than one language." [correct]
>
> **EXAMPLE 3**
> In 1998, Gomez redefined and broadened the term *bilingualism* as follows: "any conversation involving individuals who are able to speak more than one language." [correct]
>
> **EXAMPLE 4**
> In 1998, Gomez redefined and broadened the term *bilingualism* as: "any conversation involving individuals who are able to speak more than one language." [incorrect]

In Example 1, the short quotation is incorporated into the sentence and is not preceded by an independent clause. Thus, no colon is needed before the quotation.

In Example 2, the short quotation is incorporated into the sentence, and introduced with a comma.

In Example 3, the short quotation follows an independent clause and a colon.

However, Example 4 is incorrect because the text that precedes the colon is not an independent clause. Thus, no colon should be used before the quotation.

Long Quotations The MLA and APA formats for direct quotations are presented in Appendices 1 and 2. Quotations that are longer than four lines (MLA) or 40 words (APA) are usually introduced with an independent clause, followed by a colon, indented on a line below, and presented without quotation marks.

> **EXAMPLE 1**
> In 1998, Gomez redefined and broadened the term *bilingualism* as follows:
>
> > The way that we understand bilingualism has been too narrowly defined. Bilingualism does not have to involve a conversation with two languages; instead, it should also be understood as any conversation involving individuals

> who are able to speak to each other using more than one language but who decide to use only one language. (Gomez, 1988, p. 126) [correct]

EXAMPLE 2

In 1998, Gomez redefined and broadened the term *bilingualism*:

> The way that we understand bilingualism has been too narrowly defined. Bilingualism does not have to involve a conversation with two languages; instead, it should also be understood as any conversation involving individuals who are able to speak to each other using more than one language but who decide to use only one language. (Gomez, 1988, p. 126) [correct]

EXAMPLE 3

In 1998, Gomez redefined and broadened the term *bilingualism* as:

> The way that we understand bilingualism has been too narrowly defined. Bilingualism does not have to involve a conversation with two languages; instead, it should also be understood as any conversation involving individuals who are able to speak to each other using more than one language but who decide to use only one language. (Gomez, 1988, p. 126) [incorrect]

Examples 1 and 2 are correct. In Example 1, the phrase *as follows* is used to form an independent clause, which is followed by a colon. In Example 2, the colon follows an independent clause.

However, Example 3 is incorrect because the text that precedes the colon is not an independent clause.

To Separate the Main Title from a Subtitle

Colons are often used in book and essay titles to indicate the focus of a text.

EXAMPLE 1

Japan: A history of its language and culture

EXAMPLE 2

Natural causes of climate change: Are the skeptics wrong?

Example 1 is a book title. The colon separates the general topic of the book, Japan, from the specific focus, which is a historical study of Japanese language and culture.

Example 2 is an essay title. The general topic of the essay is the natural causes of climate change; the specific focus is an analysis of the arguments used by climate skeptics (i.e., that climate change is a natural phenomenon and not caused by human activity).

In Examples 1 and 2 above, the word following the colon is capitalized. In British academic writing, lower case letters often follow colons in titles.

Other Common Punctuation Errors

Punctuation and Such As

When *such as* introduces a defining phrase, no punctuation precedes the term. However, when *such as* introduces a non-defining phrase, that phrase is set off with commas. A colon is not used after *such as*.

> **EXAMPLE 1**
> There are many famous Japanese dishes such as sushi, tempura, and teriyaki.
>
> **EXAMPLE 2**
> Many Japanese dishes, such as sushi and tempura, are famous around the world.

In Example 1, the phrase introduced by *such as* is defining, so no punctuation precedes the term.

In Example 2, the phrase introduced by *such as* is non-defining, so that phrase is set off with commas.

Punctuation and for Example

The term *for example* is used with a comma, a semicolon, or a period, depending on the grammatical structure of the sentence.

> **EXAMPLE 1**
> Many Japanese dishes are famous around the world, for example, sushi, tempura, and teriyaki.
>
> **EXAMPLE 2**
> Many Japanese dishes are famous around the world; for example, many people are familiar with sushi, tempura, and teriyaki.
>
> **EXAMPLE 3**
> Many Japanese dishes are famous around the world. For example, many people are familiar with sushi, tempura, and teriyaki.

Note that in Examples 1 to 3, *for example* appears after an independent clause.

In Example 1, *for example* appears mid-sentence before a list of items, so it must be set off with commas. If it is followed by another independent clause (as in Examples 2 and 3), it is preceded by a semicolon or period, with a comma after it.

Punctuation and Ambiguity

Some writers do not like to use a beginning comma after an introductory phrase. They feel that such commas break the flow of the writing. Although this approach is acceptable, sometimes it can confuse readers.

Let's look back at the sentence you have just read, with the beginning comma and without it.

> **EXAMPLE 1**
> Although this approach is acceptable, sometimes it can confuse readers. [with a comma]
>
> **EXAMPLE 2**
> Although this approach is acceptable sometimes it can confuse readers. [without a comma]

Example 1 includes a comma after the introductory phrase. However, the omission of the comma in Example 2 creates ambiguity. The sentence could be read as having the same meaning as Example 1. However, it could also be read as meaning that it is acceptable to do this *sometimes*. In such cases, the beginning comma should always be included to avoid confusing the reader.

TASK 6

Punctuate the sentences in the following paragraphs according to the rules learned in this appendix.

Japanese food

Japanese food is healthy it is also delicious. Many traditional Japanese dishes can now be eaten in restaurants around the world for example sushi tempura and teriyaki. Three staple foods of the Japanese diet are fish rice and vegetables. In recent years however Japanese families have begun to eat large amounts of meat such as beef and pork and dairy products for example milk and cheese.

Without doubt when most people hear the words *Japanese food* they think of one thing sushi. Sushi means vinegared rice. There are many different kinds of sushi but the most common forms that are eaten outside of Japan are the following *maki sushi* and *nigiri sushi*. Maki sushi which can now be found on the lunch counter in local stores all around the world is a combination of vinegared rice fish or vegetables and *nori*. Nori is the sheet of seaweed that is wrapped around the rice. Nigiri sushi another very recognizable type of sushi usually has a piece of raw fish on top of vinegared rice that has been moulded into a round shape. When sushi is served at a restaurant it usually arrives at the table with *wasabi* a paste derived from a type of Japanese horseradish and soy sauce.

Japanese food is considered to be one of the healthiest cuisines in the world however not all Japanese food is so healthy. With high levels of fat some dishes may not after all be so healthy. One such example is tempura dishes which are usually seafood fish or vegetables deep fried in a light batter and which have a high fat content. As the Japanese saying goes *hara hachi bu* or eat only till you're 80 percent full.

APPENDIX 5

Improving Style in Academic Writing

There is no such thing as standard style in academic writing. Academic writing style can vary significantly depending on the *genre* of writing, the *audience,* and the *context.*

There are, however, ways to improve style in academic writing that can be applied to different types of text. There are also some common stylistic problems in academic writing that writers should seek to avoid.

MODERN ENGLISH: TWO WAYS TO SAY ONE THING

Many people are unaware that the language that this book is written in, Standard Modern English, did not exist a thousand years ago. A thousand years ago, most inhabitants of the British Isles spoke either Anglo-Saxon, a Germanic dialect of settlers from Saxony in Germany, or a Gaelic language such as Welsh. In fact, the roots of Modern English can be traced back to 1066, when the Norman French, under William the Conqueror, defeated the Saxon King Harold at the Battle of Hastings. Thereafter, the French language became the language of higher social status, the language of the court and of the aristocracy. Most of the words that we use in Modern English today have their roots in these two languages: Anglo-Saxon and French, the latter originating from Latin.

Many ideas in Modern English can be expressed in two ways: in informal English that is dominated by short words, many of which originate from Anglo-Saxon; and in more formal English, whose words originate mostly from Latin. One very notable feature of written academic English is the use of words that originate from Latin.

An Anecdote

A famous British soccer player, Player A, was once asked what he thought about the increasing number of foreign players in the English Premier League. He started his answer as follows:

> *"Well, like, because there's loads of foreign lads coming over here, like, it's a lot harder for our young lads to get picked for games."*

In the same interview, a famous French soccer player, Player B, who played for the same team, answered the same question as follows:

> *"I suppose that, as a consequence of the rapid internationalization of British football, it is more difficult for the young players to gain selection for games."*

A local newspaper ran an article lamenting the lack of education of British soccer players, suggesting that players from countries like France, Spain, and Italy were given more academic support while they were playing on professional youth teams. The journalist compared the two interview responses to prove his point.

TASK 1

Do you agree with the journalist's conclusion that Player B is better educated than Player A? Why or why not? Write your answer in the space below.

____

____

____

____

____

____

USING FORMAL VERBS

In less formal English, short one-syllable verbs (e.g., *get*, *bring*, *take*) are commonly used. They are often used as phrasal verbs with one or more prepositions (e.g., *up*, *about*, *on*) to create a new meaning.

The following are examples of less formal phrasal verbs:

> *Get by*—Many people in developing countries *get by* on less than two dollars a day.
> *Bring about*—The protests failed to *bring about* a change of government policy.
> *Take in*—The government has *taken in* many refugees from conflicts around the world.

Each of these sentences could be expressed in an alternative way by using longer single verbs, which often sound more formal and academic.

TASK 2

Rewrite the two sentences below using an alternative single verb that adds formality to the sentence.

1. Many people in developing countries *get by* on less than two dollars a day.

   ____

2. The government has *taken in* many refugees from conflicts around the world.

____

When you are choosing which words to use in your academic writing, use what you consider to be appropriate style for your audience, genre, and context. Remember: if you use too much formal vocabulary, your writing may become overly formal. Make sure that you find the right balance of formal and less formal language.

USING THE PERSONAL "I"

It is not always clear whether or not you should use the personal "I" in academic writing. Using the personal "I" does not mean that your writing is informal. However, in many subject areas, the personal "I" is discouraged, as it is seen to be too personal. Deciding whether you should use it depends on the genre of the writing, your audience, and the context of your writing. If you are unsure, ask your instructor or analyze the style of the academic books and articles in your particular subject area.

PERSONAL AND IMPERSONAL WRITING

In the following example of writing with the personal "I," the writer uses a direct and personal style.

> **EXAMPLE**
> **1** In this essay, I will discuss the advantages and disadvantages of quantitative easing as a tool for central banks. **2** My analysis will include a comparison of central banking policy in Japan, Canada, and the UK during 2009, and the central banks' use of quantitative easing to stimulate economies in recession.

The above example could be written in a more impersonal style. Doing so would be advisable if the writer had received guidelines from an instructor stating that personal language should not be used for the writing task.

There are three common techniques for avoiding the personal "I" that appears in Sentence 1.

Sent. 1 In this essay, I will discuss the advantages and disadvantages of quantitative easing as a tool for central banks.

a) **Use a passive voice structure.**
In this essay, the economic advantages and disadvantages of quantitative easing as a tool for central banks *will be discussed*.

b) **Change the personal subject pronoun to an impersonal subject.**
This essay will discuss the advantages and disadvantages of quantitative easing as a tool for central banks.

c) **Use an impersonal phrase such as "The focus of this essay is."**
The focus of this essay is the advantages and disadvantages of quantitative easing as a tool for central banks.

In Sentence 2, you can avoid using the personal "my" by replacing it with an impersonal determiner such as "the."

Sent. 2 My analysis will include a comparison of central banking policy in Japan, Canada, and the UK during 2009.

a) *The* analysis will include a comparison of central banking policy in Japan, Canada, and the UK during 2009.

TASK 3

Make the following sentences **less personal.**

1. In this essay, I have analyzed the pros and cons of private health care. I argued that private health care should be limited in order to protect the public system.

____

____

Make the following sentences **more personal.**

2. The discussion so far has focused on the benefits that the jury system brings to criminal law cases. The following four important benefits were highlighted.

____

____

12 COMMON EXAMPLES OF WEAK STYLE

Listed below are 12 common examples of weak style. The key words in each example are underlined.

1. Repetitive Writing: Vocabulary

Using the same words repeatedly can reduce the effectiveness of your academic writing by making it seem simple and lacking in sophistication. The reader may feel that the lack of variety in vocabulary weakens your argument.

EXAMPLE
Effective <u>academic writing</u> is essential for success at university. However, <u>academic writing</u> is not always easy for university students, as <u>academic writing</u> has many rules and conventions that need to be learned.

2. Repetitive Writing: Sentence Structure

Using the same sentence structure repeatedly in your academic writing can also reduce the effectiveness of your writing. For example, avoid starting each sentence with a linking word (e.g., *therefore, however*), then continuing with a simple sentence structure (e.g., subject-verb).

> **EXAMPLE**
> Firstly, violence on television is often shown before nine o'clock. Therefore, many children see violent programs in the early evening. However, children do not always copy what they see.

3. Too Many Compound Sentences

Academic writing may also seem weak if the writer uses too many compound sentences. Compound sentences are made by using any of the FANBOYS coordinators (i.e., *for, and, nor, but, or, yet, so*) to link independent clauses (i.e., clauses that have a subject and main verb and can stand alone). This type of sentence is very common and very appropriate in everyday spoken English, and in academic writing when describing equal ideas. However, such sentences seem simple when you are comparing or describing relationships between ideas or processes, for example, cause and effect. (See Appendix 6 for more on complex and compound sentences.)

> **EXAMPLE**
> The government increased the number of police on the streets of New York, and the crime rate fell.

4. Overly Long Sentences

Avoid writing sentences that have too many clauses and ideas. Overly long sentences can make it difficult for the reader to put everything together. They can also reduce the effectiveness of an argument or discussion.

> **EXAMPLE**
> There are many serious problems that patients are facing in public hospitals today, which are mainly the result of a lack of government funding and systemic weaknesses, which should be addressed not only by politicians but also by members of the public from all walks of life.

5. Simple Words

In many forms of academic writing, words that have their origins in Latin are used as alternatives to shorter simple words (e.g., *get, find out, a lot of, thing*). Latin-origin words are longer and seem more academic.

> **EXAMPLE**
> The United Nations should look into ways of letting developing world countries get easier access to NAFTA and EU markets.

6. Spoken Language That Would Not Normally Be Used in Writing

Some phrases and expressions that are used in spoken language can seem out of place in academic writing. Such language can reduce the effectiveness of the writing.

> **EXAMPLE**
> In this section, I am going to be talking about three key theories; then I will be having a look at their applications.

7. Contractions

Contractions (e.g., *don't, haven't*) are shortened forms of words that are very common and appropriate in everyday conversation, and in less formal writing. They are less common in most forms of academic writing as they can make the writing seem chatty or conversational. While some academic writers do use contractions, the standard convention would be to use the complete form.

> **EXAMPLE**
> English grammar isn't very easy to learn because there are so many exceptions to rules.

8. Addressing the Reader as "You"

It is unusual to address the reader as "you" in most forms of academic writing. This can make the writing seem chatty and conversational.

> **EXAMPLE**
> One skill that you need during the first year of university is the ability to become independent.

9. Gender-Exclusive Language

In recent years, many writers in universities have changed their writing style to avoid gender-exclusive language. This type of language uses terms that exclude one group on the basis of gender: for example, educational articles may traditionally have referred to the learner as "he"; now most use alternatives such as "he or she" or "they."

> **EXAMPLE**
> The language learner should spend as much of his time as possible in the company of native speakers.

10. Verbs + Stranded Adverbs

In some writing, an argument or main idea is presented in a long sentence with an adverb added on to the end. Adverbs should be placed next to the verbs they modify.

> **EXAMPLE**
> Many teachers are supporting the government's new policies to develop public education actively.

11. Rhetorical Questions

Rhetorical questions are questions that are asked to make an idea or argument stronger; the reader is not expected to form an answer. Such questions are useful in public speaking but are usually avoided in academic writing.

> **EXAMPLE**
> Climate change is an issue that politicians have yet to act upon in parliament. What will happen in the future if the issue is left any longer?

12. Inappropriate Metaphors

Metaphorical language is common in literature, for example, in novels and poetry. A metaphor compares one thing with another, often for dramatic effect, for example, describing life as a "journey." In many forms of academic writing, metaphors are not commonly used.

> **EXAMPLE**
> Jameson's theories are ancient dinosaurs in today's political world.

TASK 4

Rewrite the example sentences from the list above in a way that improves their style.

1. Effective academic writing is essential for success at university. However, academic writing is not always easy for university students, as academic writing has many rules and conventions that need to be learned.

2. Firstly, violence on television is often shown before nine o'clock. Therefore, many children see violent programs in the early evening. However, children do not always copy what they see.

3. The government increased the number of police on the streets of New York, and the crime rate fell.

4. There are many serious problems that patients are facing in public hospitals today, which are mainly the result of a lack of government funding and systemic weaknesses, which should be addressed not only by politicians but also by members of the public from all walks of life.

5. The United Nations should look into ways of letting developing world countries get easier access to NAFTA and EU markets.

6. In this section, I am going to be talking about three key theories; then I will be having a look at their applications.

7. English grammar isn't very easy to learn because there are so many exceptions to rules.

8. One skill that you need during the first year of university is the ability to become independent.

9. The language learner should spend as much of his time as possible in the company of native speakers.

10. Many teachers are supporting the government's new policies to develop public education actively.

11. Climate change is an issue that politicians have yet to act upon in parliament. What will happen in the future if the issue is left any longer?

____

____

____

12. Jameson's theories are ancient dinosaurs in today's political world.

____

____

____

APPENDIX 6

Sentence Structure 1: Independent and Dependent Clauses, and Complex and Compound Sentences

WHAT IS A CLAUSE?

A clause is a group of words that can form a whole sentence, or part of a sentence. There are two important types of clauses you need to be able to recognize and use in academic writing: independent clauses and dependent clauses.

INDEPENDENT CLAUSES

Independent clauses are also sometimes called *main clauses*. An independent clause can stand alone as a sentence—that is why it is called independent. Independent clauses form a complete thought and contain a subject and a corresponding verb. As you will see later in this appendix, on its own an independent clause forms a simple sentence. Below are examples of independent clauses.

EXAMPLES

Climate change **has led to** rising sea levels.

subject **verb**

Police in the city **arrested** hundreds of violent demonstrators.

subject **verb**

DEPENDENT CLAUSES

Dependent clauses are also sometimes called *subordinate clauses.* A dependent clause does not form a complete thought and cannot stand alone as a sentence—that is why it is called dependent. A dependent clause must be joined with an independent clause for it to become a complete sentence. If it stands alone, it is a fragment, or a grammatically incomplete sentence. Dependent clauses are commonly formed with subordinators (linking words such as *although, despite, unless*) or relative pronouns (linking words such as *which, that, who*. (See Appendix 3.)

Following are some examples of dependent clauses. Standing alone, these dependent clauses are fragments (incomplete sentences). The subordinators are marked in italics.

EXAMPLES

1. *Although* most people accept that climate change is caused by human activity
2. *Despite* the evidence showing links between carbon emissions and climate change
3. *Unless* action is taken to reduce carbon emissions
4. *Which* was drawn up in December 2009
5. *That* are fair to both developing and developed countries
6. *Who* drew up the deal in the final hours of the climate summit

If the dependent clauses above ended with a period, they would still be grammatically incomplete sentence fragments.

EXAMPLE

1. *Although* most people accept that climate change is caused by human activity. [fragment]

For a dependent clause to become a grammatically complete sentence, it needs to be connected to an independent clause as illustrated below. If the dependent clause comes first, a comma is used to separate it from the independent clause. If it comes second, there is no comma.

EXAMPLES

1. Although most people accept that climate change is caused by human activity, *there may also be natural causes such as volcanic and solar activity.*

   dependent clause — *independent clause*

2. Despite the evidence showing links between carbon emissions and climate change, *climate skeptics remain unconvinced.*

   dependent clause — *independent clause*

3. *Seas may rise to unprecedented levels* unless action is taken to reduce carbon emissions.

   independent clause — dependent clause

4. *The controversial Copenhagen Accord,* which was drawn up in December 2009, *is seen by most people as a starting point in a long process.*

dependent clause
independent clause

5. *Solutions* that are fair to both developing and developed countries *are required for future agreements.*

dependent clause
independent clause

6. *The politicians* who drew up the deal in the final hours of the climate summit *reached a compromise agreement.*

dependent clause
independent clause

TASK 1

Add independent clauses to the following dependent clauses to make them complete sentences.

1. ______________________ even though they didn't have enough money.
2. In spite of the terrible weather, ______________________
3. If you don't study hard, ______________________
4. Barack Obama, who was born in Hawaii, ______________________
5. ______________________ that I can read during the flight.

TYPES OF SENTENCES

- An independent clause on its own forms a *simple sentence.*

EXAMPLE
Barack Obama became the first African-American to be elected president of the US.

- Two independent clauses separated by a coordinating linking word form a *compound sentence.*

EXAMPLE
Barack Obama served as a senator in Illinois from 2005 to 2008, *and* he became the first African-American president of the US in January 2009.

Compound sentences are used to join together ideas of equal importance. As you learned in Appendix 3, compound sentences can be formed by connecting two or more independent clauses with coordinating linking words. Recall that the seven coordinating linking words are represented by the acronym FANBOYS: *for, and, nor, but, or, yet, so.*

- When an independent clause is joined with a dependent clause, a *complex sentence* is formed.

> **EXAMPLE**
> While he was in his first year in office, Barack Obama was awarded the Nobel Peace Prize based on his world vision.

Complex sentences are commonly used to emphasize that the idea in one clause (usually the independent clause) is more important than, or the result of, the idea in the dependent clause. In a complex sentence, the dependent clause commonly begins with a subordinating linking word (e.g., *although, despite, unless*) or a relative pronoun (e.g., *which, that, who*). (See Appendix 3 for a list of subordinating linking words.)

CHOOSING THE RIGHT BALANCE OF SENTENCE TYPES

It is important to have a good balance of sentence types in academic writing. Paragraphs are considered unbalanced if they have either too many simple sentences or too many compound sentences; a balanced paragraph contains a good mix of the two.

PARAGRAPHS WITH TOO MANY SIMPLE SENTENCES

The following paragraph is written with too many simple sentences.

Paragraph 1: Informal digital communication

1 Informal digital communication is very different from academic writing. **2** Informal digital communication takes place when people communicate online by text messaging, email, or on social networking sites such as Facebook. **3** It has its own abbreviated forms. **4** In informal digital communication, writers commonly use forms such as lol (laugh out loud), u r (you are), and smiling faces -:);^). **5** The conventions for informal digital communication are constantly changing. **6** Academic writing also changes in different contexts. **7** However, academic writers generally have to follow much stricter conventions about structure and style.

Every sentence in Paragraph 1 is a simple sentence. Writing with too many simple sentences can make writing appear as follows:

- **Repetitive:** The writer is repeating the same sentence structure, which could make the reader lose interest.
- **Lacking flow:** The writing can seem to start then stop abruptly. The lack of flow makes it difficult for the reader to read smoothly.
- **Lacking coherence:** If ideas are not joined together with a variety of sentence structures and linking phrases, a paragraph may seem less coherent.

TASK 2

Rewrite Paragraph 1 on page 258 to improve the style by reducing the number of simple sentences. You should form compound or complex sentences to avoid the weaknesses listed above.

PARAGRAPHS WITH TOO MANY COMPOUND SENTENCES

Read the following paragraph on bilingualism. The paragraph is written with too many compound sentences. The coordinators are in bold.

Paragraph 2: Bilingualism

1 Virtually all of the world's population has one first language, **and** most people can understand or speak at least a few words of another language. 2 Most people in the world speak more than one language, **so** it would seem to be safe to state that the majority of the world's population is bilingual. 3 This majority may be able to speak more than one language to some limited degree, **but** can we define them as bilingual? 4 The answer to the question depends on how we frame our definition of *bilingualism*, **yet** the term *bilingualism* is not always used by scholars to mean the same thing, **and** some scholars use terms such as *multilingual* or *plurilingual* as alternatives. 5 Bilingualism is a complex and multifaceted linguistic phenomenon, **and** it changes according to individuals' abilities, perceptions, and local contexts.

Every sentence in Paragraph 2 is a compound sentence. Compound sentences work well when the two independent clauses that make up the sentence are of equal importance or when the writer wants to give equal emphasis to the ideas. However, as is the case with using too many simple sentences, writing with too many compound sentences can make writing appear too simplistic and repetitive, and lacking in flow and coherence.

TASK 3

Rewrite Paragraph 2 to improve the style by reducing the number of compound sentences. It may not be necessary to change every compound sentence, especially where you find ideas of equal importance or that merit equal emphasis. Where this is not the case, find alternative ways to express the ideas by using complex sentences or simple sentences. Practise using *subordination*, that is, forming complex sentences with subordinating linking words, wherever appropriate.

APPENDIX 7

Sentence Structure 2: Relative Clauses and Participle Clauses

Relative clauses and participle clauses define or describe a term or an idea in an independent clause. This appendix focuses on the following:

- The difference between defining and non-defining relative clauses
- When to include or omit the relative pronoun that introduces a relative clause
- The difference between present and past participle clauses

THE DIFFERENCE BETWEEN DEFINING AND NON-DEFINING RELATIVE CLAUSES

Defining Relative Clauses

A defining relative clause provides essential information about someone or something in an independent clause. It tells the reader "who" or "which one." Without the defining relative clause, who or what is being referred to may not be entirely clear to the reader.

EXAMPLE
The projector *that's in room 5048* is broken.

In the sentence above, the independent clause is "The projector is broken." The defining relative clause is in italics: "that's in room 5048."

Why is the defining relative clause included? Whether the defining relative clause is included depends on the context between the speaker and listener, or reader and writer.

Imagine that a teacher is teaching a class to a group of students in room 5048. In this context, it would not be necessary to add the defining relative clause "that's in room 5048" because the students would understand which projector the teacher is talking about. The teacher could just tell them "the projector is broken." However, if the teacher were to call the maintenance department about the projector, it would be essential to include the defining relative clause so that a technician would know which projector to fix.

Remember these two rules when writing defining relative clauses:

- Do not use a comma before the relative pronoun (e.g., *that, who, where, when*) that introduces a defining relative clause.
- When describing a thing, typically use *that* instead of *which* at the beginning of a defining relative clause. Using *which* seems very formal.

Non-defining Relative Clauses

A non-defining relative clause provides additional, non-essential information about someone or something in an independent clause. If the non-defining relative clause were taken out of a sentence, the basic meaning of the sentence would remain the same. A non-defining relative clause can give additional, non-essential information about the following:

1. **A noun or noun phrase in the independent clause**

   EXAMPLE
   Yesterday, I took the **university placement test,** *which wasn't too difficult.*

   In this example, the non-defining relative clause "which wasn't too difficult" is additional, non-essential information about the test. The writer is saying, "Yesterday, I took the university placement test, and by the way, in case you're interested, I don't think the test was very difficult."

2. **The whole idea in the independent clause**

   EXAMPLE
   Yesterday, I took the university placement test, *which really stressed me out.*

   In this example, the non-defining relative clause "which really stressed me out" is additional, non-essential information about the whole idea of the independent clause, that is, the experience of taking the exam. In this case, the writer is saying, "Yesterday, I took the university placement test, and by the way, in case you're interested, the experience of taking the exam was really stressful for me."

Remember these three rules when writing non-defining relative clauses:

- Use a comma before the relative pronoun (e.g., *which, who, where, when*) that introduces a non-defining relative clause.
- When describing a thing, use *which* instead of *that* at the beginning of a non-defining relative clause.
- Use a comma before and after a non-defining relative clause that appears in the middle of an independent clause.

TASK 1

In each of the sentences below, underline the relative clause. Then circle whether the relative clause is defining or non-defining.

1. Yesterday I met a student advisor, who recommended that I get some work experience this year.
Defining/Non-defining
2. Yesterday I met the student advisor whom you recommended to me earlier in the year.
Defining/Non-defining
3. The lab class, which was really interesting, lasted for three hours.
Defining/Non-defining
4. The lab class that I missed last week was on how to write lab reports.
Defining/Non-defining
5. Do you know anyone who can proofread my essay for me?
Defining/Non-defining

WHEN TO INCLUDE OR OMIT THE RELATIVE PRONOUN IN A DEFINING RELATIVE CLAUSE

In some defining relative clauses, it is possible to omit the relative pronoun that introduces a relative clause, while in others it is not. It depends on whether the someone or something being defined is the subject or object of the relative clause.

Subject-Defining Relative Clauses

EXAMPLE
The teacher *who taught me the most* was Miss Smith.

EXPLANATION
In the sentence above, the relative clause is "who taught me the most." It is a dependent clause that appears in the middle of the independent clause "The teacher was Miss Smith."

The relative clause "who taught me the most" is a *defining relative clause.* The relative clause is defining the teacher in the independent clause, telling the reader "which one," that is, Miss Smith, not another teacher.

This relative clause is also a *subject-defining relative clause.* It is a subject-defining relative clause because the person that the relative clause is defining, the teacher, is the subject of the relative clause.

subject	*verb*	*object*	
↓	↓	↓	
Miss Smith	*taught*	*me*	*the most.*

In subject-defining relative clauses, it is not possible to omit the relative pronoun. So, the sentence can be written in only one way:

✓ The teacher *who taught me the most* was Miss Smith. [including the relative pronoun *who*]
✗ The teacher *taught me the most* was Miss Smith. [not possible to omit the relative pronoun *who*]

Object-Defining Relative Clauses

EXAMPLE

The school *that I remember most fondly* is St. John's.

EXPLANATION

In the sentence above, the relative clause is "that I remember most fondly." It is a dependent clause that appears in the middle of the independent clause "The school is St. John's."

The relative clause "that I remember most fondly" is a *defining relative clause.* The relative clause is defining the school in the independent clause. Here, the speaker is referring specifically to the school remembered with most fondness, not any other school.

The relative clause is also an *object-defining relative clause.* It is an object-defining relative clause because the thing that the relative clause is defining, the school, is the object of the relative clause.

subject	***verb***	***object***	
↓	↓	↓	
I	*remember*	St. John's	*most fondly.*

In object-defining relative clauses, it is possible to omit the relative pronoun. So, the sentence could be written in two ways:

✓ The school *that I remember most fondly* is St. John's. [including the relative pronoun *that*]
✓ The school *I remember most fondly* is St. John's. [omitting the relative pronoun *that*]

In everyday speech, people tend to omit the relative pronoun wherever possible. In academic writing, the decision to omit the relative pronoun in an object-defining relative clause is more a question of personal style and preference. For example, in North American academic writing, relative pronouns tend to be omitted in object-defining relative clauses. This approach is less common in British academic writing.

If in doubt, include the relative pronoun. It is never an error to include the relative pronoun, as long as it is the right one.

TASK 2

In the sentences below, carry out the following tasks.

1. Underline the defining relative clause.
2. Circle whether the sentence includes a subject-defining relative clause (which requires the relative pronoun) or an object-defining relative clause (which does not require a relative pronoun).
3. Circle *yes* or *no* to indicate whether the sentence can be written without the relative pronoun.

The first is an example.

EXAMPLE

1. I'm looking for a dictionary that includes etymology and a thesaurus.
   Subject/*Object*
   *Relative pronoun can be omitted? Yes/**No***

2. The class that interests me most is Twentieth Century History.
Subject/Object
Relative pronoun can be omitted? Yes/No
3. He's the instructor that I told you about yesterday.
Subject/Object
Relative pronoun can be omitted? Yes/No
4. The course that I got the best grades in this term was Sociology.
Subject/Object
Relative pronoun can be omitted? Yes/No
5. That's exactly the idea that I was trying to express in my essay.
Subject/Object
Relative pronoun can be omitted? Yes/No

PARTICIPLE CLAUSES

Participle clauses can be used to provide information about an independent clause. They make your writing more economical because they allow you to say something with a reduced number of words. Moreover, participle clauses add variety to the sentence structures you use in your writing.

A participle clause is often used as a shorter alternative to a relative clause.

EXAMPLE 1
Bisphenol A, *which is used in many plastic products*, has been banned in baby bottles in Canada. [with a non-defining relative clause]

EXAMPLE 2
Bisphenol A, *used in many plastic products*, has been banned in baby bottles in Canada. [with a participle clause]

In Example 2, the participle clause is used for stylistic purposes to say more briefly what is said in the relative clause in Example 1.

The Difference between a Present and a Past Participle Clause

There are two kinds of participle clauses: present and past. The difference between the two has nothing to do with time, as the names would suggest. Present participle clauses are used when the verb in the independent clause is active, and past participle clauses are used when the verb in the independent clause is passive. (See Appendix 9 for more on the passive voice.)

- **Present participle clauses**

  The following underlined clauses are present participle clauses. Notice how they can be used for any time idea and how they are used with independent clauses in the active voice.

EXAMPLE
The central bank, <u>hoping for a fall in inflation</u>, will raise interest rates later today.

EXPLANATION
<u>Hoping for a fall in inflation</u> means *because the central bank is hoping for a fall in inflation*. The independent clause has an active voice structure: the subject (*the central bank*) undertakes the action (*will raise*). In this example, the participle clause provides a reason for the action taken in the independent clause.

EXAMPLE
I ran out of the room, slamming the door as I left.

EXPLANATION
Slamming the door as I left means *and I slammed the door as I left*. The independent clause has an active voice structure: the subject (*I*) undertakes the action (*ran*). In this example, the participle clause provides additional information about the action taken in the independent clause.

- **Past participle clauses**

The following underlined clauses are past participle clauses. Notice how they can be used for any time idea and how they are used with independent clauses in the passive voice.

EXAMPLE
The interest rate rise, confirmed earlier today, was supported by bankers.

EXPLANATION
Confirmed earlier today means *which was confirmed earlier today*. The independent clause has a passive voice structure: the subject (*interest rate rise*) receives the action (*was supported*). In this example, the participle clause provides additional information and a shorter alternative to a relative clause.

EXAMPLE
Romeo and Juliet, adapted numerous times for the stage, was written by William Shakespeare.

EXPLANATION
Adapted numerous times for the stage means *which was adapted numerous times for the stage*. The independent clause has a passive voice structure: the subject (*Romeo and Juliet*) receives the action (*was written*). In this example, the participle clause provides additional information and a shorter alternative to a relative clause.

TASK 3

Reduce the following underlined clauses by changing them to participle clauses.

1. I apologized to my friend and explained that I couldn't lend her any money.

____

____

____

2. The local council increased the number of police officers, which led to a reduction in street robberies.

____

____

3. The dissertation award, which is given to the best graduation thesis, is worth $150.

____

____

____

APPENDIX 8

Sentence Structure 3: Sentence Fragments and Comma Splices

SENTENCE FRAGMENTS

Sentence fragments are incomplete sentences. All sentence fragments lack a key component that would make them into independent clauses, and thus complete sentences.

Something Is Missing in a Sentence Fragment

A sentence fragment occurs when something is missing from what is intended to be an independent clause. Sentence fragments usually occur in four contexts:

1. **When a subject is missing from a sentence**

   > EXAMPLE
   > Went to the college bookstore to buy the course textbook.

2. **When a verb is missing from a sentence**

   > EXAMPLE
   > The textbook back in stock in three days.

3. **When a subject and verb are missing from a sentence**

   > EXAMPLE
   > The book as soon as possible.

4. **When a group of words is a dependent clause and, thus, cannot stand alone as a sentence**

   > EXAMPLE
   > Although the textbook is out of stock.

TASK 1

Look at the four examples of sentence fragments below. Correct each one to make a complete sentence.

1. *When a subject is missing from a sentence*
   Went to the college bookstore to buy the course textbook.

   ____

2. *When a verb is missing from a sentence*
   The textbook back in stock in three days.

   ____

3. *When a subject and verb are missing from a sentence*
   The book as soon as possible.

   ____

4. *When a group of words is a dependent clause and, thus, cannot stand alone as a sentence*
   Although the textbook is out of stock.

   ____

COMMA SPLICES

A comma splice occurs commonly in two forms:

1. **When two independent clauses are separated with a comma**

EXAMPLE

✗ I just had my first lecture this semester, there were over 200 students in the lecture theatre!

independent clause — *independent clause*

CORRECTION

The easiest way to correct this type of comma splice is to replace the comma with a period or semicolon.

✓ I just had my first lecture this semester. There were over 200 students in the lecture theatre!

✓ I just had my first lecture this semester; there were over 200 students in the lecture theatre!

Note: You cannot correct a comma splice by removing the comma and replacing it with nothing.

EXAMPLE

✗ I just had my first lecture this semester there were over 200 students in the lecture theatre!

This is a run-on sentence, which is also grammatically incorrect, as there are two independent clauses with no punctuation separating them. It is even worse than a comma splice!

2. **When two independent clauses are separated with a comma followed by a conjunctive adverb such as *however* or *therefore***

EXAMPLE

✗ It was only my first biology lecture this semester, therefore, I couldn't understand everything.

independent clause — *independent clause*

CORRECTION

A comma splice that has a comma followed by a conjunctive adverb, such as *however* or *therefore,* can be corrected as follows:

Keep the comma and replace the conjunctive adverb with a coordinating linking word (*for, and, nor, but, or, yet, so*). Doing so makes a compound sentence.

✓ It was only my first biology lecture this semester, so I couldn't understand everything.

Or, you can keep the conjunctive adverb and replace the first comma with a semicolon or period.

✓ It was only my first biology lecture this semester; therefore, I couldn't understand everything.

✓ It was only my first biology lecture this semester. Therefore, I couldn't understand everything.

Or, you can form a complex sentence with a subordinating linking word.

✓ As it was only my first biology lecture this semester, I couldn't understand everything.

Using a Relative Clause to Correct a Comma Splice

If the second clause in a comma splice provides *defining or additional information* about the first clause, the comma splice can be corrected by revising the second clause to a *defining or non-defining relative clause.* The relative clauses below are highlighted in bold.

1. **Correcting a comma splice with a defining relative clause**

EXAMPLE

✗ Drug-dealing is a serious crime, it affects a wide cross-section of society.

CORRECTION

✓ Drug-dealing is a serious crime **that affects a wide cross-section of society**.

Reminder
In a defining relative clause, no comma appears before the relative pronoun (*that*, in this case). When describing a thing, typically use *that* instead of *which* at the beginning of a defining relative clause.

2. Correcting a comma splice with a non-defining relative clause

EXAMPLE

✗ Government funding for the arts is still too low, it has not increased enough in recent years.

CORRECTION

✓ Government funding for the arts, **which has not increased enough in recent years**, is still too low.

Reminder
In a non-defining relative clause, a comma appears before the relative pronoun (*which*, in this case). When you are describing a thing, use *which* instead of *that* at the beginning of a non-defining relative clause.

When a Comma Splice Is Acceptable

The occasional use of comma splices is acceptable in some genres, such as literary, narrative, and poetic writing, and some forms of journalistic writing. Comma splices also appear in less formal writing (e.g., email, personal correspondence), in which writers do not follow the formal rules of academic writing.

TASK 2

Identify which of the following sentences are comma splices by circling *yes* or *no*. Correct the sentences where necessary.

1. I went to the library, took out four books, had a quick lunch, and went to class. (*Yes/No*)

____

____

____

2. The government increased interest rates, mortgages became more expensive. (*Yes/No*)

____

____

____

3. The experiment involved all three members of our group, it was a collaborative effort. (*Yes/No*)

4. Sea levels may rise 50 cm over the next 20 years, as a result, coastal regions may become flooded. (*Yes/No*)

5. The polar bear is at risk from climate change the species will have to adapt to survive. (*Yes/No*)

APPENDIX 9

The Passive Voice

The passive voice is commonly used in many forms of academic writing, especially scientific writing. In other writing genres, it is less common.

Using the passive voice can change the emphasis in a sentence and can give your writing an objective tone.

One way to recognize the passive voice is by comparing it with the active voice. Consider the following two sentences:

EXAMPLES

Active voice William Shakespeare wrote *Romeo and Juliet*.

Passive voice *Romeo and Juliet* was written by William Shakespeare.

The passive-voice sentence gives greater emphasis to the *agent*, or the person or thing that performs the action (William Shakespeare, in this case) than the active-voice sentence.

HOW TO FORM THE PASSIVE VOICE

The passive voice can be formed in a number of ways.

- **By using transitive verbs**

  Only *transitive verbs* can be used to form the passive voice. Transitive verbs are verbs that require an object. Some verbs are always transitive (requiring an object).

  EXAMPLE

  ✓ I **will take** *the files* to the library.

  In this example, the verb is "will take" and the object is "the files." The verb *take* is a transitive verb that can be used only with an object after the verb. It is not grammatically correct to state the following:

  ✗ I will take to the library.

  Many verbs can be used either transitively or intransitively, depending on the context.

  EXAMPLE 1

  ✓ I passed the exam! [the object is explicitly stated]

  EXAMPLE 2

  ✓ I passed!

In Example 1, the verb "passed" is used transitively. As a result, the writer states the object of the verb explicitly, probably to make the sentence completely clear.

In Example 2, the verb "passed" is used intransitively. In this example, the object is not stated, perhaps because the writer feels the reader will implicitly understand the context of the statement. Perhaps the reader has just asked the question in an email message, "Did you get your results for the exam?"

- **By moving the object to subject position**

To change an active-voice sentence to the passive voice, move the object of the transitive verb in the active-voice sentence to the subject position in the passive-voice sentence.

EXAMPLES

	subject	verb	object
Active voice	William Shakespeare	wrote	***Romeo and Juliet.***

Passive voice ***Romeo and Juliet*** was written by William Shakespeare.

- **By changing the verb to past participle form**

The verb from the active-voice sentence is rewritten with a form of the verb *to be* followed by the past participle of the verb (often a form ending in *ed* or *en*).

EXAMPLES

	to be	*past participle*
wrote →	***was***	***written***

Active voice William Shakespeare **wrote** *Romeo and Juliet.*
Passive voice *Romeo and Juliet* **was written** by William Shakespeare.

- **By stating the agent after *by***

If it is necessary to state the agent, the agent is stated after the preposition *by*.

EXAMPLE

Romeo and Juliet was written **by William Shakespeare.** [agent stated]
(*by* → by; *agent* → William Shakespeare)

- **By not stating the agent**

It may not be required, or possible, to state the agent, if the agent is unknown or not important.

EXAMPLE 1
Romeo and Juliet was written in the late sixteenth century. [agent not required]

EXAMPLE 2
My bag was stolen last night. [agent unknown]

In Example 1, the writer does not consider it necessary to state the agent. The writer assumes that the reader already knows who the author of *Romeo and Juliet* is.

In Example 2, the writer does not know who stole the bag. Because the agent is unknown, it is not stated.

TASK 1

Identify the following sentences as active or passive by circling the correct answer.

For practice, rewrite the active-voice sentences as passives, and the passive-voice sentences as actives.

1. The local council rejected planning permission for the new shopping mall.
   Active/Passive

   ____

   ____

2. The orchestra was given a three-minute standing ovation by the adoring audience.
   Active/Passive

   ____

   ____

3. Many people think that life exists elsewhere in the universe.
   Active/Passive

   ____

   ____

4. You should return or renew all library books before the term ends on December 18.
   Active/Passive

   ____

   ____

5. The bus stop was damaged by vandals for the third time this year.
   Active/Passive

   ____

   ____

TASK 2

Look at the two passive-voice sentences below and answer the question that follows.

1. My bag was stolen last night at the train station. [agent not stated]
2. It was stolen by two teenagers who threatened me. [agent stated]

Why do you think that the writer states the agent in Sentence 2 but not in Sentence 1?

____

____

____

____

____

WHY USE THE PASSIVE VOICE?

The passive voice is used for a variety of reasons.

- **To give emphasis to the object in a sentence**

  EXAMPLE 1
  Patients should take *a dose of two teaspoons (10 ml)* three times a day. [active voice]

  EXAMPLE 2
  A dose of two teaspoons (10 ml) should be taken three times a day. [passive voice]

  Example 2 places more emphasis than Example 1 on the dose that the patient should take because "A dose of two teaspoons (10 ml)" has been moved to the subject position in the passive-voice sentence.

- **When the agent is unknown and not important**

  Writers can use the passive-voice structure when the agent is unknown.

  EXAMPLE
  The book was delivered to my office yesterday afternoon. [no stated agent]

  The writer does not know who the agent is, that is, who delivered the book, so the passive rather than the active voice can be used. Also, the sentence carries the connotation that it is not important who delivered the book—the time of arrival is more important. In this sentence, it would seem odd to state the following:

  EXAMPLE
  The book was delivered by someone to my office yesterday afternoon. [unknown agent is stated]

  The reason that the sentence seems odd is that adding *by someone* takes the emphasis away from the time of arrival and places it on the unknown agent. In this case, it seems like the writer is trying to find out who delivered the book.

- **To emphasize the stated agent**

  In some cases, the passive voice with stated agent can be used to emphasize the agent. This form of the passive voice is especially useful when writers want to highlight an agent they feel the reader may be unaware of.

  EXAMPLE 1
  Edward the Second was written by Christopher Marlowe, not William Shakespeare.

  EXAMPLE 2
  Romeo and Juliet is one of many famous plays written by William Shakespeare. The playwright was born in Stratford-upon-Avon in England in 1564 and was to become the most famous poet and playwright in the English language.

  In Example 1, the writer corrects a mistake by emphasizing that one agent (Christopher Marlowe) rather than another (William Shakespeare) was the author of the play mentioned.

  Similarly, in the first sentence of Example 2, the writer emphasizes the agent by using the passive voice. The reason is not to inform the reader that Shakespeare wrote *Romeo and Juliet*; instead, it is to link the agent to the sentences that follow in the paragraph, which are about the playwright rather than the plays he wrote.

- **To add an objective tone to writing**

  In some academic disciplines, the passive voice is preferred to give writing what is considered to be a more distant, objective tone.

> **EXAMPLE 1**
> In this essay, I have analyzed the non-anthropogenic causes of climate change.
>
> **EXAMPLE 2**
> The non-anthropogenic causes of climate change have been analyzed in this essay.

In Example 1, the writer uses personal language and the active voice: "I have analyzed . . ."

In Example 2, the writer depersonalizes the sentence by using a passive-voice structure with no stated agent: "The non-anthropogenic causes of climate change have been analyzed . . ."

In academic writing, it is necessary to make informed decisions about whether personal language or passive-voice structures are appropriate in different subject areas. Find out what the most common practice is in the different subject areas that you study.

TASK 3

Rewrite the following active-voice sentences as required.

1. *Use the passive voice when the agent is unknown or unimportant.*
   Someone told me to come here to register.

   ____

   ____

2. *Use the passive voice to emphasize the stated agent.*
   A ticket inspector stopped me, not a policeman.

   ____

   ____

3. *Use the passive voice to add an objective tone to writing.*
   I will analyze the pros and cons of higher taxation in three areas: income tax, sales tax, and property taxes.

   ____

   ____

USE OF THE PASSIVE VOICE IN SCIENTIFIC WRITING

In scientific writing, it is more common to use the passive voice than in many other disciplines. For example, use of the passive voice is very common in lab reports. By using the passive voice, writers of lab reports are emphasizing the scientific process rather than their own actions as agents.

EXAMPLE 1
I observed the diffraction pattern five times during the experiment. [active]

EXAMPLE 2
The diffraction pattern was observed five times during the experiment. [passive]

In Example 1, the writer uses the active voice to explain that she observed the diffraction pattern five times during the experiment. The personal language and active voice make the style personal and direct. This style is less common in many forms of scientific writing.

In Example 2, the writer uses the passive voice with no stated agent. Here, the writer is the agent, but uses the passive voice without stating her agency, keeping the focus on the scientific process and not her. This style is much more common in scientific writing, especially when describing processes and methods. Scientific writing styles can vary, so find out whether your instructor requires you to use the active voice or the passive voice in your scientific writing.

THE PASSIVE VOICE WITH NO STATED AGENT: PROBLEMS

Some instructors, especially in the arts and humanities, discourage use of the passive voice with no stated agent. They consider this form of the passive voice to be poor style due to their philosophical stance about how knowledge is constructed. They argue that all knowledge is constructed by agents, including the results of scientific experiments. Thus, they would disagree that using the passive voice with no stated agent is a way of showing objectivity.

Sometimes writers use the passive voice with no stated agent because they do not know, or are unsure about, who the agent is. This use of the passive voice is considered by many instructors as analytically weak.

EXAMPLE 1
It is recognized that reading bedtime stories helps children's literacy development.

EXAMPLE 2
The health care bill was supported mainly because it would extend health care to more of the population.

If the sentence in Example 1 appeared in an essay, an instructor would typically ask, "By whom?" In this sentence, the writer must state clearly who actually supports this view.

In Example 2, the writer explains what he feels is the main reason for the health care bill gaining support. However, he fails to state the agent(s), that is, who supported the bill. In a subject like health care, where different opinions often cause very heated debate, it is necessary to be specific about who supports what.

PASSIVE VOICE WITH *GET* AND *HAVE*

The passive voice can also be created with *get* and *have*, instead of a form of the verb *to be* before the past participle of a verb. Meaning can change in subtle ways by using *get* or *have*.

- **Using *get* for unexpected or unpleasant events**

> **EXAMPLE 1**
> My bag *was stolen* last night.
>
> **EXAMPLE 2**
> My bag *got stolen* last night.

Get is often used instead of *to be* to describe unexpected or unpleasant events that have happened or will happen in the future. Example 2 emphasizes the unexpected or unpleasant nature of the theft more than Example 1.

- ***Having*** **or** ***getting*** **something done**

> **EXAMPLE 1**
> I'm servicing my car tomorrow. [active voice]
>
> **EXAMPLE 2**
> I'm *getting* my car *serviced* tomorrow. [passive voice with *get*]
>
> **EXAMPLE 3**
> I'm painting my house tomorrow. [active voice]
>
> **EXAMPLE 4**
> I'm *having* my house *painted* tomorrow. [passive voice with *have*]

In Examples 1 and 3, the subject is the agent doing the mechanical work on the car, or doing the painting.

In Examples 2 and 4, someone else is the agent: the car is being serviced by a mechanic and the house is being painted by a painter.

TASK 4

Read the excerpt below from the Chapter 6 expository essay "What is bilingualism and how do people communicate bilingually?" Underline any examples of the passive voice that you can find. Then, in the margin, make a note of whether the agent is stated or not stated: mark examples where the agent is stated **S** and where it is not stated **NS.**

Margin Notes

8 In everyday conversations, the term *bilingual* is used when referring to people who can speak two languages, and usually with reference to people who can speak two languages very well. **9** However, scholars disagree on what it means to be bilingual. **10** Perhaps the most open definition of bilingualism was offered by Edwards (1994), who originally suggested that virtually everyone could be considered bilingual, even a speaker with a passive understanding of a number of terms in another language. **11** That would mean that someone who goes on holiday to Mexico and understands and speaks limited Spanish such as *por favor* (please) and *gracias* (thanks) could be considered bilingual. **12** This academic definition is far from the "everyday" understanding of the term that most people have, which is associated with having a high degree of competence in more than one language. **13** This more traditional view of bilingualism is more in line with historical definitions such as those given by linguists Bloomfield, Weinreich, and Haugen. **14** According to Bloomfield (1933, p. 56), being bilingual requires "native-like control of two languages," while Weinreich describes bilingualism as "the practice of alternately using two [or more] languages" (1953, p. 1). **15** Haugen (1953, p. 7) suggests that bilingualism begins when the speaker of one language can produce "complete meaningful utterances in the other language" (in Romaine, 1989, p. 10). **16** An example of these more traditional definitions of bilingualism would be the children of immigrants in North America who speak a family language and the national language (English, French, or Spanish) equally well.

TASK 5

In the paragraph above, there are three examples of passive-voice structures with no stated agent and two examples where the agent is stated. Explain why you think the writer is stating the agent in some sentences but not in others.

____

____

____

____

APPENDIX 10

Articles and Noun Phrases

To use articles (i.e., *a*, *an*, and *the*) correctly in noun phrases, it is necessary to understand the following: the difference between *countable* and *uncountable* nouns, the difference between *general* and *specific reference*, and the idea of *shared knowledge*.

COUNTABLE AND UNCOUNTABLE NOUNS

Nouns can be broadly separated into two groups: countable and uncountable.

Countable Nouns

Countable nouns are nouns that have both a singular and a plural form. For example, the noun *computer* is countable: it can be used in the singular form with the indefinite article *a* to refer to one computer or as a plural by adding *s* to refer to more than one computer.

EXAMPLES

For a birthday present last year, I got *a computer*. [singular form]

Computers are getting faster and cheaper every year. [plural form]

Uncountable Nouns

Uncountable nouns are nouns that do not have singular or plural forms. For example, the noun *milk* is uncountable: it cannot be used with the article *a* or as a plural by adding *s*. (It is possible to say, "I would like a milk"; however, this means "I would like a glass of milk.") Uncountable nouns are also known as *mass nouns* because they refer to a mass rather than a singular or plural object.

EXAMPLES

I try to make sure to drink *milk* every day to stay healthy. [uncountable]

I never have *milk* with my coffee. [uncountable]

Nouns That Can Be Both Countable and Uncountable

A small number of nouns can be used in either countable or uncountable form, depending on the context. One example is the noun *hope*.

EXAMPLES

Hope is a human emotion that allows some people to never give up. [uncountable]

I have many *hopes* and fears about the future. [countable]

GENERAL AND SPECIFIC NOUN PHRASES

A *noun phrase* is the part of a sentence in which the main component is a noun. It can be a single noun, a single pronoun, or a group of words that function as a noun. Speakers or writers can refer to things in general (with a *general noun phrase*) or to specific things (with a *specific noun phrase*).

EXAMPLE 1

Laptop computers have come down in price recently. [general noun phrase]

In Example 1, the noun phrase "laptop computers" is a general noun phrase because it refers to all laptop computers, or *all members of the group*.

EXAMPLE 2

The computer in my office is not working. [specific noun phrase]

In Example 2, the noun phrase "the computer in my office" is a specific noun phrase because it refers to one specific computer, or *a specific member of a group*.

Rules for Describing Things in General and Specific Noun Phrases

FIGURE 1

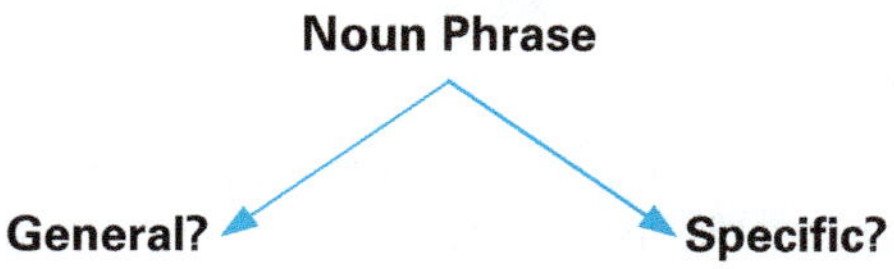

Figure 1 illustrates the first question to ask yourself when you want to describe a thing in English: Do I want to refer to it in general or specifically?

If you want to describe *any* or *all members of a group*, use a general noun phrase.

If you want to describe *a specific member* or *specific members of a group*, use a specific noun phrase.

FIGURE 2

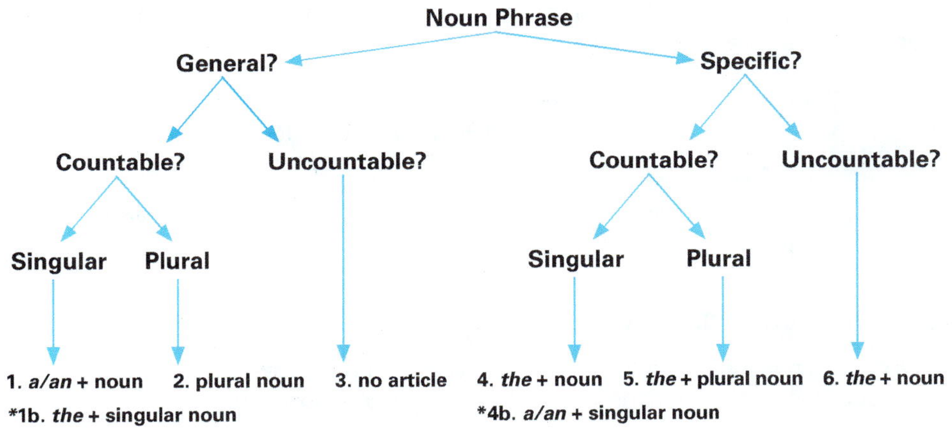

Figure 2 illustrates the second question to ask yourself when you want to describe a thing in English: Is the thing countable or uncountable?

The answers to these questions will lead you to six main options for article usage: three for general noun phrases and three for specific noun phrases. Options 1b and 4b (marked with an asterisk) are exceptions, and will be discussed later in this appendix.

ARTICLE USAGE IN GENERAL AND SPECIFIC NOUN PHRASES

The following options for article usage in a noun phrase correspond with numbers 1 to 6 in Figure 2 above.

General Noun Phrases

Option 1

If the noun is countable and singular, use the article *a* or *an* with it.

> **EXAMPLE**
> Having *a good laptop computer* can make life a lot easier for self-employed people.
>
> **EXPLANATION**
> The noun phrase "a good laptop computer" refers to laptops in general, that is, any laptop computer, or *any member of the group*.

Option 2

If the noun is countable and plural, use the plural form of the noun with no article.

> **EXAMPLE**
> *Computers* are a lot faster and cheaper than they were 10 years ago.
>
> **EXPLANATION**
> The noun phrase "computers" refers to computers in general, that is, all computers, or *all members of the group*.

Option 3

If the noun is uncountable, use the noun without an article and without a plural marker such as the letter *s*.

> **EXAMPLE**
> *Milk* is high in calcium and, therefore, a healthy drink for children.
>
> **EXPLANATION**
> The noun phrase "milk" refers to milk in general, that is, *any or all types of milk.*

Specific Noun Phrases

As a general rule, use the article *the* with specific noun phrases. This rule is applicable in most cases; the exceptions will be discussed in the next section.

Option 4

If the noun is countable and singular, use the article *the* with it.

> **EXAMPLE**
> I need to return *the computer that I bought yesterday*.
>
> **EXPLANATION**
> The noun phrase "the computer that I bought yesterday" refers to a specific computer, that is, the one that I bought yesterday, *one specific member of the group*.

Option 5

If the noun is countable and plural, use the article *the* with it.

> **EXAMPLE**
> *The computers in Lab 3152* need to be upgraded.
>
> **EXPLANATION**
> The noun phrase "the computers in Lab 3152" refers to specific computers, that is, the computers in Lab 3152, or *more than one specific member of the group*.

Option 6

If the noun is uncountable, use the article *the* with it.

> **EXAMPLE**
> *The milk that you bought yesterday* isn't very fresh.
>
> **EXPLANATION**
> The noun phrase "the milk that you bought yesterday" refers to specific milk, that is, the milk that you bought yesterday, not *any or all types of milk*.

TASK 1

Read the underlined noun phrases below. Use the numbers (1 to 6) in Figure 2 on page 281 to identify the option for article usage that applies.

1. The air in Toronto is often hot and humid in summer. Option _____
2. Wide-screen televisions are bad for the environment as they consume so much electricity. Option _____
3. On the day that I got married, I woke up at 5 a.m. Option _____
4. Honesty is the greatest human virtue. Option _____
5. If you buy a satellite navigation system, it will help you to find your way around the city. Option _____
6. More action is needed to protect the Amazonian rain forests of Brazil. Option _____

All Good Rules Have Exceptions! Options 1b and 4b

Look again at Figure 2 on page 281. The two exceptions to the six main options for article usage in general and specific noun phrases are 1b and 4b.

Option 1b

In the example sentences above, all of the specific noun phrases use the definite article *the* to identify them as specific. The general rule is to use *the* for specific reference. However, *the* is sometimes used with a singular noun in a general noun phrase.

EXAMPLES

1. *The tiger* is in danger of extinction.
2. *The computer* has revolutionized the modern workplace.
3. In Canadian secondary schools, what is the role of *the language teacher*?

EXPLANATION

In Example 1, the noun phrase "the tiger" refers to tigers in general, that is, the species, or *all members of the group*. The idea could be expressed with the same meaning by using Option 2 in a general noun phrase as follows: "Tigers are in danger of extinction." We can use the 1b form when we are referring to a *species*.

In Example 2, the noun phrase "the computer" refers to computers in general, that is, all computers, or *all members of the group*. The idea could also be expressed with the same meaning by using Option 2 in a general noun phrase as follows: "Computers have revolutionized the modern workplace." We can use the 1b form when we are referring to *an invention*.

In Example 3, the noun phrase "the language teacher" refers to language teachers in general, that is, all language teachers, or *all members of the group*. The idea could also be expressed with the same meaning by using Option 2 in a general noun phrase as follows: "In Canadian secondary schools, what is the role of language teachers?" We can use the 1b form when we are analyzing *something important in our field of study*: for example, teachers' role in society, their relevance, or their impacts.

Whether you use the 1b form is partly a question of style. Generally speaking, use of the 1b form for general noun phrases is common in many academic fields. It can also make your writing style seem more formal and analytical.

Option 4b

There is another exception to the general rule regarding the use of the article *the* with specific noun phrases. In some cases, the article *a* or *an* is used with a singular noun in a specific noun phrase.

EXAMPLES

1. There has been an accident on the Port Mann Bridge. *The accident* is in the left lane heading west.
2. This morning I reported that I had a problem with my email account. Luckily, the technical support people fixed *the problem* within an hour.

EXPLANATION

In Example 1, the noun phrase "an accident" refers to a specific accident. This sentence would typically be heard on a radio travel report soon after the accident has happened. We can use the 4b form for specific noun phrases when we are *introducing new information*. Thereafter, we can switch to Option 4, which uses *the*. Notice that in the following sentence, the radio reporter says, "*The accident* is in the left lane heading west." Here, *the* is referring to the accident mentioned in the previous sentence. From the context, the listeners know which accident the announcer is describing. It is implicitly understood.

In Example 2, the noun phrase "a problem with my email account" refers to a specific problem. Again, we can use the 4b form for specific noun phrases when we are *introducing new information*. And again, in the following sentence, the writer uses Option 4 in "*the problem*" to refer to the problem mentioned first in the previous sentence. The reader knows which problem the writer is describing. It is implicitly understood.

TASK 2

Before each of the nine sentences below, the context of the sentence is explained. Each sentence contains one underlined noun phrase. First, read each sentence and indicate whether the underlined noun phrase is general or specific by circling the correct answer. Then identify the option for article usage based on Figure 2 on page 281. The sentences include examples of Options 1b and 4b. The first sentence has been done as an example.

EXAMPLE

1. **Context: Child to parent**
   "Mommy, I want a toy tiger for my birthday."
   General/Specific. ***Option 1***

2. **Context: Child to parent after opening the birthday present**
   "I got a tiger! Thank you."
   General/Specific. Option ____

3. **Context: Child to parent**
   "I've decided to call the tiger Tigger."
   General/Specific. Option ____

4. **Context: Encyclopedia**
The tiger is in danger of extinction.
General/Specific. Option ____

5. **Context: Encyclopedia**
Tigers are in danger of extinction.
General/Specific. Option ____

6. **Context: Sign at the zoo**
Don't feed the tiger!
General/Specific. Option ____

7. **Context: Sign at the zoo**
Don't feed the tigers!
General/Specific. Option ____

8. **Context: Conversation after lunch**
The food in the student cafeteria is really expensive!
General/Specific. Option ____

9. **Context: Magazine article**
Organic food is pesticide-free but usually more expensive.
General/Specific. Option ____

SPECIFIC NOUN PHRASES AND SHARED KNOWLEDGE

Whenever you write a specific noun phrase using the definite article *the*, you share knowledge with your reader. To share knowledge successfully, you need to give enough information or be sure that the context makes the meaning of the noun phrase clear. Shared knowledge can be *implicit* or *explicit* in specific noun phrases. Look at the examples below:

EXAMPLE: Explicitly stated shared knowledge
On the day that I got married, I woke up at 5 a.m.

EXPLANATION
The underlined noun phrase in the example is "the day that I got married." This is a specific noun phrase in which knowledge is shared explicitly. This means that the writer has added "that I got married" as specifying information to make the context clear to the reader. If the writer wrote only, "On the day, I woke up at 5 a.m.," the reader might be confused as he or she might not know which day the writer is describing.

EXAMPLE: Implicitly stated shared knowledge
I planned everything for my wedding day. On the day, I woke up at 5 a.m.

EXPLANATION
The underlined noun phrase in the example is "the day." This is a specific noun phrase in which knowledge is shared implicitly. The writer has not added any specifying information as the context can be implicitly understood from the previous sentence. The reader understands that "the day" is the writer's wedding day. Where the context is clear and can be implicitly understood, writers tend to avoid specifying information.

TASK 3

In the following sentences, state whether the shared knowledge is expressed explicitly or implicitly in the underlined noun phrases. Circle the correct answer. The first is an example.

EXAMPLE

1. The assassination of President Kennedy occurred on November 22, 1963, in Dallas, Texas.
   Explicit/Implicit

2. The assassination changed US history.
   Explicit/Implicit

3. Teacher: "I need some technical assistance. The video-conferencing machine isn't working."
   Technician: "Which one are you talking about?"
   Explicit/Implicit

4. Teacher: "I need some technical assistance. The video-conferencing machine in EDF25 isn't working."
   Technician: "I'll send someone over to help you in the next 10 minutes."
   Explicit/Implicit

5. Reporter: "We are receiving reports of a power outage in the south east of the city."
   Explicit/Implicit

6. Reporter: "The outage is thought to be the result of a lightning strike."
   Explicit/Implicit

SUMMARY

The rules for article usage in noun phrases in English are complex. Accurate usage depends on understanding the following:

- The difference between countable and uncountable nouns
- The difference between general and specific noun phrases
- The difference between explicit and implicit shared knowledge

TASK 4

The sentences below are from a paragraph about a group of scientists who are investigating the use of honey as a vaccination for hay fever sufferers. Each sentence has one or more underlined noun phrases. Some are correct (i.e., they use articles as they should), while others need to be corrected. Read each sentence and state whether the noun phrases are correct or not by putting a ✓ (correct) or an ✗ (incorrect) above the underlined noun phrases. If the sentence has an incorrect noun phrase, rewrite the sentence using the correct form. Corrections can be made in more than one way.

1. Have you ever suffered from an allergy?

____

____

____

2. Several studies have shown that the allergies are becoming increasingly common in the world today.

3. The scientists and pharmaceutical companies are researching new ways to help allergy sufferers.

4. The group of scientists in California are trying to develop a vaccination for hay fever, also known as *allergic rhinitis*.

5. The vaccination for people suffering from hay fever will use local honey.

6. In order for the honey to have a vaccinating effect, honey should be produced by local bees.

7. It is thought that local honey will have traces of the local pollen that is triggering allergic reactions.

8. The scientists are currently looking for volunteers for a controlled experiment.

9. There is the potential problem, however.

____

____

____

10. The problem is the following: in many parts of North America where harmful pesticides have polluted local environments, the common honey bee appears to be in danger of extinction.

____

____

____

INDEX

A

D

E

Q

R

S